Praise for

Joan Chittister: Her Journey from Certainty to Faith

"Sister Joan Chittister is one of the most powerful women I know. Her power does not come from wealth, celebrity, or office. It is a power that comes from her presence, from values, from beliefs, from within. In this biography, Tom Roberts reveals the long journey she took to find that power. It's a must-read for anyone expanding their faith."
—Maria Shriver

"I love the stellar witness of this woman! A more faithful, authentic, sustained voice calling for full inclusion of women in the Catholic Church cannot be found. And what a fascinating bud-to-flower woman's life story lies within these pages. I read it deep into the night, long after good sense told me to go to sleep. That's Chittister for you—waking us up and keeping us awake to the radical call of the Gospel." —**Sister Helen Prejean, CSJ, author,** *Dead Man Walking*

"Simply put, Sister Joan Chittister is one of the great spiritual voices, and great prophets, of our time."
—**James Martin, SJ, author,** *Jesus: A Pilgrimage*

"Sister Joan Chittister is one of the most consequential and courageous Catholic women of her generation, a prophetic and inspiring voice. Tom Roberts is one of our moment's wisest, best informed, and eloquent Catholic writers and thinkers. That they have come together here is an enormous blessing and a gift to readers, Catholic and non-Catholic alike. This is an essential book for understanding Catholicism in our time." —**E. J. Dionne Jr., author,** *Souled Out*

"With keen journalistic acumen, Tom Roberts chronicles the life of one of the most beloved spiritual leaders of our times. Along the way, we learn not only about Sr. Joan Chittister's graced journey but also about the evolution of the Erie Benedictines, post–Vatican II religious life, and the struggle for women's equality in the Catholic Church. Roberts has the biographer's gift of invisibly shaping his material, allowing Chittister's piercing, prophetic life to illuminate—and inspire. A wonderful book!"
—**Christine Schenk, CSJ, Founding Director FutureChurch**

"Tom Roberts' highly readable new biography will certainly surprise you in its frank depiction of events Joan Chittister had kept to herself until now. In telling her story, he's also tracing the complicated history of the American church over the last century in the most human way possible, through the life one extraordinary woman has spent both serving and shaping it."
—Melinda Henneberger, Senior Writer, *Bloomberg Politics*

"This is the story of a remarkable visionary—theologian, religious leader, feminist, voice for justice and renewal, peacemaker—brilliantly told by Tom Roberts, who captures both her struggles and her triumphs. Joan Chittister is a woman of her times—a woman who has learned the importance of becoming and evolving, guided always by the lessons of Jesus and his ministry to those on the margins of society. Through her own experience she shows us what is needed for spiritual growth and a purposeful life."
—Melanne Verveer, Former US Ambassador for Global Women's Issues

"Joan Chittister brings to life all that matters most in faith. Out of the stormy years of her prophetic ministry, Tom Roberts seizes the lightning of that witness, and he lets it shine—a source of warmth and illumination. This book lays bare a special person, and a challenging age. A fine writer, a man of faith himself, Roberts is a biographer fully worthy of his brilliant subject."
—James Carroll, author, *Christ Actually*

"Tom Roberts captures the remarkable Sr. Joan Chittister in an extraordinary manner. Joan's life of determination, courage, her humor, her extraordinary talents are revealed from her early years, right to the present. Among Joan's qualities, the gift of endurance is pivotal—the genius of prophets from ancient times until the present. I endorse this publication with great pride and support; it captures the woman Joan, as she follows her 'Impossible Dream!'"
—Theresa Kane, RSM, former president, Leadership Conference of Women Religious

"Untold numbers of people know Joan Chittister as a public person. Here is a book that enables everyone to get to know her as an extraordinarily, deeply human person. In opening up her personal life to Tom Roberts, Joan shares her vulnerabilities, her doubts and struggles as she follows a prophetic call to proclaim a message of justice with a special emphasis on full equality for women in the Church and society."
—Bishop Thomas Gumbleton, Detroit, MI

JOAN CHITTISTER

JOAN CHITTISTER

Her Journey from Certainty to Faith

TOM ROBERTS

ORBIS BOOKS

Maryknoll, New York 10545

ORBIS BOOKS
Maryknoll, New York 10545

Founded in 1970, Orbis Books endeavors to publish works that enlighten the mind, nourish the spirit, and challenge the conscience. The publishing arm of the Maryknoll Fathers and Brothers, Orbis seeks to explore the global dimensions of the Christian faith and mission, to invite dialogue with diverse cultures and religious traditions, and to serve the cause of reconciliation and peace. The books published reflect the views of their authors and do not represent the official position of the Maryknoll Society. To learn more about Maryknoll and Orbis Books, please visit our website at www.maryknollsociety.org.

Roberts, Tom (editor-at-large)
  Joan Chittister : her journey from certainty to faith / Tom Roberts.
      pages cm
  Includes bibliographical references and index.
  ISBN 978-1-62698-148-5 (Cloth)
  ISBN 978-1-62698-198-0 (pbk.)
  1. Chittister, Joan. 2. Benedictine nuns—Pennsylvania—Biography. I. Title.
BX4705.C4748R63 2015
271'.97—dc23 [B]
2015014798

*To the Franciscan and Dominican sisters
at St. Aloysius Elementary School
and St. Pius X High School in Pottstown, Pennsylvania,
who tried their best to educate this difficult case.
To the women religious who often are
the sole remaining Catholic presence in our inner cities
and in parts of the globe where few others venture.*

———————————

*In memoriam:
To William J. and Anna L. Roberts*

CONTENTS

INTRODUCTION

This book had an unexpected beginning. I went to Erie in July 2011 for the *National Catholic Reporter* to update our file on Sr. Joan Chittister, OSB, who had long been associated with the paper as a board member and a columnist. On that July morning Chittister and I met in a sitting room outside her small office in the same building she once inhabited as a young nun. She was seated on a small sofa, I in a stuffed chair at a right angle to her. In front of us, on a coffee table, was a digital recorder. Thus began a series of interviews that continued over several years and in a variety of venues. Some were done via Skype from locations in Ireland and the Cayman Islands, where she annually retreats for several months to write, and others in person during subsequent visits to Erie and as I accompanied her to a wildlife refuge in northern Kenya for a gathering of religious figures from around the world.

The initial interviews, however, were key to this project. They were conducted over a few days, mostly in that sitting room outside her office, and they opened up a vista onto Joan's life that I and most others had never known existed but that further illuminated many areas with which her readers were already familiar. I don't know why I started the interviews as I did. I had not originally intended to conduct a deep inquiry into her life. There existed already an abundance of autobiographical material in her books and a running commentary of her thoughts on current issues in the columns she regularly wrote. But for some reason, before we began the session, I said that though I had known her as a writer and a friend over a number of years, I really didn't know a lot about her other than her public life. "So," I said, "tell me who you are and where you come from. Let's begin at the beginning."

We did, and during that first day she spoke for hours, and I recorded what turned out to be forty-three pages of transcribed text. She began peeling away layers of covering that had served for decades as a buffer against the raw reality of a childhood lived in devotion to a mother who sought the best for her while at the same time subjecting her to the kind of flinching uncertainty that came with a violent and alcoholic stepfather. Joan loved them both, her mother with a fervor that later turned to motivation in a lifelong advocacy for women; her stepfather in the skittish way one proceeds when exposed to the kind of relationship that presents itself as protective one moment and the next willing to destroy every bit of domestic tranquility at the slightest provocation. It was a reality the details of which she had hidden, even from her closest friends and associates in her community, for more than sixty years.

The interviews that first day were interrupted for a lunch on Erie's waterfront and a drive around the city to view the spots where she had done most of her growing up.

We ended late in the afternoon. I remember it as an exhausting day, and I wasn't certain that she'd want to continue. The information I'd heard was so fresh and compelling that I needed an evening to sit with it, to begin to understand what I'd heard. I had known the public, self-assured Joan Chittister, the one who could hold audiences of hundreds, thousands even, spellbound, the writer who confidently kept prodding and articulating both the glories and the inconsistencies of the institution to which she'd given her life. I had not before seen the Joan of deep vulnerability and personal anguish.

When we met the next morning to continue the interview process, I asked if she was okay. She said yes, but that the night had been difficult. She said she had not disclosed to anyone before in such detail the domestic violence she had witnessed as a youngster and into young adulthood. I asked her, "Why now?" She responded, "It's time."

As we continued the interviews for a total of four days, the text of which would eventually fill more than 160 pages, relating details of those early years to later developments in her thinking and vocation, it became clear that we had gone well beyond updating an obit file. There are considerable downsides one might anticipate in venturing into a project such as this about another writer, particularly one as inventive and prolific as Joan Chittister. The upside to the work is that there are certain shared instincts. At some point talk about a book became part of the conversation. She was quite agreeable to the project.

I, too, was enthusiastic at the prospect, but had several reservations. The first I expressed immediately. If I were to do a book about her, she had to recognize that though we were friends I would be asking, at times, questions that a friend might not normally ask. "I know exactly what you have to do," she said. "I'll give you my list of enemies." It never really came to that. If there are "enemies" or anything that comes close, they exist in competing ideas about the meaning of religious life, its future, what the church means, the place of women in the church, and other such matters.

The second reservation had to do with the community that calls itself the Erie Benedictines. It was clear that any extended treatment of the life of Joan Chittister could not be done apart from the life of this disarmingly powerful and deeply spiritual group of women whose influence extends well beyond the bounds of one of Pennsylvania's gritty cities, a place that has seen far better days.

I told her I would not do a book unless I had the cooperation of the community and especially of two of her most trusted long-time friends, Sr. Maureen Tobin and Sr. Mary Lou Kownacki. I met individually with each of them and discussed the possibility, letting them know that while I was openly admiring of Chittister and the community, my reporting would not back away from unpleasant or unflattering aspects of community life that I might uncover and deem essential to the writing of the story. They each endorsed the project enthusiastically and agreed to be interviewed. In the intervening years, I've spent stretches of time at the order's primary location, Mount St. Benedict. Sr. Anne Wambach, the prioress, extended gracious hospitality. I dined with the sisters, joined them in morning and evening prayer, interviewed many of them at the Mount and in other locations in Erie, and have had countless other conversations with members of the community.

A third reservation having to do with maintaining sufficient journalistic distance to tell the story with integrity was soon answered, given the content of the initial interviews and the fact that my reservation was based, in a real sense, on confronting Joan with language that fit my perception of a reality that she initially posited in rather neutral terms. I was further encouraged on this score when one of the agreements reached easily and early on was that she would have no prior approval of what was written. In fact, she was so adamant about not interfering in the writing and ensuring that there would not even be the appearance of her having prior approval that when I gave a lecture in April 2013 at the opening of her archive—a lecture that she would respond to—she refused to look at the speech beforehand. Instead, she took notes during its delivery. She told me she did not want anyone to be able to say we had "colluded" in any of this in any way. Of course, there was "collusion" of a sort. She and others made themselves available to answer ongoing questions through to the end of the process. "A writer has to be able to write with freedom," she said. I have not felt at all constrained. I've asked one member of the community to read the manuscript prior to publication, essentially to judge the accuracy of my depictions of certain aspects of community life and history. She has had no veto power over any of the material but has proved extremely helpful in such matters as confirming dates and correcting language and terms specific to religious life and to the history of the Erie Benedictines.

In assembling the story of Chittister's life from extensive interviews, I have, for the sake of a coherent narrative, recounted her conversations with others and among others, many of them long dead, as she recalled them. In those instances, where I could verify her perception of conversations with others, I did so and those are documented in footnotes. I have also used the terms "nun" and "sister" interchangeably. Though canonically a meaningful difference once existed between the two, the distinction rarely exists today in practical terms and has become nearly meaningless in the public imagination. Further, Chittister herself and many of her sisters in the community used the terms interchangeably during interviews and conversations.

While the attempt here is to draw as complete a portrait as possible of Chittister's life and career, the effort is circumscribed by the boundaries of time, space, and the limits of my own expertise. If there is one certainty with which I finish this project it is that I leave behind a universe of horizons left to explore in the life of Joan Chittister. The sheer volume of her written and spoken corpus is daunting. It includes more than fifty books, countless essays and lectures on the spiritual life, religious community, the place of women in the church and society, issues of peace and justice, deep reflections on the nature of God, and even on the relationship between humans and animals.

In her printed resume, honors and awards go for nearly two pages, single-spaced. They include twelve honorary doctorates as well as her own earned doctorate in speech-communication theory from Pennsylvania State University.

In the world of women religious, she was elected early to leadership positions, first as president of the Federation of St. Scholastica in 1971; president of the Conference of American Benedictine Prioresses in 1974; president of the Leadership Conference of Women Religious in 1976; and prioress of the Benedictine Sisters of Erie in 1978, a tenure that lasted until 1990. She has lectured at conferences and special appearances throughout the country and she is still scheduled out more than a year in advance. Her international travels as lecturer, participant in symposia, activist for women's causes and for peace, as well as a chronicler of events, have taken her to more than thirty countries, some of them repeatedly over decades—from the former Soviet Union to South Africa, from the Philippines to India, from the whole of Western Europe to Haiti and parts of South America.

She's been hailed as a prophet, as courageous, as funny, "a treasure to the world community of faiths." Sr. Helen Prejean, the death penalty abolitionist, once wrote, "She has a razor wit and a full-throttle laugh. She tells a good joke. After a working session she relaxes with you, delights in good wine, belts out a solo of 'I am woman, hear me roar,' in a Karaoke bar. She writes in a way that ordinary people can understand.

She lives what she teaches. She makes Jesus come alive in the twenty-first century. When she misspeaks or is insensitive, she apologizes."

Religion scholar Phyllis Tickle, who developed the religion section of *Publisher's Weekly*, wrote that Chittister "has left her mark upon America's book reading public in ways that few writers could ever hope to do and most can only envy."

Joan has also been criticized from all angles and points on the ecclesial spectrum and vilified in the wilds of the Internet universe. She has been taken to task repeatedly from more conservative corners of the Catholic community for pushing the limits too far, for abandoning tradition, for hastening the ruination of religious life as we've known it. Others would say that she's not gone far enough, that she's been too considerate of tradition and too cautious while working within the ecclesial structure. She and her community once went toe to toe with the Vatican's guardians of orthodoxy and came away a bit battle worn for the experience but overall not much the worse for it.

The extent of her influence on individuals and groups around the globe and across cultural and religious lines is extensive. The index of subjects her questions raise for the church, for religion generally, for the world at large provides a virtually inexhaustible supply of material. I am privileged to present an early take that I hope will prove helpful to further exploration of this huge life that, as of this writing, is still being lived with remarkable energy and creativity. This book begins with a depiction of Chittister in a circumstance in which most might encounter her today—in full voice, an accomplished and celebrated author and speaker delivering a powerful reflection on the evolution of her thinking about God. Most of the book, however, is concerned with what I call Chittister's private existence: the years from childhood through high school and her introduction to the Erie Benedictines; the years of formation in the order and her election to various leadership positions; the struggles with renewal and her years as prioress of the community. One chapter on Chittister's advocacy for women covers much of her history in the order and includes her confrontation with the Vatican over the issue.

Whatever the future holds for religious life within the church and for life in general within the larger Catholic community, it is reasonable to presume that Chittister's contribution to it will be significant. Her life and career to this point arc over one of the most tumultuous periods of modern church history. The tension among some segments of the global Catholic community is, at times, palpable and seemingly insurmountable. Yet no matter how much some might wish for a return to an ill-defined golden era of Catholic practice and certainty—and no matter how hard some might work to reestablish such a period—the church has changed enormously over the past sixty years. All indications suggest that it will continue to change, to evolve, to develop, sociologically, politically, dogmatically, ecclesiologically. That became particularly evident when, midway through the research and writing of this book, Pope Benedict XVI resigned and the college of cardinals elected Cardinal Jorge Mario Bergoglio, who quickly upended papal customs, relocated the papacy, took the name Francis, and embarked on a reign marked by an emphasis on pastoral theology and on "the art of accompaniment." The church has changed, and will continue to do so, in its capacity to understand itself in an increasingly pluralistic world where old monarchies, whether divinely inspired or otherwise, have long ago outlived their usefulness. As much as any individual Catholic thinker and writer might, Chittister has been both a part of and a fashioner of that change.

PART I

Benedictine Sisters of Erie in the 1950s, proceeding to chapel.

ONE

THE GOD OF LIGHT

S he was an unlikely figure in an unlikely place. A Benedictine nun from a poor neighborhood in Erie, Pennsylvania, standing at the front of an imposing Protestant church located in the heart of one of the wealthiest sections of Kansas City, Missouri. Placing herself at the intersection of forces and themes that ordinarily don't meet is a hallmark of the long career of Sr. Joan Chittister, and the confluence of events and places that had led to her appearance on an autumn day in 2009 seemed fitting to the topic of her talk, "The God They Never Told Me About: A Convergence of Opposites." It was an odd hour for such a gathering, 9:30 on a Saturday morning, but people poured into the Country Club Christian Church, more than nine hundred of them, filling the pews and the choir loft and overflowing out the rear doors into the vestibule.

The talk—like a reduction that has been patiently rendered over low flame—represented the essence of Chittister's long journey from trauma-tized child to articulate voice for those seeking God from the margins. Some might reasonably argue that religious life provided a welcome es-cape from a world that, especially during her early years, had shown it-self too often to be brutal and unforgiving. It may in fact have been an es-cape, at least in part, during her early years in the Benedictines. However, the restlessness with which she pursued God, her rigorous and persistent search for an almighty not bound to the limited imaginations of a certain century or the needs of an institution, her ultimate conviction that a monastery's purpose is not to shelter its occupants from the world, weren't consistent with the notion of escape. She knew, too, as the ful-crum tipped her toward the latter stages of life, that the stakes were high.

All the debates and questions that had established her in some quarters as a "dissident," the brushes with authority even to the highest levels of the Vatican, all of those iconic "Joan" moments aside, what really mattered was this God whom she now dared approach—and who had persistently pursued her. The stakes were high, she would acknowledge, because she had come to the conclusion, over years, "that it is precisely our idea of God that is the measure of our own spiritual maturity. What you and I believe about God colors everything we do in the name of God. It forms everything we think about other people."

Belief in God is not a terribly exceptional matter, she said that morning as sun poured through stained glass windows. "Every people on earth, in fact, has come to the juncture where only God is an answer to questions for which there are no answers." In fact, belief in God may be the least important fact in considering this matter of God. "It is not the idea of God that sets us apart in the history of humanity," she noted. "It is the kind of God in which we choose to believe that in the end makes all the difference."

That question—What kind of God did she believe in?—was the motivation, sometimes unseen and perhaps at times even unknown, behind the rest of life. In the end, it was the search for the answer to that question that made sense of the hours of prayer every morning, at noon, and in the evening, the endless recitation and singing of psalms. It is what drove her to keep exploring new initiatives, new ventures, and to endure endless travel to other countries and cultures, meeting people outside the Catholic family who often found great solace in her wisdom and experience. So much of the world made room for her, often warmly opening its arms to her, and frequently when the leaders of her own church, to which she had devoted her life, were viewing her more with suspicion than with trust. Her God, the one revealed through all this effort over decades and the one she preached now with passion, provided great consolation to many of the faithful within the Catholic family. More than simply a source of comfort, this God she preached was often a point of renewed connection for Catholics, especially women, who had considered leaving the community altogether. The sentiment that "Joan has kept me in the church," was repeated countless times among those in the long lines that formed to greet her after talks or among those who gathered to read and study her written works, or who signed in for her on-line conversations and courses.

Her convictions made her at times a threatening presence to the men who ruled the Catholic community with unassailable authority and unwavering confidence in their knowledge of the mind of God. The God of their history, the God imagined and defined over centuries by a celibate, all-male priestly culture, had bestowed on them remarkable, even super-human, powers. According to their understanding of God and what he had called them to, the difference between members of this all-male caste and the rest of the world was no less than ontological, a difference in the nature of their very being. Youngsters were taught in Catholic schools that when priests were ordained they received an indelible mark on their souls and that, in relation to the rest of the community, they stood in the place of Christ himself, alone possessing the power to forgive sin and to make Christ fully present in the bread and wine of the Eucharist. This was a mighty God indeed, in a well-ordered religious universe designed and overseen by men.

As Chittister put it on another occasion, "Women don't question theological truths that have been defined without half the world's spiritual insights because men say that God does not want women to decide what God wants. They have made the all-spiritual God male—a very clever heresy—and so they have made themselves closer to God, and made God hostage to sexism, and left a sacramental church without sacraments and, because it is their will, say it is God's will."[1] She was describing the static God that, over time, she would cast off in search of another, a God who, in the words she used that morning in Kansas City, "has been a changing, moving, inviting, disturbing, and totally engrossing mystery."

Along the way she would discard "God the persecutor who created life in order to trap us in our own ignorance," as well as "God the mighty male...to whom obedience, subservience, and deference were the only proper response for a woman." She came to the conclusion "after a lifetime of looking for God" that she was looking in the wrong places, "that a divinity such as this is simply a graven image of ourselves, that such a deity is not a god big enough to believe in."

She had known, she said, "all of those gods in my own life: God the angry, God the indifferent and remote, God the magician, God the implacable judge, God the tease," adding that "all of those gods have failed me. I learned that law-keeping did not satisfy my need for meaning ...I learned that fear of wrath did not seduce me to love. I learned that God the distant doer of unpredictable and arbitrary magic failed to engage my soul, let alone enlighten it. I learned that life was surely about far more important things than walking around in a darkened funhouse, sometimes bumping into the God who does good things, and sometimes the God who does bad."

---

1. Von Hügel Lecture, St. Edmund's College, University of Cambridge, May 21, 1966.

She had used all of those gods and more at different times in her life, often as a shield to protect herself from life's unpleasantness. "As a result, I failed often to take steps to change life either for myself or, worse, perhaps for all those others on my television screen, on my block, in my club, when injustice masked itself as God's will for them and oppression as God's judgment on them." God was always "out there," said Chittister, and thus she became "blind to the God within me."

The irony in that ever-increasing crowd of godly images was that they ultimately "blocked the image of the presence of God in life" for her. Worse, they actually "made a mockery of the very definition of God, the fullness of being, the one who, having created us, wills us well and not woe, good and not grief, and all of us fullness of life, not some of us inert and invisible nothings."

If, as she contends, "we grow in the image of God we make for ourselves," she is proof herself that our notions of God can change radically, that raising questions about God and how God is formed in our imagination also exposes us to endless consideration of who God is and what influences our conceptions of God.

Chittister's evolution in thinking about God springs in part from the context of contemporary Christianity, where there seems, as Sr. Elizabeth Johnson notes, something in the air of this era that is generating new searches for God. And if that morning in Kansas City—when hundreds of people gathered to hear Chittister speak and, following her talk, many lined up, with some waiting for more than an hour, to meet and talk to her—was any indication, the search remains quite alive in the early twenty-first century, particularly among women. Struggles to understand God in new ways, Johnson writes, have arisen out of such disparate forces as efforts to understand the evil of the Holocaust; the struggles for social justice; concern for women's issues; involvement in facing environmental challenges; and "from Christianity's encounter with goodness and truth in the world's religious traditions."[2] Chittister would add to those forces her deep roots in the Benedictine Rule as well as the influences of science and globalism, and "feminism that came to crumble, wash away, and replace a God made small by puny ideas cast in puny images." From the Rule of St. Benedict, written in the sixth century, she finds a path to her modern understanding of God in "chapter seven on humility, which is Benedict's great spiritual theology." Humility begins, says Chittister, with "what the ancients call the fear of God," and what today we understand as "the sense of God, the

2. Elizabeth Johnson, *Quest for the Living God* (New York: Bloomsbury, 2011), 14.

awe of God, the awareness of God, the consciousness of the presence of God always before our eyes, here and now, this moment in this place, in you, in me, and in the people next to us."

Chittister sets out on her quest for God from what Johnson describes as "a settled country," a view centuries in the making that "envisions God on the model of a monarch at the very peak of the pyramid of being. Without regard for Christ or the Spirit, it focuses on what Trinitarian theology would call the 'first person,' a single powerful individual who dwells on high, ruling the cosmos and judging human conduct." Even when benevolent, she writes, "He, for it is always the ruling male . . . is essentially remote."[3]

Chittister takes a close look at that view and comes up with some unsettling thoughts. If God is personal, she notes, we have reasoned that God is then, necessarily, a person "simply written a bit larger than ourselves, and we have seen in that limited conception both the best and the worst, both the most limitless and the most partial of ourselves." We've absolutized that version with its limitations, she says, and in doing so, we've substituted our own limitations for the unlimited nature of God. The imagined God goes nowhere beyond who we are, so that "until I unmask the God who lives in my own heart, regardless of the endless panoply of other god images around me, I will never understand another thing about my own life."

Layers of masks waited to be removed, she discovered, as "a confluence of things . . . began to converge newly in my own spiritual life. I began to see God grow, or maybe I saw me grow and couldn't tell the difference.

"So I have abandoned God the stern father who has no time for human nonsense and little time for women either. I have abandoned God the cloud-sitter who keeps count of our childish stumblings toward spiritual adulthood in order to exact fierce retribution from humans for being human. And I have seen all those fragments of the face of God dissolve into the mist of the impossibility of a God who is not godly." All of those gods, she has become convinced, "do not exist, never did exist, must not exist if God is really God."

If an inadequate God of small ideas and limited imagination is rejected, what God of big ideas might we substitute? "I have become sure," she tells her audience, "that if all I know about God is that my God is the fullness of life and the consummation of hope, the light on the way and the light at the end, I will live my life in the consciousness of God and goodness everywhere. Obscure at times? Yes, but never

---

3. Ibid.

wholly lacking. Now God, at this stage of life, that old rascal, is doing it again. I am moving in my heart from God as a trophy to be won or a master, however benign, to be pacified, to God as cosmic unity and everlasting light."

In the Benedictine tradition, she says, the first step toward union with God "is knowing you already have God. The first degree of humility is to keep the presence of God always in mind. You already enjoy God. You're living God right now. You've been living there all your lives, the life that is God. God is here in us now. The Rule of Benedict says don't forget it. If you start by forgetting that, you'll get nowhere else. The God you seek is already here."

Benedict, then, is the starting point of her realization that God is not to be pursued or coveted, can't be won like some spiritual trophy to be possessed, placed on the shelf and glanced at should doubts arise. Once that point is established, that one need not keep a continuous ledger to determine whether one is on this or that side of God's favor—indeed, that such a project is an exercise in futility, that God's love is unearnable and as impossible to possess as the wind itself—one can stop trying to fashion the God of previous expectations and limits.

The saint and his rule are almost always the starting point, the touchstone from which Chittister advances, no matter the ideas or the cause. As will become clear, she arrived at the monastery door a youngster whose dreams of religious life rested in the certainties of traditions she then considered unchanging. More than that, she saw no reasons for change and was more resistant to them than might be expected from someone to whom the label "dissenter" was so readily assigned later in life.

In her Kansas City talk, Chittister said she was revealing for the first time something that occurred when she was thirteen, a girl moving toward adulthood who had already given serious thought to religious life. She was in a darkened church illuminated only by a sanctuary light, when she "had an experience of intense light" and was "totally convinced that that light, whatever it was, wherever it came from, was the presence of God. I had seen it that night."

In later years, she said, she reasoned it could have been a janitor working late or a faulty switch of some sort, "but I do know that it was a startling insight given young, given gratuitously, and I came to understand that I had to look for that God who was light."

The image served her well as the search went on. "Whenever God was shrunk to meet someone's then-current need to control or frighten or cajole...Whenever God the theological Santa Claus didn't give me what I wanted and God the judge let evil go by unchallenged, I knew down deep that God, the God I had experienced, was bigger than that.

You can't trap light. You can't box it, buy it, earn it, or be sure of it. I was never able to stop feeling the undiminished light within."

She came to a deeper understanding of the God introduced to Moses as "I am who am"; of the God of mercy upon mercy of the Jonah story; of the God of light of the Mount of Transfiguration. "This was a God without a face of any color or gender, a God who did, indeed, come in fire and light, God with us, Emmanuel, but unseen, God with us but hidden in the obvious. The God I knew lived in the light and the light I could feel was inside of me. Then all the thinking stopped and the knowing began, and the light burned the puny, punitive, paltry images away."

This is God, finally, who reveals rigid hierarchies and a men-only culture of authority and control as inadequate products of limited imaginations. It is the God who can stand up to the tests and questions emanating from science, from cosmology, from the increasingly blurred borders between nations, cultures, religions, genders.

In a segment heavy with echoes of Teilhard de Chardin's insights into the "irresistible rise...of an evolutive God of the Ahead"[4] she writes, "The God of design and plans becomes the God of evolution and the working out of creation with us as we go." It is hardly surprising that the work of the visionary French Jesuit should echo loudly through the speculation of women imagining aspects of God previously unrecognized by men charged with determining the nature of the deity for the Catholic community. Teilhard inspired a new universe of thinking about the nature of God and dared to suggest a "refashioned Christology" appropriate to an age of ever-increasing scientific discovery. What he conveyed through these new imaginings was a God unbounded by a static universe. As N. M. Wildiers notes in his foreword to Teilhard's *Christianity and Evolution*, "In a static world, the dignity of human labor does not qualify for expression in the same terms as it does in a world in evolution."[5] In Teilhard's construct, humans are in cooperation with and essential to the "great work of evolution," which, in turn, requires a new and even holy love for creation.

"What you and I do not do in this world, this world cannot become," says Chittister. "As nature grows and experiments and unfolds and selects and adjusts and adapts, so you see must we. Growth, not perfection, becomes the purpose of life." That last sentiment takes on significance in Chittister's life when the reality of her early years, which

---

4. Pierre Teilhard de Chardin, *Christianity and Evolution* (New York: Harcourt Brace Jovanovich, 1969), 10.

5. Ibid., 12.

she kept hidden from even her closest friends for most of her life, finally is revealed. The notion of becoming, of journey, of movement, is extremely important to her thinking about religious life in transition from old forms that have become ossified to something newly dynamic. It is essential, too, to her understanding of herself and her personal movement from her early years of searching for certainty and stability to her current status as a public religious person and advocate of change.

Creation, then, is "the very process of human growth," and not "human puppetry in the hands of a disinterested, distant, and demanding God." In that same vein, life is not "a program of expectations" to be figured out "before it gets too late to succeed at it. In an evolving world, God becomes becoming, the one who stands by, the one who stands with us, the one who companions us as we grow from one self to another, from one level of insight to another, from one age and awareness to another. God, we come to understand, is not the God of fixed determinations...The past is no longer a template of forever." This God, perhaps Teilhard's God of the Ahead, becomes, in Chittister's words, "the God of the future, beckoning us beyond ourselves, beyond the present into the eternal growth into God."

What is true for the individual, she believes, is true corporately, for religious life and for the church at large.

TWO

THE EARLY YEARS

Save me, O God,
For the waters have come up to my neck.
I sink in deep mire,
where there is no foothold;
I have come into deep waters,
and the flood sweeps over me.
—Psalm 69

One morning in April 1946 as Joan Chittister left home for St. Veronica's School where she was in fourth grade, her mother made a puzzling comment. She said that Sr. Patricia Maria would be dismissing Joan early that day but didn't explain why. When the youngster arrived home that afternoon, a moving van was parked in front of the building on Merchant Street where she lived with her mother and stepfather.

Joan's mother, Loretta, had cleared out all of her own and her daughter's belongings from the second-floor apartment in Ambridge, a small industrial town in western Pennsylvania, leaving her husband only his Civilian Conservation Corps locker. Loretta had been physically abused for years by Harold "Dutch" Chittister, and this was her attempt to escape. Joan, who was just about to turn ten, had been unaware of her mother's plan until the two of them climbed into the truck with a driver and got ready to take off, minutes before her stepfather was due home from work.

"She had clearly been planning this for a while," Chittister recalled. Her mother had borrowed money from her sister to help with the move, a daring escape for a woman in the mid-1940s. "Now that the time had come," she said, "I found myself in the cab of the truck between the driver and my mother. I remember the anxiety I felt. My little heart was pounding because I was so frightened. My stepfather would get home from work by five after four and it was ten to four and we were still sitting in front of that building. My mother was very slow about things all her life. She was always late for things, and I just knew that we were not going to get away."

But they did get away, setting out on the long drive from Ambridge, just northwest of Pittsburgh, almost due north to Erie. After driving through the rest of the afternoon and half the night (a trip that would take between two and three hours today), they finally arrived at a relative's home in Erie around midnight.

Chittister's mother and stepfather died years ago. What Chittister recalls about that day—the sense of threat and dread, the ongoing and pervasive emotional tug of war over her feelings about her stepfather, the constant possibility of danger—are emotions that in fact colored her entire young adulthood. The day she escaped with her mother, the person who was to forever remain a singular reference point in her life, would be one of the ineradicable memories of her childhood.

Chittister's narrative is woven through with a perpetual struggle between loving the man who had stepped in and provided materially for her and her mother and fearing him at the same time as a constant threat to their safety and security. Her life as a youngster and beyond was constantly disrupted by Dutch's outbursts of violent temper, which always seemed to simmer non-stop beneath the surface. Chittister's mother looms large in her daughter's adult recollections as an anchor in Chittister's life, a woman who was both shaped by and who pushed back against the conventions of the day. She became, over time, a source of insight into essential issues involving women as well as an inspiration for much of Chittister's later work. Theirs was an unusually close mother-daughter relationship, and some of that attachment undoubtedly grew out of their shared struggle for survival. They were often lone allies in protecting themselves from Dutch. The chaotic circumstances in their home required Loretta to disclose some of life's realities to her daughter long before most children learn of such things.

During three days in June 2011 Chittister and I sat for hours outside her office in Erie as she told me her story. While talking about her early years, she spent extended periods staring at the floor, speaking into some space that seemed removed from the moment. She seemed to be unwinding a personal history from deep inside, a history driven by powerful themes and long-held feelings as well as by chronology. In my experience with her, it was an unusual posture and approach. During ordinary discourse she is always ready to engage, looking you in the eye, her blue eyes at times almost ablaze, a smile always at the ready. Her energy can seem inexhaustible. Her story lines are usually crisp and unambiguous, delivered in a strong voice with a laugh to match. This was different. This wasn't her usual storytelling or a discussion of ideas or issues, but a deliberate and methodical calling on memory, a process at times laborious, at times painful. When she did look up, her gaze was distant, her expression sad. She was unearthing and disclosing years of disturbing recollections. The image from Psalms that she used to describe her feelings was one of drowning. As we began the second day, she said the previous session had "stirred up an awful lot in me that I haven't paid any attention to for years, if ever. It stirred up a lot. It did. I woke with it."

She referenced the beginning of Psalm 69, some translations of which use the image of a person up to her neck in seawater, desperate for rescue. "Well, I could feel the seaweed lapping around my neck again," she said. "I haven't felt it for a long time. It's another world, another person, another life, and I don't carry it."

It became apparent, however, from those initial days of conversation and from many that followed that she does, in some ways, still carry "it," that the memories are deeply embedded and that she was disclosing most of the details of her early years for the first time. Some of her memories are from the earliest edges of possible recollection. Many of them are likely a mix of actual remembrance of events with what she was later told, often repeatedly, as the telling of those events evolved into family lore shared by her mother. All of the memories, from the most primitive to those of young adulthood and beyond, are intimately knitted into this complex and influential life.

In hours of interviews that stretched into days, her telling of her story constantly moved from a kind of major-key recitation of the ordinary, of what one might expect of a conventional and happy childhood, to a darker, minor-key intrusion of an alternate reality. The deeper and longer the conversation, the more frequent the appearance of the alternate reality. Her childhood days were constantly menaced by the possibility of violence, a fact she kept hidden for years because, she explained, she didn't want her teachers and religious superiors or her peers in community to know that "I didn't come from a perfect Catholic family."

Joan Chittister was born on April 26, 1936, in DuBois, a small borough in western Pennsylvania, to Loretta Cuneo and Daniel Edward Aloysius Daugherty (also spelled Dougherty[1]). Daniel was all Irish.

---

1. He spelled the name Daugherty, with an "a," a spelling used by his grandfather with whom he was very close. That is the spelling her mother used on at least one official document—Joan's adoption papers. Chittister, however, says that everyone else in the family seems to have spelled the name with an "o."

Loretta's background was either French or Italian. One family story explains her surname as the corruption of the name of a French town, perhaps Cugnaux, located in the Pyrenees. According to another story, the name is Italian, and a more compelling argument might be made in that direction since Cuneo is both a province and a capital city in Italy's northwest Piedmont region near the border with France. Chittister surmises that the specifics of who was from where got blurred through earlier migrations. On the Irish side, Chittister represents the third generation in the United States. For much of her life she had little connection with either extended family, though an aunt on her father's side stayed in touch and her children have occasionally contacted Chittister.

She hardly knew her biological father, who died less than three years after she was born. She came to learn that he had been practically "the boy next door" in terms of her mother's family, that he and her mother had been friends since childhood, and that her mother always thought of him as the love of her life. He was a bright young man, considered good humored by accounts she heard later in life. Daniel had graduated from high school and intended to be an engineer. Chittister's mother was twenty years old and he was twenty-one when they married on September 26, 1935.[2] He died May 10, 1938, in a tuberculosis sanitarium where he'd been for only three days. Chittister has a photo of his tombstone on her desk. Her mother, she said, "was a twenty-three-year-old widow with a baby at the end of the Depression with no job, and undereducated.

"I used to have—and my heart breaks to tell the story—I had a tiny little children's notebook, about three inches wide and five inches long.

---

2. During the initial interviews Chittister was uncertain of the precise age of her parents when they married and of the precise date of the wedding. It was only when research for this book turned up the marriage license that she learned her parents had been married only seven months before she was born. The probability was obvious that her mother may have been pregnant before she was married, a fact that would have been far more significant in the 1930s in a Catholic ghetto made up primarily of Italians and Irish than it would be today. Chittister, in an email, responded to a question about whether anyone had ever mentioned anything to her about a premature birth or whether her mother was pregnant at the time she was married: "Not a word. This is a real shock to me, too. Given her age and the era in which they lived, I'm not surprised that, on the one hand, she might not have told anyone. But I thought she always told me everything. All I am really sure of is that she never loved anyone but him and never stopped loving him ever. You couldn't play 'Danny Boy' in front of her." In a later email she wrote: "I've been thinking about the dates all day, of course. And kind of smiling. After all, if it was good enough for Jesus, it's good enough for me."

In it there was a note written by my father, saying to his brother-in-law, 'Dear Ogden, they brought me in here on Tuesday, and it's Thursday, and I'm in a side room already.'

"That was code for being taken out of the TB ward into a private room to die, so the family could come." The note continued: "Please take care of Tootsie and the baby. I'm very tired. Dan." It was the only thing she possessed that he had written, "and in one of the moves of my life," she said, "something happened to it." Daniel was six-foot-three, and Chittister's mother would describe how she'd walk under his arm. Chittister has photographs that show her mother was "a tiny little thing, and he was this big, thin, lanky Irish kid."

Joan pressed her mother at times for more information, and she learned that her father was funny and loved to dance. Did he drink? she asked. "No, not then," her mother would answer. Joan learned that he liked a game of poker.

Loretta wouldn't say much more. "My mother was a woman of great wisdom. She would tell me, 'Joan, you don't need to make a shrine to your father. Danny was a wonderful man, but he was very young. He was hardly a man when he died.'" She wouldn't allow Joan to build imagined monuments to her father. "Your father loved you very much," she would say, "and that's enough."

By counting forward from her first year in elementary school, Chittister arrives at 1946 as the year of the escape from Ambridge to Erie. Dutch came home that day to an empty house. No note, no explanation. By that point, the patterns had been set. On weekends, especially, he would go out drinking and come home raging drunk. Whatever demons were at work in him would take out their vengeance on Joan's mother.

Dutch was also from the DuBois area. He had apparently had his eye on Loretta for some time before she married Daugherty. When Dutch learned that Daniel had died, he quit his job on Neville Island, a small municipality on the Ohio River near Pittsburgh, and returned to DuBois to wait for Loretta. "I used to use the language, 'When we marry Dutch,' 'When Dutch was courting us,'" recalls Chittister. "I was a little kid when I was using that language. I have a picture in my mind of my stepfather coming up the stairs to the second floor of my grandmother's house, carrying a box of chocolates under his left arm and a watermelon on his right shoulder. The chocolates were for my mother, and the watermelon was for me. He definitely courted us. There was no question about it."

Loretta married Dutch on August 26, 1939. She would later tell her daughter that she married Dutch to give her a father. The tensions were evident from the start. In order to marry Dutch Chittister, a Presbyterian, Loretta Dougherty had to marry outside of her denomination, no minor

matter in the culture of that era. Joan says she remembers hearing that
Loretta and Dutch were married in a quiet ceremony that she believes was
held at the Chittister homestead. It was performed before a "minister of
the gospel" named Austin V. Hunter, according to the marriage certificate.

A few years into the marriage and at Loretta's urging, they decided
to have the marriage "fixed," in Dutch's term. Chittister, who was
around six at the time, recalls sitting in their car in the parking lot of
St. Veronica's Church in Ambridge while her mother and Dutch went
through the ritual to have the marriage recognized by the Catholic
Church. The brief ceremony was held in the sacristy because "mixed
marriages" could not be celebrated inside the church.

At some point after the marriage was blessed by the church, Dutch
considered converting. The couple consulted a priest in a parish somewhere in or around Ambridge, but the initial session ended badly. During the discussion, as the story was told, Dutch asked a pointed question
of the priest: "Are you telling me that my mother is not going to go to
heaven?" The priest picked up a pamphlet explaining Catholic teaching
at the time, which saw no salvation outside of the church. The priest
pushed it in front of Dutch and said, "You can read. You read it."

"My father picked it up," says Chittister. "He put it down and he
said to my mother, 'Loretta, I'm getting out of here. I refuse to stay here
one more minute. You make a decision: Are you staying here with him
or are you going with me?' My mother got up and left, and after that,
she very seldom went to Mass. I went by myself all my life."

The issue of the church put further strain on an already shaky marriage. Joan described it as "unbearable in both directions." Her mother,
seeking counsel in the church, was told by priests that if her husband
drank, he must be unhappy, and she must be at least partially the cause.
If he was violent, it was because she wasn't doing something right.
Loretta would eventually tell Joan that when she explained to priests that
she had no desire to sleep with Dutch because of his violent behavior,
they would tell her that she had to "perform her wifely duties."

"So she went to confession for a while," said Chittister, "and then
she just said, 'That is enough.'"

As the turmoil increased, the child would ask: "'Mom, why don't we
just go and live by ourselves?' Now, I obviously had no awareness of
the fact that she couldn't support us alone, but her answer was, 'Because we're Catholic. We're Catholic, and we don't get divorced.'" It
was an answer in line with the ethos of U.S. Catholicism of the 1940s
and '50s. Expectations were clear, and certain things simply weren't

done. But when her daughter asked her about going to Mass, Loretta responded, "My marriage is more important than being in their church on a Sunday. I don't need to go to their church."

It is difficult to overstate the strains that a mixed Catholic and Protestant couple might have experienced at that time, especially if their religious affiliations were important to them. It would be another two decades before the revolutionary changes in church teaching on other faiths would come out of the Second Vatican Council, a series of meetings of the world's bishops in Rome conducted over four years (1962–1965). Those meetings led to significant reforms in the Roman Catholic Church. Among the most notable for the world beyond the church were the council's decrees on ecumenism and on interfaith relations, which opened wide the doors to new cooperation and dialogue with other Christian denominations and with other world religions.

Loretta and Dutch were attempting to navigate the difficult cross currents that ran between Christian denominations before Vatican II. At the time they sought to "fix" their marriage, the non-Catholic partner had to face the humiliation of being told that he or she was the reason the Catholic partner was not permitted to be married in the church. The message to non-Catholics was fairly direct: their Christianity was inferior. The consequence was a marriage ceremony conducted in the shadows of the community.

Moving away from the church must have been an especially wrenching decision for Loretta, a lifelong Catholic who once had ambitions herself to enter religious life. "She told me she had planned to be a Sister of Mercy in Erie—in all the great ironies of life—" said Chittister, "and that she had begun to make her own habit, which was the custom those days for the Mercies." Loretta's education had ended after eighth grade. "She never got to high school. She was a girl," said Chittister, and so "there was no reason for her to go any further."

Loretta, the youngest of thirteen children, was needed at home to help care for a father who had severely injured his back in the coal mines and who also suffered from black lung, a disease common to miners. Her mother, a tiny woman, was exhausted from multiple pregnancies and trying to care for her husband. "She was a worn-out woman and she had no intention of letting my mother leave home." Chittister thinks Loretta was sixteen or seventeen when her mother found the nearly completed sister's habit hidden under her bed. She told Loretta that she needed her at home, and she burned the garment. A few years later, Loretta married Daniel Daugherty and, seven months later, little Joan arrived.

Chittister said she never asked her mother why she wanted so badly to be a sister. "The interesting thing is, I never asked because I was so crazy about the sisters myself. It was a given. I didn't need another reason. I didn't know the Mercies, but I just loved the sisters. I just took it for granted, and when I look back now, I say to myself, 'It had to have been obvious to a lot of women of that age that being a sister was a dignified, worthwhile, important kind of life, and it could save you from a hell of a lot of beatings, poverty, misuse, and burdens.' I hate to put it like that, but I'm pretty convinced that when we talk about the social and cultural dimensions of a vocation it changes from century to century."

While women in the last century were beginning to become more educated and have a higher literacy level than women in earlier centuries, "nobody expected them to use it," Chittister says. "It was supposed to make them good mothers, not good thinkers, not strong women, certainly not good leaders. But down deep, for maybe a hundred years, this was beginning and they were growing up in the whole suffragette movement; they were finding another sense of possibility or another goal. You simply cannot dismiss the power and presence of the women's movement in the church."

The attraction to religious life for Chittister, however, was awakened, in her recollection, long before she gave any thought to women's issues or was influenced by sociological forces. That attraction, she is convinced, more than seven decades later, had to do with a moment of deep transition in her life and one that, in retrospect, was profoundly religious.

After Daniel died, Loretta took the child, not yet three years old, to her father's viewing. The story was told to Chittister repeatedly later in life, and she related it as one would a well-known bit of family lore. Some members of Loretta's family strongly objected to taking a child to view the body. To the objections, Loretta replied: "What the hell is wrong with your heads? She has lost a father just the way I lost a husband. She has to grieve for him just as I have to grieve for him. What am I supposed to tell her? He just disappeared? He just walked out and never came back?"

Joan is convinced she has direct memory of the scene in the funeral home. "I'm on her shoulder so that I can see him. Well, the family was furious. This baby should not see this corpse. She had me touch it. 'You and I are going to touch Daddy, and then any time you think of it, it'll just be sweet, just be sweet.'

"I reach over like this but I have my hands around her head, you know, a little kid's hands. I can feel the wet on her face. I know this is not good. I keep saying, 'Daddy, get up. Daddy, let's play. Daddy, wake up. Let's play.' She's holding me very tight.

"This is the first image I have of sisters. Down at the foot of this casket were three of the strangest creatures I'd ever seen in my life, and I said not 'Who is that?' but 'Momma, what is that?' She answered,

'Those are very special friends of Daddy's.'" They were the Sisters of Mercy from St. Catherine's School from which he had graduated. "Those are very special friends of Daddy's and very special friends of God's. When the angels come tonight to take Daddy's soul, they'll say, 'This is Joan's daddy, and he was a perfect daddy. Take him straight to God.'" The sisters immediately became wonderful people in Chittister's young imagination, and they would grow in importance during her years in school, often providing a calm balance to the furor at home.

The story of her mother's homemade religious habit and its destruction contains, of course, an inherent regret. Loretta was not permitted to pursue her early dream. Chittister says her mother expressed that regret. "I thought she was right. It never translated to me as, 'I wish I'd never had you,' because we were very close, and I adored her.

"I was the hope of her life, there was no question. I was raised with a couple of mantras, and one was, 'You've got to be educated, Joan. You've got to be able to take care of yourself.' It took me some years to fill in the blanks after that: 'You have got to be able to take care of yourself. I know because I couldn't, and I married Dutch Chittister to give you a home.' Boy, I tell you, I made those connections in a big hurry."

The connections, however, were not made until she had grown beyond childhood. Her earlier years were a mix, in memory, of bitter and sweet, safety and danger. Early on, she learned some of the rhythm and patterns of the dysfunction she witnessed.

Dutch was extremely violent at times, and Chittister has vivid memories of seeing and hearing him strike her mother, who often bore visible bruises from the beatings. "Weekend after weekend. He couldn't handle drink and he couldn't stop drinking." Holidays could be especially brutal. The drinking and the violence went on, she said, "all our lives." Chittister grew to hate weekends and holidays.

Joan formally became a Chittister (a fact wrapped in a measure of ambiguity) the day her adoption by Dutch was finalized. It was preceded, she said, by "a lot of family talk over my head by aunts and uncles." One group, which included her mother, saw adoption as a good thing, because they then would both have the same name. The other group protested that the child was not a Chittister but a Dougherty, and that adoption wasn't necessary.

Her mother's view prevailed, and they ended up in Clearfield County Court on July 25, 1942, but not before six-year-old Joan put up a protest. "I can still feel the pressure of her hands on my two wrists," she said, extending her arms as she spoke. "I didn't want to get out of the car. I knew what was going on and I didn't want to get out of the car."

Although she finally did get out, she continued protesting. At one point Dutch picked her up and carried her. He asked her mother for all the change she had, grabbed the coins, headed to a vending machine, and started popping in coins and pulling levers. The youngster had never been offered so much candy at once, and the bribe worked to quiet her temporarily.

Once inside the courtroom, this effect quickly wore off. After the judge spoke to the adults, he turned his attention to the child. When he asked her how she felt about being adopted, little Joan burst into tears. "I don't want to be adopted," she remembers saying. "I don't want to be adopted."

The judge looked at the two adults and suggested that he and the child have a discussion in private. The two went into the judge's chambers where, she said, he asked her how she was doing, how she liked her new daddy, whether she thought he would be a good daddy. She answered yes to all the questions, and the judge, satisfied that all would be well in the long run, returned her to her parents and approved the adoption.

After signing the adoption papers, the judge instructed the parents to go to a nearby office to obtain a new birth certificate. That was a step too far for Loretta, and she refused. As the family story goes, Joan's mother said, "That's the damnedest, dumbest thing I've ever heard. What do you mean, a new birth certificate? You can't give anybody a new birth certificate. She's got a birth certificate."

The judge tried to explain that it would make it a lot easier in the future for the child if her name were officially registered as Chittister. Her mother was adamant. The child's name had been changed by the adoption, and there was no need for a new birth certificate.

Some three decades later, when the adult Chittister applied for a passport for her first trip out of the country, the passport office in Philadelphia responded that it couldn't issue one in that name because a person of that name didn't exist. She dug out the adoption papers, which say that she would "hereafter...be known by the name of JOAN CHITTISTER." She eventually received the passport, and ever since she has carried a copy of her adoption papers with her whenever she travels.

The name, however, never became a fully settled matter in her life. She remembers kids teasing her because of her name. Teachers, through graduate school, were unable to remember or pronounce it properly. As she grew older, the ambiguity of how she felt regarding the name was magnified by her complicated relationship with Dutch. At one point she was about to look into changing it, and her description of her feelings at that moment capture the swings of sentiment she still carries about her stepfather:

"I was getting ready to ask people how to do this. I was alone in my office, and I had my hand on the phone, ready to call somebody at the courthouse or anybody I could think of to begin this process of going back to my own name. And I could not do it. I put the phone down, and I said, 'This man raised me. He loved me outrageously, even though he had lots of problems in life himself. I can't do this to him. I simply can't. His love is the only thing I know that proves the gratuitous love of God.

"He loved me, and he didn't have to. He had nothing to do with me. We had the religion problem. We had the drink problem. We had every problem in the book, but he loved me. He was clear about it, and he was good. He had his weaknesses, but he was a good man: paid every bill, never missed a day of work, was as honest as the day is long, was generous beyond his means. He was a good man, but what an arm wrestling match it was."

Chittister made that decision as an adult, as one who had survived the bursts of drunken temper and come to some peace with an extremely generous assessment of his life. She had found her path as a nun, as a leader among women religious, and she was increasingly finding her voice as a writer. She had long ago won the arm wrestling match. Though Dutch mellowed a bit over time, he apparently would never find the degree of tranquility that his stepdaughter managed to achieve.

After Dutch and Loretta married, the three of them moved from DuBois to a series of small towns in and around Pittsburgh. There was plenty of post-war work for Dutch, an accomplished welder. Their home life, however, was a rolling series of upheavals.

Chittister is no longer certain of the succession of moves, but they lived briefly in three or four locations near Ambridge, including in Baden and Oakhill. "We moved from place to place because other people couldn't handle him," she says. The family faced eviction when Dutch's angry eruptions would lead to broken bottles and dishes, a noticeably bruised wife, and holes in the walls.

When they were living in Baden, Chittister was about five, and she came down with a severe case of scarlet fever. She remembers her mother soothing her with cold compresses and she recalls that her bed was surrounded by candles. "She's making such beautiful sounds and tones over me and taking care of me, but there's a tension with him going on in the room at the same time, and my mother says, 'Dutch we have to have electricity.'" The power had been turned off because the landlord was trying to force them out. Dutch eventually went downstairs to the landlord and, as the family lore has it, threatened to take the place apart if the landlord didn't turn the power back on. The electricity was restored, Joan got better, and the family then moved to a second-floor apartment on Merchant Street in Ambridge. They stayed there for nearly four years, from the time she was six until she was nearly ten years old.

Soon after Dutch and Loretta were married she became aware of the deep hostility the Chittisters harbored toward her and her daughter. Chittister said her mother had learned of a letter from her mother-in-law responding to an earlier letter from Dutch saying that he and Loretta had purchased a desk and other items for the child's bedroom. The letter from Dutch's mother said that he should not be spending money on a Catholic child, that he should not have married a Catholic to begin with, and that this was, after all, not his daughter. The letter said Dutch could feed Joan, but that Loretta should take care of her; that he should save his money for children he might father with Loretta.

One Christmas early in the marriage there arrived for the youngster a large box of gifts—books, toys, and clothes—from the Doughertys. Dutch wasn't having it. He told Loretta that he couldn't compete with a ghost. Whatever the child needed, he said, he would provide. He was enormously jealous of the memory of Daniel and suspicious of the Dougherty family. He made Loretta return the entire box of presents. In later years, Chittister remembers, Loretta began to insist on certain matters over Dutch's objections. The wider family learned that the child had become a voracious reader and she began receiving large, beautiful books each Christmas from Aunt Helen on the Dougherty side of the family. Though Chittister said she didn't see any of the Doughertys again until she was in high school, two of the books from Aunt Helen made a permanent impression. One was a child's book of poetry, and Chittister said she had memorized every poem in it. The second book was titled, *Little People Who Became Great*, by Laura Antoinette Large, a collection of short biographies of famous people first published in 1920.

That second book "just carved in my head that it didn't make any difference where you came from, what kind of life you had. It didn't make any difference. You had to do something worth being alive for, and I got that at seven, eight, nine, ten years old." As an older adult she still marvels at the "almost overwhelming" influence the book had on her.

The strains caused by religious differences, by Loretta's decision to leave the church, by Dutch's alcoholism and jealousies, by his mother's opposition to the marriage, and by the persistent fear of violence would have been enough to push any couple to the limit, but Ambridge added one more layer of discontent. Chittister says her mother hated the town. She had been raised in rural, green Pennsylvania. This was heavy-industry Pennsylvania, its air thick with dust and the smell of foundries and manufacturing plants, and here she was far from her family.

While the marriage survived in a sense, Chittister thinks the letter from the grandmother and the isolation from the Dougherty family were particularly significant in exacerbating an already difficult situation.

Other people in Dutch's family were more congenial. Years later, during a visit to the Chittister family on her way home from Pennsylvania State University, where she was doing doctoral studies, Chittister was treated with admiration and acceptance. She was greeted by an aunt who had become the matriarch of the family. Other relatives were called in, and as the clan gathered, the aunt instructed one of her sons to retrieve a large manila envelope from a drawer. When Chittister opened it she found that the aunt had been clipping every story she could find about her niece. (This was long before the age of home computers.)

"I said, 'What in God's name are you doing with these? Why do you have these?'"

Her aunt responded, "This is family. We're very proud of these."

"The tears just rolled down my face."

The aunt who saved the clippings was Dutch's sister, the oldest of seven siblings.

While Dutch apparently found ways to keep peace with the landlords on Merchant Street, the tension within the marriage kept escalating. One point of contention was that Loretta insisted on enrolling Joan in a Catholic school over Dutch's strong objections. Other strains, generalized in Chittister's memory, were constant. She recalls a car ride during which an angry Dutch, yelling about something, began speeding recklessly. She remembers her mother screaming for him to stop until he finally did. She got out of the car with Joan and got back in only after much pleading from Dutch and promises to Loretta that he would drive responsibly.

In Ambridge, the relationship between her mother and stepfather apparently became so frayed, and her mother's sense of foreboding so great, that Loretta began hiding money under carpets and included two addresses with the hidden cash: the address of the generous Aunt Helen in New Jersey and the address of the local convent. "She would move the money from week to week or month to month so he wouldn't find it," Chittister recalls. The instructions from her mother were clear, she says. "If anything happened to her, no matter what hour of the day or night, I was to take that money, get those addresses, and get out of that house. I was not to allow any Chittisters to take me. I was simply to go to the sisters and say, 'Call my Aunt Helen. Put me on a bus. I have the money.'"

The child was about eight when her mother gave her those instructions. They kept her awake at night, as she tried to imagine exactly how she would accomplish such a mission. If the worst occurred at night, she was to "go down and get a ticket if you can't get to the sisters. You will have the money for the ticket. Have them put you on a bus and call this number."

The youngster knew where the money was at all times. She knew the addresses and telephone numbers. Lying in bed at night she would wonder about how she would be able to get from the bus station in New Jersey to Aunt Helen's home. She wondered what it meant when they said Aunt Helen lived in "the Oranges" in New Jersey. And what if Aunt Helen wasn't home when she arrived?

At the same time, she knew she would be able to do it, had to do it. There was no alternative. She and her mother were alone. There were no other family members nearby, no long-time friends or neighbors to call on. "I knew I could do it, and I knew somehow or other that there was an aura around me, that somehow or other I lived in this little bubble," Chittister said, recalling that time in her life. "That might come with being an only child, especially if you don't know family and there is no grandmother's house for Sunday meals. If there is none of that stuff— there is no dog or bird or anything—you're on your own and you have got to be able to pull it off. I was cautious, and I would lie in bed and try to figure it out. Where do you go to get cabs? Who would you ask? How would you know you were being taken to the right place? I thought it all through, every single thing. How would I know if I should go right or left? I would think it out. I'd get it set and I'd rehearse it to myself."

It was an unusual burden for an eight- or nine-year-old and one she believes connects her, at least on a level of some understanding and empathy, with abused and abandoned children. She reacts deeply to their circumstances. The question that always occurs to her when she encounters stories of abuse and abandonment is, "Who lets them know, 'We know you're terrified?' I am no good with children at all but I have a real feeling for them, for the child who is abandoned in the middle of the crowd."

For years, she remained that abandoned child in the middle of the crowd, the child alone with her secrets. "I was ashamed. I didn't want people to know what kind of a house we had. I knew it was wrong and there was nothing anybody could do. I knew that. We were trapped. That was it."

Trapped, yet trying to convince herself even as an adult that "it wasn't all bad." It is the kind of claim that kept poking through the telling of this tale of terror, attempts even at the distance of decades to overlay the story with some degree of normalcy. For instance, during a brief talk at the event of the opening of her archives in April 2014 at Mercyhurst University, she spoke of the time her family moved to Erie. It was the way she normally spoke of it, as if it were nothing out of the ordinary, a move to a new job for her stepfather. There was no hint, in that moment and before that small gathering of mostly long-time friends and community members, that the move to Erie had been a desperate escape from the constant threat of violence. In fact, in one of her books she reflects on being an only child and paints a rather idyllic picture of such a child as one who is "center of the universe, the one carrier of all the hope in the family, the one mirror of a parent's life, the only complete picture of themselves that a parent has." You get all of their attention, she writes, and they give you all of theirs.[3] None of that is untrue, and she was, indeed, her mother's hope. As a description of her own circumstances, though, it falls short. Somewhat like a painting in the primitive style, it lacks shadow and complexity. Still, in the context of the point being made, the shadows and complexities would have been far too much to go into.

Over the course of our conversations, however, attempts to laminate the narrative with a degree of regularity, to blur or smooth away the harsher aspects of the story failed. The truth was that as a child she had experienced ceaseless fear.

"Every day wasn't tragic. The real problem in my life was that every day could turn into a tragedy, and you never knew which day it would be," Chittister said. "So that was always hanging over me. It might not rain but the clouds were there, and you knew it was going to happen again. I never remember saying to myself, 'This is wonderful. It's all over. This will never happen again.'"

The fear that the worst could happen at any moment, pervasive as it was, seems to have become particularly acute just before the escape from Ambridge. That year in school she recalls that a neighbor, the mother of a child Chittister played with regularly, showed up at the classroom door one day. On seeing her, Chittister instantly called out: "What happened to my mother?" The neighbor and Sr. Patricia Maria assured her that nothing had happened to her mother. The neighbor was simply delivering something to her son and had come to the wrong classroom.

Chittister traces some of her attraction to the sisters and religious life to those years. In hindsight, she believes the sisters knew more than they let on about what was going on at her home. Her mother's flight from danger obviously involved some planning with the sisters, and Chittister remembers them being especially kind to her.

She believes those years had a strong influence on the formation of her spirituality. When she was a child there was a glow-in-the-dark rendering of Jesus walking on water hung on a wall at the foot of her bed. It became a source of great consolation for her. "That picture, the whole notion that in that storm, Jesus was there and things would be

---

3. Joan Chittister, *In Search of Belief* (Liguori, MO: Ligouri/Triumph, 1999), 69.

all right," affected her deeply, she says. "I didn't have to be afraid. I was going to make it somehow."

An elementary school teacher who read Bible stories to her class at recess also made an enormous impression. "She would ask us questions about the people in those stories. I was in second grade and I adored her, and that was all I wanted, those Bible stories. I could have gone to school my whole life and just had people tell me Bible stories, and I swear I would have gotten the same education I got anyway."

At some point she began to view the situation at home as her cross. "Somehow or other I was supposed to bear this cross and I'd be all right. The cross always has another side to it. You go through the cross and on the other side is where you are supposed to be."

From a distance of nearly seventy years it is easy to imagine Chittister's insights into human nature, the passionate concern for the oppressed, especially women, and her understanding of the Christian mystery and a life in God as constituting the other side of the cross.

In the spring of 1946, however, salvation meant getting away from Dutch. When she and her mother arrived in Erie, they stayed for a while with one of Loretta's nephews. As far as Chittister knows, there was no contact between her parents, though her stepfather was aware that Loretta had relatives in Erie. They had been in there less than two months and the school year was nearly over when Dutch showed up. She was coming out of St. Patrick's School, where her mother had enrolled her. "I'm running down the steps with a couple of kids and—Jesus!—there he is. He said, 'Hi Joan. Are you going to talk to me?' I said, 'Hi, Dad,' and I kept on going, I was running like hell, trying to get home to tell my mother. Of course he's following me . . . He's following me every step of the way."

She remembers trying to throw him off track by going down wrong streets and through yards. "But I'm a little kid, just ten years old. I get home and warn her, 'He's coming. He found me.' My mother says, 'That's all right. Don't be afraid. It's all right.'"

Her mother and stepfather eventually went inside and she recalls that they talked for hours.

She remembers sitting on a ledge and looking out over Presque Isle Bay, a body of water along the city's northern edge separated from Lake Erie by a naturally occurring isthmus. "They're inside for hours. It's starting to get dark and then, all of a sudden, I hear my mother calling me, and I go up the hill. I don't see him and she calls me into our room. She pulls me over to her and she says, 'Your father wants to come here to be with us.'

"I say, 'Okay.'

"She says, 'How do you feel about that?'

"I say, 'It's your marriage.'" Chittister remembers feeling that she didn't have a right to weigh in on the matter even though she opposed the reunion. "I didn't want this to happen."

Her mother assured her that things would change and told her she thought it would be better for her if she were part of a family. Chittister recalls telling her, "Don't do it for me."

She believes it was that same night that Dutch approached her and tried to reassure her. "He said, 'Snooks, I'm sorry. It'll be better. We'll be better. We'll be all right.'

"I said, 'I hope so.' It lasted a year, I guess. The great peace lasted about a year."

The Chittisters soon moved to a room in one of the worst sections of Erie. It was just after the war, and with men returning and lots of new, young families starting out on their own, apartments were at a premium. They lived in one room for her fifth- and sixth-grade years and then moved to a home at 23rd and Holland where, it seems, she had some of her happiest moments as a child. Though in recent years, 23rd and Holland has deteriorated and become, in Joan's words, "the drug center of Erie," back in the late 1940s it was a lively and well-kept predominately German neighborhood. She recalls it as a place with lots of trees and other kids to play with. "It was a nice little neighborhood. We had a yard, and that was a big thing."

Dutch did little in the way of disciplining her; her mother was the one who established rules for her. They were few, and in her recollection the disputes over such matters were rare. "I kept those rules. I was not a brat. I was not defiant, and I adored my mother. She asked very little of me, and I could negotiate most of it."

The closeness between mother and daughter undoubtedly was the product of countless influences, but part of it also had to do with the kind of conspiracy for mutual protection evidenced when Loretta hid the money and addresses for Joan should things go terribly wrong.

Such possibilities eventually arose again in Erie. The calm, as Joan noted, lasted for about a year. By age twelve she had learned a technique for keeping herself awake at night. She remembers having figured out that if she sat on the floor of her bedroom with her back against one wall and her feet propped up on the bed, she could remain awake. "I'm one of these people who feel everything has to be perfect to sleep, and that would keep me awake." She stayed up to get between them if he came home drunk and in a rage. She said she stepped between them for years. "I used to be afraid he would murder her. I was terribly afraid."

Chittister believed that her role regarding her mother "was to take care of her and make sure she'd be all right." There were moments of calm and even happiness. "When he wasn't drinking, he was kind of a solemn guy. He needed the drink, and if he only had so much drink, he was pleasant and fun. He played the mandolin and loved a good party. He loved kids. He was very good with kids. He was a good man but, boy! As far as he was concerned, he didn't have a problem."

She somehow maintains those thoughts of "a good man" while simultaneously holding memories of scenes in which she witnessed, just prior to her teen years, the deep bitterness that had developed between Loretta and Dutch and the disdain that her mother in one violent incident expressed toward her husband. During lunch in November 2011 in a sandwich shop a few blocks from her home in Erie, Joan spoke of the one time her stepfather came directly at her. Recalling that time, she set her jaw and took on that same faraway gaze that would come over her when she revisited that troubled era of her life.

Her parents had been fighting near an open second-floor window on a hot summer night in Erie. Dutch was hitting Loretta and Joan was trying to get between them, as she had so often tried to do. Dutch grabbed her arm and shoved her. She "would have gone through that second-floor window," she said, if her mother had not grabbed her and pulled her back, while screaming at her husband. Joan remembers then getting behind Dutch, picking up a heavy ceramic pitcher, and pulling it way back, preparing to strike him in the back of the head when her mother called out: "Joan! Don't! He isn't worth it!"

In the aftermath, her mother sat her down and in short bursts put the explanation in stark terms. Joan wasn't to think about doing anything like that, and it wasn't out of concern for Dutch, but for her own sake. "They'll just send you to juvenile detention, and you're too smart for that," her mother said. "You have more to do with your life. They'll only send you to the detention center."

The hellish childhood, she is convinced, contained a grace of desperation. "God was my salvation and refuge, everything the psalm was saying. I wasn't going to daily Mass because some nun had told me to. Nobody ever told me to go to daily Mass." The trouble at home moved her, precociously, in an interior way toward God. "There is no doubt I was a very spiritual young woman. Spiritual but not pious. Though I went to daily Mass, I did not see that as piety. That was literally my strength, as if I were an adult. I didn't even know why I was there, but I knew I couldn't not be there."

No other outlet existed. She didn't want to further burden what she saw as her already overburdened parents. Indeed, in hindsight it is easy to imagine the futility of even trying to consult her parents, caught up as they were in vicious cycles of violence. She never told anyone else of what she was living through, her own burden. She didn't say a word of it to relatives or friends, teachers or priests, anyone. In her understanding at that time, God alone knew what she knew.

The events of her early years forever colored her disposition in other ways. "Death, loss, fear, loneliness, determination, independence, initiative," were the words she used in a string to describe how she "grew up very fast." She lived with the reality of death from the time she was a toddler. "I'm comfortable with it, and loss I take for granted. That's probably the darkest side of my personality. I expect things to go bad, but I don't dwell on them, and I don't plan that way. I don't think that way, meaning it's never stopped me in my tracks. It doesn't paralyze me."

One of the items she inherited from her birth father was a little prayer book he owned. "There was a verse in it that I memorized at about the age of eight and I carried all my life: 'I have only just a minute, only sixty seconds in it, forced upon me, didn't choose it, can't deny it, must not lose it.' That's what I remember of it now, seventy years later. That whole notion that whatever is now may not be sixty seconds from now, get ready for it. It's out there. It's all right. That probably is the single, greatest lesson. This too will pass away. However good or bad, this too will pass away."

She says she has long been comfortable with understanding that loss and change are part of the process of life. As a result, she adds, "I don't rest anywhere, I don't come down with any kind of a sense that this will always be. I just don't." Even the community with which she has spent her life, certainly an example of constancy, has also been, paradoxically, an example of the process of change she has come to view as integral to life in all of its phases.

It is significant, perhaps, that as she aged, her expectations did not emanate exclusively from "the darkest side" of her personality. Even as a youngster, when she was becoming so regularly acquainted with the reality of loss and change resulting from bleak circumstances, she also experienced a number of bright—arguably even life-forming and life-changing—patches along the way.

Any sweet memories of childhood would include Sr. Patricia Maria, a Sister of St. Joseph, her fourth-grade teacher in Ambridge. She was the sister who, one day when Joan accidentally spilled ink on a new skirt (Catholic school girls didn't wear uniforms at the time), quietly took her aside, gave her a coat to wear, and took the skirt to the convent. Chittister said she was terrified to tell her mother because it would only mean causing more trouble at home. The skirt came back from the convent later in the day all cleaned and pressed. Sr. Patricia Maria assured the youngster that she wouldn't have to bother her mother with that story.

If Sr. Patricia Maria was especially compassionate, she was also aware of a budding superior intellect in the class. Chittister remembers with great fondness the arrangement that her teacher made with her. One day Sr. Patricia Maria took the youngster and placed her in the last seat of the last row. Then she had a bookcase filled with books set up in the back of the classroom by Joan's desk. Finally came the best part, a separate deal with young Joan: whenever she completed an assignment she was allowed to read any of the books. By the time she made the escape with her mother to Erie, she had read through a fair number of children's classics.

"She just kept that book shelf packed, and she said, 'But you may not tell any of the other children what you're doing.' She didn't have any special education programs, but she knew she needed one. So she decided that books were my thing." Sr. Patricia Maria kept the bookcase loaded and Joan waited, especially for geography assignments, because she could always finish them quickly and then grab the latest book she was reading.

Once in Erie, she told her mother she wouldn't go to school "unless she could find my sisters, and my sisters were the Sisters of St. Joseph." In Ambridge the St. Joseph's sisters were from Baden, a town in western Pennsylvania near Pittsburgh. "They were a dear lot, friendly, funny. When I came to Erie, I had teachers from the same order but a different community."

At the time, she said, she had every intention of becoming a Sister of St. Joseph. But her school experience in Erie from the end of fourth grade through the end of eighth grade was anything but pleasant. School in Erie did not present the same kind of sanctuary she had known in Ambridge. She was the new kid in town and the new kid in school. She said she experienced bullying and rejection. "If you were the odd person out, getting in was very difficult. It taught you a lot as a child, but it also confused you a lot as a child. I'm in a new city. We are trying to build a renewed family. Nothing is stable in my life. Nothing is familiar. Nothing is the same. I had no niche anywhere."

She went from being singled out as the brightest child in class with special privileges to being the outsider, a misfit. Those years for her, she said, were good years academically but not socially. She took piano lessons from the sisters at their mother house in Erie. But otherwise, except for one or two sisters, she felt that she "never got close to their lives."

The isolation she felt was apparently a class issue as well as a matter of being the new kid in town. Most of the children in her school at the time were "from the best parts of town...old cathedral families, and I was the outsider looking in." What made it worse was that for several years her family lived in cramped quarters and not in one of the best parts of town. "I couldn't take any kids home. There was no place.

We lived in one room, so there was no home to take them to. There was no yard to play in."

The teenager made it clear to her mother that she did not want to follow the Cathedral family kids to high school. At the same time, her mother was insisting on a Catholic school and Dutch was strongly resisting. "He was not going to pay a penny for Catholic education, absolutely not. That's why we had public schools. 'She can go to any public school for free, and I am not paying to send her to a Catholic school.'"

Hearing that declaration, Chittister became determined to go to a Catholic school even though she didn't know where and had no money.

She was in seventh grade when she got a job at the local YWCA handling registration when people showed up at the pool. "I gave them towels and took their dimes for their towels. Then, when all the kids had been registered, I could swim as much as I wanted. So I could use the pool, and I didn't have to pay a membership fee to belong, and I made money."

When she was in eighth grade, she got a job tending to a child for a local family who put some money away for her. "So I had a little money. I figured I could pay my way through school." But she didn't figure out where she would go to school until it was nearly too late. It was the end of August of her eighth-grade year and she had not yet enrolled anywhere when an acquaintance mentioned St. Benedict Academy.

Joan knew nothing about the place. She and her mother investigated. The tuition—she recalls it as $75 a year at the time—was affordable. She enrolled, and within two weeks of the start of school she felt perfectly at home. She was among kids from Erie's East Side, the section of town historically inhabited by the working poor and middle class. It was the Benedictine side of town. It was where they first set up their monastery and school and where they've remained in ministry to the present day.

In those first weeks, Joan's academic star began to shine again. She was in an algebra class when she was called out by a sister who was her English teacher. The sister wanted to know about an essay this new student had handed in. "I don't remember what it was. It certainly wasn't a 'what I did on my summer vacation' paper, but it was a get-to-know-you essay." The sister was convinced that someone else had written it. She asked if her mother had actually done the work or helped her write it. Chittister kept responding that she was the only one who had worked on it.

The teacher persisted, asking if anyone had dictated, wanting to know—yes or no—if Joan had written every word of the essay. "Yes," Joan answered, "I wrote that paper."

If that was the case, said her teacher, Joan was to show up after school in the "J" (for journalism) room in the basement because she was going to become a member of the journalism club. Joan had intended to sign up for the basketball team that night, but she went to the journalism room instead. "And that was it. I lived there, writing articles, making sure that the paper got out. At first I was editor of this, and then I was editor of that. Then I did this column, then I did a humor column, and then I did an editorial—you know, the whole show. Before long I was editor in chief, and I was handling everything."

Eventually, she was spending long days at school, sometimes until 7:30 at night, when the sisters would all leave to go into the monastery, which was attached to the school, and chant Compline. Often she would walk the fifteen blocks home to 23rd and Holland Streets, saving up the bus money her mother had given her so she could stop for treats with friends while walking to school. Some days, when the student paper deadline was nearing, she would stay with Sr. Mary Jude Sarifinski until nine and ten at night. Those nights she would regularly take the bus home.

Her love of the school and of the journalism program and other extracurricular activities began to run up against a harsh reality. The time needed to be editor in chief at the school newspaper was making it difficult to keep up with her job at the YWCA.

When Sr. Mary Jude said she wanted her to stay and work on the paper at nights, Joan finally had to tell her that she wouldn't be able to because she had a job. The sister pressed her. Why would she have a job when she was going to school?

Joan told her she needed it to pay for tuition. "Sr. Mary Jude didn't blink. I didn't get any, 'Well, your mother and dad will pay your tuition.' She just acted like it was very normal information. She said, 'Oh, it's for tuition?'

"'Yes,' I answered.

"'Well, you just wait here. We'll talk about it in a minute.'"

She left and came back with an offer. Joan could have a job right there at the school, cleaning the J room and the basement from the end of the school day at three in the afternoon until three-thirty and then begin her work for the journalism club. On the spot, she had a work-study program that would cover her tuition.

That evening she went home and told her mother she had a job that would cover things. "What I didn't tell anybody is that it didn't cover lunch. So I stopped going to lunch. I decided I didn't need to go to lunch because I didn't have any money to pay for lunch. Now I didn't have any money at all except bus money," which her mother provided. Dutch would not put up a cent for costs associated with Catholic school, and he would not allow her mother to work. He told her that if she started working, he would quit. Her place was at home.

It wasn't long after the agreement was reached with the newspaper monitor that Sr. Rita O'Sullivan, who was in charge of the lunchroom, realized that Joan was no longer coming to lunch. Sr. Rita confronted the teenager, and Joan told her she was "just around," that she didn't need lunch and "would just as soon read."

Sr. Rita finally got Joan to admit that she didn't have money for lunch. The nun left and consulted with the principal, Sr. Theophane. She returned in a little while with another offer: if Joan could clean the stairs up to the third floor, lunch would be provided. Joan quickly agreed, and began showing up in the cafeteria for lunch.

"So I go in every day now, and Sr. Rita, the old Irish biology teacher, knows that this little kid is coming through with no money. I take a little bit of this and a little bit of that. Rita picks up the tray and goes down that line and says, 'You can't live on that' Bang! Here's this and here's that. Every day, there is something extra on my tray. Every single day there is something extra."

The sisters realized that Joan was staying at school through the dinner hour most days, so they began to set aside food for her from the convent and leave it in the cafeteria. After she'd finished cleaning hallways and stairways, she was told to go into the cafeteria and pick up the food they had left.

"So I've got it all handled, now. All bases are covered. I've got tuition. I've got lunch, and they'll even bring me a sandwich at night when I'm working. They'll bring something from the convent. So I just loved them."

Often when she stayed late at school, as she was cleaning or working on the paper, she would hear the sisters next door chanting evening prayer. The sounds resonated deeply. These women had taken care of her, recognized her talent, found a way for her to do this work that she loved. This was a place of peace and tranquility, a place of respite from the fear and the chaos she had known for so long. This was it. Home.

THREE

THE MONASTERY

They may not have been aware of it, but in their kindness to the new student the Benedictine sisters had sealed the deal. Before her freshman year of high school was completed Chittister knew she would become one of them. The moment couldn't arrive soon enough. At the end of her first year, Chittister rang the prioress's bell at the school. "How did I know you weren't supposed to ring the prioress's bell? They were forever ringing bells, and I saw they had a card there with the sisters' bell numbers, so I just went and hit '1.' That was the prioress."

Mother Sylvester, the prioress, came out of her office. She looked a bit bewildered at seeing this youngster in front of her. Chittister got right to the point. "I said, 'Mother, I would like to talk to you about being a Benedictine.'"

She didn't get beyond that. The prioress asked her age, and when Joan said fifteen, the nun told her that the order did not take girls younger than sixteen.

Chittister went back to classes at the academy and the following April showed up once more at the monastery. Mother Sylvester again answered the door. Chittister announced that she was now sixteen. The nun, who by this time knew Chittister, looked puzzled; she had obviously forgotten the previous year's encounter. "Last year, I came to ask you about being a Benedictine," Chittister said. "You told me I had to be sixteen." She explained that she had just had a birthday and wanted to talk about entering the community.

The response was a shock. Mother Sylvester told her once more that she would be unable to join the community.

"I said, 'Why not?'

"She said, 'Because you're an only child. We don't take only children.'

"I said 'Why not?'

"She said, 'Because some day your mother is going to need you, and it's not fair to her and it's not fair to you. No, dear, we do not take only children.'

"I was stunned. I just stood there. She didn't say another word. She simply turned to go back in her office and closed the door in my face. I finished whatever I was doing. Then I ran all the way to 23rd and Holland, as fast as my legs could take me."

She wanted to get there before Dutch got home from work so that she could tell her mother about her conversation with Mother Sylvester. She was worried about her father's reaction to her desire to become a nun. When Loretta heard why the Benedictines had turned her down, she told her daughter to call the monastery and request an appointment with Mother Sylvester.

That evening, Loretta and Joan were led into the large parlor of the monastery on 9th Street. Loretta asked Mother Sylvester if the child's understanding of the conversation that afternoon was correct. Mother Sylvester confirmed the order's rule, one that, from her point of view, was considerate of the family. Loretta had a different view.

She told Mother Sylvester that it wasn't Joan's fault that she was an only child and that, as her mother, she did not want her daughter's life affected by that fact. She said her child was free do whatever she wished and that her ambitions had nothing to do with her mother. "I did not have her to use her as a domestic nurse when she got older," Loretta told Mother Sylvester. "She has a life to live."

She said if the order did not want Joan in the community for other reasons, she could understand. But she also put Mother Sylvester on notice: "When that kid makes up her mind to do something, she does it. Now she's going to enter somewhere, and it does not have to be here, but she's going to enter because if she wants that, that's where she's going."

Mother Sylvester asked Loretta if she meant all of that, and Loretta assured her that she did. "I don't want my life hung around her neck," Loretta said. She wanted her daughter to be happy.

The prioress responded, "Well, the entrance date is September 8th. Maybe we should begin to talk."

"That was it," said Chittister. "I wound up here, and the rest is history."

She finished the school year and took up a hectic schedule that summer. Most days began with seven o'clock Mass, followed by a catch-up Spanish class she needed. Immediately after class she would walk a few blocks to 10th and State Streets to a florist shop, open it for the day at 8:30, and work there until noon. At noon she would walk to 10th and Parade Streets to an ice cream and sandwich shop, where she began work at one in the afternoon. She would leave the ice cream shop at five and run to 27th and Parade to work at a diner, where her day ended at eleven at night.

Chittister worked the three jobs to make money to buy a list of items she needed for entrance to the order. It was part of the ritual of the day, and Dutch, who had provided no money for Catholic schooling, was not about to pay her way into the convent. Dutch had prohibited her mother from working, so his was the only income the family had. In fact, Chittister said that she never told Dutch her plans about the convent until just before she entered.

On the list to be purchased were black shoes ("They were a big deal"), a place setting of silverware ("Damask Rose was the pattern that I bought") and blankets (purchased on a layaway plan at the local Sears & Roebuck store). She also had to purchase luggage and a big steamer trunk.

Whatever time was left in the summer was spent in normal teenage pursuits, including days at the local beach and going out with a boyfriend named Bobby. She had dated boys from the time she was fourteen, making sure in those early years to stop holding hands a few blocks from home because she knew Dutch was worried about her going out with boys. In this matter, her mother intervened sternly on her behalf and let Dutch know that what Joan was doing "was perfectly normal." That seemed to have put the subject to rest. The teenage Joan was free to hold hands and to invite boys to the house.

As the summer of her sixteenth year wore on, however, she had to take the first tangible step on the transition to life in a monastery. She had to tell the boy she was dating. "I was entering in September and now it was late July," says Chittister. "He was making plans for the next year and my mother said, 'Don't you think it's time you tell Bob that you aren't going to be there next year? Are you going to wait and let him find out on the first day of school?'"

Soon after that conversation, the two teenagers spent a day at the beach "and at some point over the baloney sandwiches I said, 'I'm entering the convent in September.'"

The shocked young man answered, "You're kidding!"

She told him she wasn't. He tried to persuade her to wait. She said she saw no reason to delay the decision. She didn't want to wait any longer to start her new life. "That was really the conversation. It got very quiet after that. It wasn't much of a fun date after all. If I remember correctly, he took me home. He wasn't going to waste any more time either."

As she notes in a history of the community that is highly autobiographical, the Erie Benedictines that Chittister joined in 1952 were fashioned by "the rigor of routine."[1] Religious life, which would undergo such drastic changes over the course of the next two decades, was at the time, and had been for years, "marked by five basic characteristics: it was reflective, regular, focused, clear, and effective."[2]

Women involved in that monastic routine were, on most practical counts, only a few degrees removed from their married and childbearing sisters of that era. They cooked, they cleaned, they had no personal money, they looked after the children in schools and, "at the highest levels of ecclesiastical jurisprudence, they lived at the mercy of male superiors," Chittister writes. "The church, the courts, and the family all gave men control of a woman's property, her intellectual development, her personal behavior, and her public participation."

In one significant respect other than celibacy, the nuns were different from most other women of that era. They lived in a world of ideas—encountering on a daily basis scripture, the psalms, writings of church fathers and other great thinkers of the tradition—and they went to college. That was a significant marker for many of them, even if they were required to take classes around the demands of classroom teaching. They were regularly assigned to teach in the order's schools before they had earned their full degrees. More than a few times in interviews, sisters of a certain generation in the Erie community mentioned the opportunity for education that they otherwise would not have had as one of the motivations for entering religious life. Though Chittister's early life was an extreme example, it also was not uncommon to hear that women who joined had arrived from abusive situations or dysfunctional or poor families. The Benedictines had a reputation in Erie as the "blue collar" community. The "Mercies," sisters of the Mercy order, were viewed as the next step up the ladder, and the "Josies" or St. Joseph sisters, occupied the top rung of the socio-economic ladder.

While those general perceptions may not precisely represent the reality of that time, it is not surprising that Chittister found herself comfortably at home with the other students at St. Benedict Academy and determined to join the order. She immediately found acceptance at the

---

1. Joan Chittister, *The Way We Were: A Story of Conversion and Renewal* (Maryknoll, NY: Orbis Books, 2005), 18.
2. Ibid., 19.

high school and a welcoming community in the convent. "I kind of dropped into a situation with people I really loved," she says. "I wasn't doing penance. I didn't go into religious life to do penance or to give things up. I really saw it as a place of peace and harmony and goodness."

Sometime in the week or two before she would enter the convent, Chittister left on a cocktail table in the family living room some brochures and other materials that made clear her intent to enter the convent. It was her way of communicating with Dutch.

She walked in on him some time after that and said, "'Dad, that's my stuff and I want you to know I'm entering St. Benedict's on Monday.'

"He said, 'I know.' There was no conversation. That was it."

Loretta told her at some later date that Dutch let her know the Friday before Joan entered that he would not be going to work that Monday but would be accompanying them instead, unless Loretta said no. She told him she would never say no, and neither would Joan. He said to Loretta, "I told them my kid was going away on Monday and I couldn't come in to work."

Early on the day she was to enter, Chittister met a good friend and the two girls attended Mass. On the way home she stopped at a vending machine and "bought a fistful of candy to get rid of the last money I had." She returned home and finished packing.

Later that morning, packed and ready to go, she came into the family living room to find Dutch, in his Sunday best brown suit, with her mother. "I went over to him and I put my arms around him and he grabbed me, he just hugged me so hard. I said to him, 'Daddy, I promise you, if I don't like it, I'll leave.'

"And he held me really tight and he said, 'Goddam it, I hope you don't.' Meaning, I hope you don't like it. And he was crying. I'll go to the grave with that memory in my heart."

He accompanied them to the monastery and waited outside in the car until the ritual of being taken into the convent ended. That was to be his practice over a number of years when he drove Loretta to visit her daughter. Most of the time Dutch would sit in the car. On the occasions when he met the sisters they were cordial and gracious to him. "The nuns were so kind to him, they were so kind to her," said Chittister. "As much as he wanted to hate them, it was pretty impossible."

Chittister entered the order on September 8, 1952, the youngest of a class of seven postulants who were beginning their education in the utter predictability of religious life: after getting up at at five, there was a half hour of Lauds, followed by a half hour of spiritual reading, a half hour to forty-five minutes at Mass, and a half hour of breakfast before heading off to school.

On that first day she and her mother entered the monastery through the front door on 9th Street. It was a big deal, because ordinary kids didn't go through the front door. They had to enter through a porch at the back of the building.

Much of the initial portion of the first day is a blur in her memory. The soon-to-be postulants and their families were ushered into a large parlor, and if there was a program of any sort, she doesn't recall the details. Before long, the new arrivals were taken off to a different part of the monastery to get dressed in the postulant's habit: a little veil and a cape, shoes, hose and a dress, all black. Then they were taken back into the parlor to say goodbye to their parents.

It was around noon when, with the goodbyes completed, the seven postulants moved off in a line down a corridor that separated the monastery from the high school, past rooms along the corridor that had large windows and past refectory doors that had stained-glass windows at the top. "What I remember about that day is that I was the youngest, and therefore I came at the end of the line. They were walking along in front of me and the shadows were bouncing along with each kid—bing, bing, bing, bing—and I looked at all those shadows and said to myself, 'I'm going to be following these kids around for the rest of my life.' We laughed about it for years, whenever anybody asks, 'Does anyone here remember anything that happened on that day?'"

That evening is clearer in her recollection. The girls were assigned to a dormitory, and for the first time in her memory she went to bed without the fear that arguments and violence might erupt nearby at any moment. She experienced "phenomenal relief, phenomenal, phenomenal relief. And happiness," she said. "And, the unmentioned emotion," she adds, pausing long seconds before continuing, "was my fear for my mother and my shame for having left her. I really struggled with that for a long time. Could I possibly be happy without her being happy?"

That night she looked at the ceiling and listened to the quiet and realized: "I had never felt that kind of security. I had never felt that safe. I was literally surrounded, you know. I was surrounded by people. I wasn't alone, for the first time in my life. And these were good people, and there was nothing to be afraid of."

That feeling would be accompanied by an awareness that "it wasn't so much security as it was certainty that the world...that this world had a genuine stability to it, that my energies were not going to have to go into protecting myself from it, enduring it, fighting it, being controlled by it."

She had only six weeks to enjoy that security and to get used to the routine before the stability of her new world was suddenly upended. It began in late October with what she thought was ordinary soreness in her back caused by lifting heavy boxes of chapel candles in the basement of the monastery with other postulants.

She woke up three or four days later with a stiff back and went to see the novice mistress. She asked for liniment. The novice mistress, she discovered, wasn't about to pamper her charges. She dismissed the request. The soreness got worse, and a few days later, as Chittister was getting out of bed, she attempted to stand and fell over. She couldn't hold herself up. She woke up the girl who slept on the bed next to hers by calling out to her, saying, "I can't get up."

She stayed in bed as the rest of the monastery went into the routine of the day. It was several hours later that the novice mistress showed up to see what was going on. Joan told her she was having trouble walking.

The novice mistress left and came back a little later to tell her she had an afternoon appointment with an orthopedic specialist. The community had no car at that time, so to get to the doctor Joan had to walk, accompanied by an older sister, more than nine blocks. "Every step, I'm more and more tired. There is something wrong. My back is killing me."

They arrived at the doctor's office at around two o'clock and waited for more than an hour. When she finally was called in to be examined, things went quickly. First one doctor, then a second, and then a third. Joan was sitting on the side of the bed and one of the doctors told her to lie down. He delivered the news quickly: "You have polio."

"That room spun. Everything went orange and spun. They were talking to me. I could see their faces and I was hanging on with everything in me, just hanging on."

Chittister, at sixteen, had become one of the 52,897 people in the United States who contracted the disease in 1952.[3] That year represented the height of the epidemic that had held parents in terror for their children's safety since the first reported cases in the United States in 1843. The disease cycled in waves every few years in increasing severity and seemed to peak each time in the summer and fall. Of the total cases reported in 1952, 21,269 were described as paralytic. In such cases the severity of nerve damage varied, but it could be so extensive that it would impair the function of limbs and, if the virus paralyzed muscles in the chest, could hinder breathing. This was the form of polio that Chittister had; her left leg and right arm had been affected and would be impaired to a certain degree for the rest of her life. She still has difficulty with stairs, can't walk long distances, and can have trouble breathing.

------

3. Figures compiled by The Historical Medical Library of The College of Physicians of Philadelphia.

No one knows how she contracted the disease. One bit of lore attached to the story suggests that she may have been exposed to the virus while eating an apple plucked from a tree that grew in an area where postulants were permitted to walk and read while professed members of the community were engaged in other activities. The reality is probably more prosaic, with fewer Edenic overtones. At the time the cause of polio was somewhat mysterious, but the disease was thought to be contagious and there was widespread fear of shared recreational facilities, for instance, especially swimming pools. In fact, the disease is highly contagious and is spread person-to-person.

The year Chittister was diagnosed with polio was the same year Dr. Jonas Salk developed a safe and effective vaccine. After extensive trials, the vaccine was made widely available to the American public. In the space of a decade, the disease was virtually eliminated in the United States.

It is unknown, of course, whether Chittister's superiors at the time recognized in the polio episode a foreshadowing of the fierce will and determination that would mark some of Chittister's later years in the community. Once diagnosed, she was told that she would be taken by ambulance to a nearby hospital. The postulant, newly arrived at a dream that she had held in general terms for most of her young life and had pursued in very specific terms for the preceding two years, would have none of it.

She insisted that the sister who had accompanied her to the doctor's office help her get dressed. The older nun at first balked, saying that an ambulance was on the way. "I can't just disappear. I can't do this," said Chittister. She told the nun, at least seven years her senior, that she was not getting in any ambulance and finally convinced her to give her the clothes. The nun "was terribly rattled, and she didn't know what to do next. I was a much more powerful personality in that room at that time."

Chittister got dressed and knew that if she could get from the examining room to the hall she could find her way to the front door. Once outside, she and the older nun started to walk home when a cabbie pulled up and asked if they needed a ride. Chittister thanked him and began to walk toward the car. He asked which convent. It wasn't the one nearby that he was thinking of, so she thanked him again and he pulled away.

A few minutes later, as they were walking down the street from the hospital, the same cab pulled up and the driver offered to take them where they needed to go. The conversation, she recalled, turned to "bad backs" and the fact that the driver, too, had a sore back. It was going on five o'clock when she got to the monastery. The Matins bell had already rung and everyone was in chapel. She dragged herself to the second floor into the section of the building called the novitiate.

"I go up there. I'm shaking like a leaf. I get to my desk in the novitiate. I sit down, and I don't know exactly what to do because I know everybody is at prayer, and I'm not going into that chapel, I can't do that."

She wasn't there long before the prioress and subprioress entered. They were carrying a box of paper tissues and covering their mouths and faces because they feared the disease was contagious. They told Chittister that she had to get to the hospital. A car was waiting—either a cab or someone the sisters had called—and she was whisked off. When she arrived at the hospital a team was waiting with a gurney.

"As they started moving me toward the door I saw my mother and father. My father was crying like a baby. He couldn't say a word. He was just staring into space and holding his mouth."

Her mother was teary eyed, "but, in true Irish fashion, she said, 'Damn it. I should have known that if anybody was going to get this, it was going to be you.'

"'I said, "It's okay, Mom. I'll be okay.'

"She said, 'You'll be okay.'"

That was her last contact with family for a while. The medical staff took her into a ward for polio patients, and no one else was allowed in. She would be in the hospital for about a month. Part of that time she spent in a "tank respirator," more commonly known as an iron lung, a contraption that helped polio victims breathe. According to the Centers for Disease Control, the vast majority of polio infections were far less severe than the paralytic type, and the milder symptoms were followed by complete recovery. Even most who have paralytic polio can recover with muscle function returning to some degree.[4]

At the time, however, the news she received was grim and the atmosphere in the hospital was dismal. Several doctors told her she would never walk again. She was aware of other women in the ward, one of whom had small children at home and cried constantly; another repeatedly tried to walk but kept falling. Chittister resisted being sent to a children's hospital in Pittsburgh, convinced that if she went there she would never get out.

In an attempt to keep her right arm functioning, the sisters collected cards and brought them and a pair of tiny scissors to the hospital. "I spent my days cutting flowers out of greeting cards with great precision." She was keeping small and gross muscle groups working. Hospital personnel were also working a bit with her leg, but it wasn't responding well and everybody knew it. At night she went into the iron lung.

---

4. Post-Polio Health International, www.post-polio.org. (All of their information is derived from the Centers for Disease Control.)

After the first week or so, she was placed in a room alone, and the staff began to bring in babies for her to exercise by moving their legs and arms. The protocol at the time, she said, was to keep patients through the quarantine period and then for a little while longer to see how much impairment had occurred. After that there was little reason for patients to be kept in the hospital and they were released. Some, like Joan, were fitted with long leg braces. She wore hers for four years and also used a wheelchair and crutches.

After being fitted for braces at the hospital, patients were taken into a room where mattresses were spread out on the floor "You would go in on your crutches and you had to walk on the mattresses. They'd come behind you and push you." After falling down, the patient had to figure her own way back up. "They just stood back and watched. They would tell you the process, but you were expected to get yourself up on the crutches, and until you could, you weren't going anywhere."

At some point while she was in the hospital she learned that some of the men were holding wheelchair races in the hall of their ward. One day she asked if she could join them, and was told she could. "So I got myself out of bed, slid into a hospital wheelchair, and got out in line with these big guys. I knew that day I was going to get well. I worked really hard. I can tell you one thing, and I've said this a million times since: I could feel it. I knew what the medical community didn't know yet about polio—nerves do regenerate. They do replace themselves, but it is so slow." Indeed, science has since learned that, apart from the spinal cord, nerves do regenerate, and it is a slow process.

Sr. Theophane Siegel, who was subprioress at the time and also a nurse, re-created at the monastery a water treatment Joan had received at the hospital. She also had someone outside the community make a "powder board," a low table used for range-of-motion exercises and massaging the legs. The sister cared for her her every night after dinner and worked the leg, "waiting for it to spark." Chittister went through three years of this and then it happened. "Once that first toe moves, once that thing generates a movement of one inch, you're on your way."

Sr. Theophane (whom Chittister, obviously with a deep personal indebtedness, once described as "the greatest woman this community ever saw") also recognized the intellectual gifts of her young patient "and mentored her, smuggling formative reading material that was not permitted in the novitiate library, but provided a solid base in Joan's spiritual development."[5] During the years of rehabilitation, from age sixteen to

5. Mary Lou Kownacki and Mary Hembow Snyder, eds., *Joan Chittister: Essential Writings* (Maryknoll, NY: Orbis Books, 2014), 17.

eighteen, Chittister did little more than read her breviary and whatever else Sr. Theophane smuggled in to her and clean the monastery. "I'm reading, I'm cleaning, I'm not kidding you. I wanted to clean. I wanted obedience, and I made coifs. I was a great coif maker."

She was fast at the task of using the machine that pleated coifs, the piece of white linen that nuns in the community once wore around their necks as part of the habit.

During those two years, the order also debated at times whether Chittister should be asked to leave. Religious orders weren't equipped to deal with serious disabilities. Some sisters, who in later years spoke to her frankly about the reservations they had had, wondered whether accepting her would be fair to Joan and to the community. Some were certain she'd end up in a wheelchair permanently. For Joan, the prospect of leaving was unthinkable. So, as her good friend Sr. Mary Lou Kownacki has written, Joan "did the impossible to keep a normal schedule, dragging her heavy leg brace down long halls and high stairwells, to attend hours of daily prayer, and meals in the refectory, and to keep up with study and chores."[6]

Chittister did everything she could to remain in the mainstream of monastery life. The only exception she allowed herself was the use of the elevator going up because when she was in the leg brace she was unable to bend her knee. For coming down the steps, she said, she figured out how to support herself on the stair bannister and swing down two and three steps at a time. She obviously convinced her superiors that she would not be an undue burden. After two years, she was strong enough to remove the brace for extended periods of time. Although she had attended high school for just over two years, the community was prepared to push her forward toward much more than cleaning and making coifs.

---

6. Ibid.

FOUR

TEACHING AND COLLEGE

The matter of education had grown in importance for the community in Erie during the successive administrations of several prioresses through to the middle of the twentieth century. "In the 1950s," wrote Sr. Stephanie Campbell in her history of the community, "Pope Pius XII had called for the sisters to become well-educated teachers."[1] The Erie Benedictines were out in front of the pope on this score. Campbell points out that emphasis on educating sisters to become fully competent teachers had actually begun with Sr. Rose Sanger, who served as prioress from 1920 to 1928 and again from 1934 to 1940. Beginning in the 1920s, all the sisters were certified to teach by the State of Pennsylvania. The first Erie Benedictine to earn a bachelor's degree was Sr. Ignatia DePuydt, who graduated in 1922 from Canisius College, the Jesuit school in Buffalo, New York.

In subsequent decades, sisters attended St. Bonaventure College in Olean, New York, and often took courses toward master's degrees in education at the University of Notre Dame in South Bend, Indiana. To this day, music holds a special place in the life of the Erie community, with its sung prayer and awareness of the importance of sacred music during liturgies. Trained musicians or those pursuing music education have been attracted to the community because of that emphasis, and sisters have attended Eastman School of Music in Rochester, New York, and the Juilliard School in New York City.

---

1. Sr. Stephanie Campbell, *Vision of Change, Voices of Challenge: The History of Renewal in the Benedictine Sisters of Erie, 1858–1990* (Xlibris, 2015), 27.

By 1962, writes Campbell, eleven sisters were studying for advanced degrees at several institutions throughout the East, including Villanova University, Boston College, and Catholic University, as well as Carnegie Mellon University and Rensselear Polytechnic Institute. "Always the emphasis was on finding the best, not the least expensive schools and colleges. And this from a community whose financial resources were always meager."[2]

Chittister had been recognized, first by the St. Joseph community in Ambridge and later by the Benedictines in Erie, as an outstanding student with great potential. Despite the constant troubles and distractions at home, the lack of resources and her stepfather's hostility toward Catholic schools, she had found ways to flourish. With the kindness of the sisters, especially at St. Benedict's, she not only achieved at a high level academically, she was also given opportunities to lead in student government and with the school newspaper. What occurred when she recovered enough from polio to be mobile on her own, however, is arguably one of those things that only nuns of a certain era would have had the clout and confidence to attempt and that only someone like the young Chittister would have been single-minded and determined enough to pursue.

She had attended high school for two years and a few weeks when the polio struck. For the next two years she worked diligently to strengthen her leg so she could become free of the wheelchair and leg brace she used to get around. In a sense, the timing was fortuitous because, polio or not, she would have spent her second, or novitiate, year almost entirely within the monastery enclosure. She is unclear today about what classes she might have been permitted to attend at the academy, which was attached to the monastery, had she not contracted polio. Others in the group of novices would not have faced that question because they had entered after completing high school. She believes much of the study would have been done in the monastery even if she had been healthy. In her case, following two years of recovery and lacking the final two years of formal high school education, the order decided it was time she got on with college. Her superiors told her she would begin classes at nearby Mercyhurst College. She objected because she had not completed high school and didn't have a full transcript. The sisters produced one filled with "A's" and explained that had she gone to high school they were certain she would have done stellar work. That's the explanation she received from Sr. Mary Michael who was taking her to registration. "I told her that they had me marked down for junior and senior year and that I hadn't gone. She said something like, 'Oh, don't worry about it.'"

---

2. Ibid., 28.

There were subjects listed on the transcript that she had never taken, marks she had never earned that implied she had made her way through textbooks she had never read. This was the era of unquestioning obedience, so if Mother said it was all right, a young nun was not going to challenge her decision. Without any complicating explanations, the community history simply states that Chittister entered in 1952 and graduated from St. Benedict's Academy in 1954.

And so, in her third year in the order, her first as a scholastic, Chittister, who had taken Sr. Mary Peter as her name in religious life, was enrolled without a hitch at Mercyhurst. She was assigned to classes based on the strength of her transcript. These classes included a second-year Spanish class, because Mercyhurst was not offering a first-year Spanish class that semester. Chittister had taken only six weeks of Spanish two years earlier, during the summer before she entered the order. She recalls memorizing Spanish vocabulary as she scooped ice cream at one of her summer jobs. Second-year college-level Spanish was quite a leap. To make matters more intense, only one other student was taking the course. There was no place to hide. "I all but swallowed that book alive," she says. She apparently became so proficient that the teacher, who would permit only Spanish to be spoken in the classroom, while impressed, was also convinced that her new student was using the incorrect word when she explained that she had had only six weeks of Spanish. She kept insisting that Chittister meant "*seis años*" when she kept saying "*seis semanas.*" Perhaps, the teacher said, she meant "*seis meses,*" six months?

With her six weeks of prior study, she sailed through and received an A in intermediate Spanish. Her next encounter with Spanish came during her doctoral work at Penn State University, where she had to brush up for a fourth-year language course to complete her requirements. As of this writing, Chittister, in her late seventies, still reads Spanish almost daily as a way of keeping up with the language and continuing to be proficient in it.

She spent her first of three years as a scholastic in Erie and attended Mercyhurst. The next year she was assigned to Immaculate Conception Elementary School in Clarion, Pennsylvania, in part to enable her to take courses at Clarion College, a state school that had a cooperative agreement with Mercyhurst. In the 1950s, Erie Benedictines couldn't attend college full time. They had schools to staff, and Chittister began teaching elementary school at age nineteen. She taught during the day and took college classes at night and finally completed her bachelor's degree in 1962, eight years after enrolling at Mercyhurst.

During the four years (1955–1959) during which she taught elementary school, she used the leg brace sparingly. The school and convent were near each other and the terrain was easy to negotiate. She didn't have to move much during the day, since elementary school students didn't change classes, so she could remain in one room.

She "hated" teaching elementary school, so much so that she often begged the prioress to allow her to simply make coifs and clean. She repeated, at different times during our interviews, that while she loved children she was not very good at working with them. Each time she approached the prioress about changing assignments, she said the prioress would tell her that other nuns had reported that Chittister was doing "just fine."

In hindsight, she believes the elementary school pupils, with their need for clarity and precision, "taught me how to teach" and that "high school kids would have eaten me alive if I had begun by teaching high school."

During the summer break of 1957, back in Erie between school years, Chittister, now twenty-one, was preparing to make her final profession.

Each year, the community would hold a festival, which served as a fundraiser, in an area behind the motherhouse on 9th Street "That was how we made our summer money." The diocese paid the teaching nuns only until the last day of May. After that, she said, "we had no money for our food bills."

The festival was always held in June, about a month before the elaborate liturgy and ceremony during which the young women would become permanent members of the community. The gathering provided a break from normal routine, with families volunteering to help out. Loretta had volunteered all the previous years and Joan was especially looking forward to seeing her mother this year, which marked a special point in her life as a young religious.

"She didn't show up the first night. I was embarrassed." When she didn't show up the second night, Chittister was annoyed. On the third night, the closing night, the scholastics had already gone back to the dormitory when word was sent to her by Sr. Mary Michael, the scholastic mistress, that someone was looking for her.

She was told that her mother was on the back porch waiting for her. "Great," Chittister thought. "It's 9:30. How wonderful."

She went down and sat on one of the built-in benches on the porch. It was dark. She was embarrassed and angry, but restrained herself.

"We started talking. I was being very patient. I never, ever showed any—we didn't argue. I just wouldn't. I wanted everybody calm.

All of a sudden, someone inside happened to turn on one of the overhead lights, and I saw the whole side of her face.

"I said, 'Mom, what happened?'

"She said, 'That's why I couldn't come, Joan. I couldn't come.'"

"I wanted to kill him," Joan said to me, referring to Dutch. "I just wanted to kill him."

"We were not then what we are now," she pointed out, referring to the community. In future decades, she explained, "I would have taken her in and said, 'You're not going back to that.'" There was no possibility of saying that in the 1950s. There was nothing she could do. "I went back upstairs after we talked. I don't even remember our conversation. Isn't it interesting, with my penchant for detail, that I can only see her face in the dark?"

When she got back upstairs she asked to speak with her scholastic mistress. "I went into her office and I said to her, 'I have to leave.'

She said, 'What are you talking about? What do you mean, leave?'"

Chittister told her she had to leave the community because her mother needed her.

"Why? What do you mean?" Sr. Mary Michael asked.

"She's not well," Chittister replied. "She's not well and she needs me. I've got to go home."

"Does your mother want you to come home? Is she asking you to come home?"

"No, she isn't, but I know that I have to go."

"What are you going to be able to do for your mother at home that we can't do here?" Mary Michael asked. "What does she need?"

"Well, it's different, what she needs." Chittister recalls telling the older nun.

Mary Michael sat with the anguished young sister for an hour and a half, and then said, "Sr. Mary Peter, you go to bed. We'll talk about this tomorrow." She told Chittister that fright in the face of final vows was, in itself, not unusual, and she added, "But we have to talk about this."

"I don't remember how we talked that out," Chittister says. On reflection, she believes that what helped her to remain was the question: "What can you do for your mother?"

"The fact of the matter was that I knew there was nothing I could do for my mother. I didn't have a job, and I didn't consider myself employable. I didn't have a college degree yet, and I was really just starting. So I could go home, and what was that going to do? Obviously I didn't go, but I remember that night like it was yesterday."

Her conversation with the community about her family situation remained cryptic, but one might reasonably presume—as she does today—that the community leaders suspected more about the domestic turmoil than the young Chittister realized at the time.

Within her family, the topic remained submerged. An unspoken taboo against discussion of the violence was firmly in place, and even as a twenty-one-year-year-old who had seen her mother's bruised face, she was unable to broach the subject. "If I had gone to him, he could have hurt her even more. There is no way I could have talked to him about it, not at all. Zero. Part of protecting her meant that everything had to look normal."

That rationale might sound jarringly dissonant in the current age, when battered women's shelters are available, when presumably most priests would not pressure women to stay in abusive relationships, and when there is significant societal sympathy for women suffering domestic violence. Counseling and support groups and women openly advocating for their own interests were still a decade or two away when Loretta and Joan were keeping the worst of their circumstances secret. No safe houses existed. Groups like Alcoholics Anonymous and the view of alcoholism as a disease were nascent, at best, and mother and daughter in the Chittister family weren't aware of them. "I'm not even sure Alcoholics Anonymous was even functioning in this town. I never heard anybody talk about it," said Chittister. Loretta sought a solution by way of subterfuge. Having read an article in "some cheap magazine," she purchased a "powder that that you were supposed to put in an alcoholic's coffee." The claim was that, having ingested the powder, the person would not be able to tolerate alcohol and would ultimately be cured.

"I don't know how much money she put into that. I used to distract him so she could get it into his coffee. It didn't work."

Chittister stayed in the community, but the mingling of guilt and peace she had felt on her very first night in the monastery lingered. "What in God's name led me to leave for the convent at the age of sixteen? The only thing I can say is that kids made life decisions earlier in those years. They were getting married before they left high school, so going into the convent at sixteen, when a lot of kids were graduating at seventeen, making life decisions...It was time for me to make a life decision. As the years went by, I said to myself, 'How did you leave her? How did you have the courage to get up and leave her?'" At the distance of decades it is not unreasonable to conclude that one motivation may have been her own survival.

Chittister made her final profession as a member of the Benedictines of Erie on July 10, 1957, in the last of three ceremonies marking different stages of entry into life in the community.

The first was an elaborate ceremony at the end of the postulant year with the young women wearing white wedding dresses. Loretta made Joan's dress, and though she no longer knows what happened to the dress she still has the pattern her mother used. "This 'bride of Christ' image was very strong at the time." But no photos were allowed, Chittister said. "You could have no pictures taken of yourself until after final profession."

At some point in the ceremony, the women left the altar and went into another room, where they exchanged the wedding dress for a habit with a white veil.

The second ceremony was held about a year later, at the end of the novitiate year, the most cloistered period of formation, the point of which was separation from the world. Visits from family members that year were limited to a few hours on one Sunday a month. "You couldn't visit parents, couldn't go home, couldn't take phone calls, couldn't go anywhere except the monastery." It was the ceremony during which first vows were taken. In this ceremony, the novices exchanged their white veils for black veils, so that in almost all appearances those who had taken first vows looked like everyone else. The one differing detail was that they did not have the ring that was reserved for those who had made final profession.

"The kids at school always knew. Every new sister that came to the school, they'd check the hands to see how young you were," she said, laughing, "and whether you had any real authority."

The April of the year she made her final profession she had turned twenty-one. Prior to the reforms that followed Vatican II, the ceremony for final profession was presided over by the local bishop. Candidates at that time also took their "name in religion" (as noted earlier, Chittister's was Mary Peter). A snip of hair was cut off, somewhat like the tonsure administered to men in certain religious orders. In the case of women, said Chittister, it symbolized "the shearing of the woman's glory. Her hair would be cut and she would be covered."

At one point during the liturgy, the sisters lay flat on their faces, much like seminarians during ordination rituals. "A funeral pall was placed over us and it was held down by four large candles, the candles that were used to accompany a coffin during a funeral. And while you were under there, they were saying the prayers about your death to the world."

While she was under the pall, Chittister experienced a twinge of doubt, wondering if she could actually make this promise for life. The candidates for final profession had been instructed that they had to commit themselves in perpetuity; otherwise the vows weren't valid.

"You were supposed to say your vows under that pall to yourself so that there was no doubt you were making this promise for life, and it would never be broken. To break it—no one ever mentioned the word 'sinful,' but you knew that there were very weighty consequences at least for your definition of yourself."

Her past experience had made her wary of long-term promises. "I had been in a situation where I thought a vow should have been changed," she said, referring to her mother and stepfather. "I just really thought it was wrong. Under the pall, I remember saying to myself that I would keep these vows with all my heart as long as I was able. As long as I was able. And I can remember worrying whether my vows were valid because I had had that little caveat in my head. At the same time, I'm still here. Somehow or other it took."

During another part of the ceremony, a crown of thorns was placed on the heads of those making final vows. It was symbolic both of suffering and triumph. "Because this was following Jesus, it was a triumphant moment as well." The women were given a ring and also a choir mantle that went over the entire habit and was worn during prayer, a symbol that the newly professed had been entrusted with the divine office of the church.

For Benedictine monastics, the vows themselves, then and now, differ from those of the traditional evangelical counsels, poverty, chastity and obedience, taken by religious in other orders. Chittister has said an argument can be made "that there really is only one vow in Benedict's Rule and that is conversion to the monastic way of life."

Even if that is the case, there are still three vows that are taken and, as Chittister enumerates them, they are:

- A vow of obedience, defined as listening to the will of God as perceived in the life of Jesus and scripture, the Rule of Benedict, the prioress, and the community itself
- A vow of stability in which one makes a commitment to a particular monastery
- A vow of conversion, a change of heart, to the monastic way of life

The first vow, for Chittister, is not meant as often interpreted in the past, as blind acceptance of authority in a life circumscribed by rules and proscriptions. In her book on living the Benedictine Rule, the chapter on obedience is titled "Holy Responsibility."[3] Given that later in her life she was regularly called a dissenter or described as defiant and often viewed

---

3. Joan Chittister, *Wisdom Distilled from the Daily: Living the Rule of St. Benedict* (San Francisco: Harper Collins, 1990).

as someone intent on rabble-rousing and overturning tradition as her career took form over decades, it is appropriate here to explore at some length her thoughts on obedience. It is the feature of religious life that inspires the most contentious debate when the subject of renewal of religious orders is raised. If there is fairly wide consensus over the meaning of chastity and a great deal of latitude in the interpretation of religious poverty, there are radically different views with regard to obedience, views that are unlikely to find common ground anytime soon.

Writers like Ann Carey, extremely critical of the direction of renewal among the majority of U.S. congregations of women religious, begins at a point very much in concert with Chittister's view regarding the need for changes in the pre–Vatican II model.[4] Carey agrees that prior to the council, sisters in the United States largely constituted an overworked, underappreciated, undereducated labor force subject to the whims of often unreasonable authorities—both male clerics and female superiors—while practicing unquestioning obedience to often capricious rules.

The rub comes when women begin to resist and to change their circumstances. Rarely is poverty or chastity the problem. The discord comes over obedience—what that term actually means and to whom one owes obedience. Carey's critique, a complex assessment of the state of contemporary religious life, will be treated in greater length later. But she generally concludes that renewal would have been less tumultuous if it had occurred in a decade other than the 1960s and if somehow the women could have put in place the needed changes while simultaneously remaining unquestioningly obedient to the mandates that derived from the male clerical culture.

For Chittister, the requirements of obedience within the context of community must be considerate of both the healthy practice of self-determination and the limits of authority. In her book, the chapter on obedience opens with a description of the post–Vatican II final vow profession ceremony. "The sister about to make vows stands up in the midst of the community gathered in chapel and announces her intention to join it forever." When called by the prioress, she brings her vow paper to the altar where the two—newly professed and prioress—sign and seal it. The new monastic then sings three times, alternating with the community, "Uphold me, O God, according to your will and I shall live, and do not fail me in my hope."

The event "says that a person has freely and independently chosen to put herself at the disposal of a group and 'under a rule and a prioress

---

4. Ann Carey, *Sisters in Crisis Revisited: From Unraveling to Reform and Renewal* (San Francisco: Ignatius Press, 2013).

for the sake of the gospel.' A woman comes to the altar alone but leaves it as a part of a community. A woman makes a decision to put herself in the hands of someone who will now become part of all the major decisions of the rest of her life. In other words, a woman stands up in public and says, 'I am not an entity unto myself.' And then, suddenly, she is stronger for it and the gospel is safer for it, too."[5]

That gesture of surrender to another and to the community cannot be a total surrender of one's own good judgment, intelligence, and person. "Authority and self-determination are two of the major problems of the spiritual life. Are we our own masters or not?"[6]

Often the antidote to rigid authoritarianism is seen as its opposite, an equally rigid egalitarianism. Chittister writes that neither model holds for Benedictines, that they are not symbolized by either the pyramid, where leadership is top down, or the circle, where no one is called leader. "On the contrary, Benedictine communities are better pictured as a wheel with a hub and spokes. In the Benedictine community there is a center to which all the members relate while they all relate to one another."

In Benedictine spirituality, neither authority nor obedience exists for its own sake. "Benedictine authority is designed to call us to our best selves by calling us, not to a system, but to the gospel . . . The fact is that the person centered in Christ lives in a system in order to transcend the system. It is the ability to think thoughts other than our own, other than the past, other than the safe, other than the acceptable that will lead us eventually to truth."[7]

A balance, precarious at times to maintain, is essential to the health of the individual and the community. Living unquestioning obedience to an authority figure results in "dependence" and "spiritual childishness."

Living to wield authority over others "is not insight and leadership; that is domination. Truth can never come without sharing authority with other members of the community. The truth that I suppress in others will limit my own growth."[8]

At the same time, defiance for its own sake results in "license," equally debilitating as blind obedience, even if one is correct. "To be

---

5. *Wisdom Distilled from the Daily*, 133–34.
6. Ibid., 134.
7. Ibid., 135.
8. Ibid., 137.

against something just to be against it, even if I am right, is not truth. It is only self gone wild with a crippling kind of isolation that will eventually make me deaf to whatever is best for me in life."[9]

Benedictine monasticism differs from the type of monasticism that was widely practiced prior to the development of the Rule of Benedict sometime during the sixth century. The Benedictine vow of stability signifies more than a life in one place. It is central, says Chittister, to Benedict's "very clear" understanding that sanctity does not reside in a set of exercises or events, but rather that it is a process requiring strong community.

Benedict's approach, she says, is about human development. He was "creating communal monasticism" during a period when the eremitical model, the solitary hermit in the desert, was the prevailing approach to monastic life. In a sense, Benedict's Rule may be part of Christianity's ongoing answer to the query St. Basil the Great, the father of Eastern monasticism who preceded Benedict by about a century and a half, posed with regard to the eremitical approach. He wondered how the solitary figure exercised charity when that virtue requires encounter with another. How does one exercise humility alone? The paradox of solitary Christianity is captured in his well-known question, popularly rendered: "Whose feet shall the hermit wash?"

In other words, says Chittister, spirituality in the Benedictine tradition, with its emphasis on hospitality, "is based on this commitment to the development of human community and to growth in it." It involves "the rubbing off of your own sharp edges," something she says married couples understand. Stability involves "blooming where you're planted. You can't run away from yourself and you can't run away from the people who know you." In the Benedictine community, she points out, others know you very well. "Every once in a while in community we'll laugh at something that will happen and we'll say, 'Ah we know one another too well. We know—we've watched each other for sixty years for God's sake."

The third vow, conversion to the monastic way of life, speaks to an interior conversion. Part of that conversion assumes the three vows of poverty, chastity, and obedience that are traditional in other orders. The vow of conversion "fleshes out the idea of the Rule, the attitudes implicit there—community, stability, stewardship, humility."

The emphasis, then, is not on a kind of rigorous physical denial for its own sake, but rather on communal growth and relationship that presumes the adherents will be poor and celibate. They will also be

---

9. Ibid., 136.

imperfect, for Benedict "doesn't set up a model of rarefied existence as the end of the spiritual life. Benedict sets up a community, a family."

It is in the "theology of community," writes Chittister, where Benedictine spirituality most departs "from the traditional norms of religious life... Of all the places where the Rule of Benedict shows us the real depth of the spiritual life, it is surely in its theology of community. 'The most valiant kind of monk,' Benedict writes from a culture of hermits, is not the solitary or the pseudo-ascetic or the wandering beggar but 'the cenobite' (RB1:12), the one who has learned to live with others in community."[10]

Benedict's insights into community, she writes, could well be his gift to the modern world.

The liturgy during which final vows are professed is the start of a new level of life within the community. "It was an exuberant day for us," says Chittister, "We were finally adults in the community." She explains, "You are taken into the professed community. That's a huge moment."

It was also the start of a three-day celebration. What came first to her memory was that they were "speaking days." The nuns who had just taken final vows, and who had previously kept silence in the monastery except for a limited period each day, could talk to each other as much as they wished. She recalls talking "all day long" and sitting at a piano and playing for hours. There were long stretches during which the newly professed were permitted to have recreation and to leave the confines of the monastery. "Three or four of the newly professed were from local parishes and we all went with them to say hello to the pastor or sit and a have a glass of Coke with the parish priest."

Now a full member of the community, with the full habit and ring signifying final profession, she returned to Immaculate Conception Elementary School. She would stay there for two more years before being assigned to teach at St. Joseph High School in Oil City. She was twenty-three. "I get sent to high school in 1959, and I get happy."

Several forces—from people she met to educational opportunities to a much pleasanter experience in her daily work—began to broaden the horizons of the young woman who had survived a violent home, polio, and four years of contending with fifth and sixth graders. By others' accounts, she blossomed as a creative teacher and found her stride among older students for whom classroom instruction could turn, at times, bold and inventive.

---

10. Ibid., 40.

Sr. Maureen Tobin, who arrived as principal at St. Joseph's the year Chittister began teaching there, would over time become one of her most trusted friends in the community and, eventually, a personal assistant who kept track of her calendar. The need for help in scheduling increased with the expansion of Chittister's role outside the community as a leader within the Benedictine world and the broader universe of women religious and as a world-renowned writer and lecturer. Tobin had a bachelor's degree in business administration and would, in time, earn a master's in school administration; Chittister eventually would become recognized as a social psychologist and budding reformer who inhabited a universe of big ideas and deep questions. Chittister would compose electrifying presentations; Tobin would make sure she got to the plane on time with the correct presentation in hand.

Tobin is nearly seven years older than Chittister. A native of Oil City, she joined the Benedictines immediately following high school. Her path was similar to Chittister's: one year as a postulant, during which she attended Villa Maria College (a school founded by the Sisters of St. Joseph that merged in 1989 with Gannon University, an institution run by the diocese of Erie) and a master's in school administration from the University of Notre Dame.

She had known about Chittister earlier because the news of her polio had circulated quickly through the community. She had encountered Chittister the young dynamo only once before the two of them arrived in Oil City. The occasion was sometime in the mid-1950s, when Chittister was asked to write a presentation for Pastor's Day, an event designed to help parish priests encourage girls to attend St. Benedict Academy, where Tobin was teaching at the time.

Chittister wrote the presentation and delivered it to Sr. Mary Jude, the high school journalism teacher who had earlier detected Joan's writing flair and who by this time was principal of the academy where the event was to be held. Mary Jude gave the program to Tobin and another sister to present. "And it was wonderful, if you knew drama," recalled Tobin. But neither she nor the other nun had any dramatic training or inclination. The presentation came complete with directions for lighting and other staged effects, because Chittister "had written the production and the instructions," said Tobin. "Whoever the other teacher was who was assigned with me wasn't that much better at doing something like that. We didn't know about this young whippersnapper."

Chittister returned to Erie from Clarion several times in advance of the presentation to help coach the two presenters, but she couldn't be there at show time. Ultimately the presentation went off without any major hitches, but Chittister hadn't made any new friends in the process.

Tobin said she didn't know Chittister well enough to complain to her at the time but that she did "have words" with Mary Jude.

Tobin's annoyance at Chittister didn't last long. By the time the two of them landed in Oil City, Tobin was aware of Chittister as a creative and energetic presence. "I could tell from that little experience that she was very able to do something, imagine something—'creative' is the word I use—and it comes out a success."

She recalled an example from the high school. Chittister was teaching world history to a class of "lower ability" students. "She was trying to teach out of the textbook, and they weren't getting anything. The next thing you know, she creates projects for them. One day, I went to her door. There was a window in the door. I looked in. All the chairs and desks had been rearranged. They were set up like a battlefield. The students were there fighting some war that she was teaching.

"That's what I mean by creative." Tobin said. "She figured out a way to get those kids to learn something with a project that they enjoyed doing. With almost anything, when you talk to her she comes up with all these ideas. Nothing is impossible to her. She figures out how she can do almost anything."

Their mutual regard, however, has far deeper roots. When Chittister began teaching high school, the physical rigors of her routine increased dramatically. High school teachers are expected to move around, and that meant climbing from floor to floor and going from classroom to classroom throughout the day. Her damaged leg, which had appeared to strengthen, gave out again.

She had to start wearing the leg brace again. Tobin consulted with Sr. Theophane, the nurse who had procured the powder board when Chittister first returned to the monastery from the hospital and who had treated her for two years to get her leg and foot working again. Sr. Theophane recommended as much rest as possible outside of the workday.

To help her even more, Tobin enlisted a few of the heftier football players to show up each morning at the convent door. "She sent those boys every single day. They came to the back door and said, 'Arms up, Sister!'" Chittister would put her elbows against her body and they'd take hold of the elbows and carry her up a hill to the school and then up two flights of stairs to her classroom. There they deposited her in a chair specially constructed behind a high lectern to compensate for the fact that she didn't have the strength to stand and teach. Tobin had had someone in Oil City build the chair and lectern so Chittister would be able to sit above the students.

Tobin and Chittister would work together at the high school level for fifteen years, first at St. Joseph, which closed in 1962 as part of a diocesan plan, and then at the new and much larger Venango Christian High School, which opened the same year and was so named because Erie Bishop John Gannon wanted the school to be "open to all faiths, free to worship God, privately in any way they wish." The name was changed to Venango Catholic High School in 2001 to emphasize its denominational identity.

"Maureen monitored my health for all those years. At St. Joe's, she changed the entire schedule so I taught in one room all day long."

Tobin was named the principal of the new high school, which also had a headmaster, Fr. Lawrence J. Antoun. Chittister speaks fondly of Antoun, though they had their differences. She saw him as a good friend and mentor, a kind of father figure. Tobin describes the two as an "intellectual match." Chittister recalls Antoun as someone widely read who enjoyed intellectual pursuits and engaging in discussion on a range of topics. He had a sister, Sr. Laureace Antoun, a member of the Sisters of St. Joseph, who was president of Villa Maria College and a very good friend of Chittister and Tobin for many years.

If Chittister had known from the time she was a toddler that she wanted to be a nun, she knew from her teenage years and the experience with high school journalism that she wanted to be a writer. As she has said, "I lived to write. I wrote all the time, I wrote in small notebooks and tiny date books and on sheets and sheets of blank white typing paper. I wrote half-sentences and long paragraphs, news stories and feature stories, editorials and humor columns."[11] And then she would wait for the paper to come out, and see her words. In secret she would write short story after short story. She never intended anyone to see these "characters and situations and places that said something to me about what I saw around me, about human struggle, about dark, driving motives and hidden pain...I simply wrote for the sheer joy of writing, the way some kids throw baseballs or practice the drums or swim laps in a pool."

She carried that love of writing and the ambition to be a writer into the monastery and it was over that desire that her commitment to Benedictine community, to the deep calling to religious life, would twice be tested in the extreme.

---

11. Joan Chittister, *Scarred by Struggle, Transformed by Hope* (Grand Rapids: Eerdmans, 2005), 4ff.

When she entered the Benedictines in 1952, she entered with one of the largest groups of that era—seven in all—and Chittister remembers them as rather lively and vital, full of questions and, in many ways that today would appear benign, challenging of the status quo. "No one ever broke a rule or questioned a direction, but we had a lot of questions about the history of religious life, the nature of religious life. We were a group on the cusp of the changes to come." She remembers that when they first entered they referred to themselves as the "seven gifts of the Holy Ghost. Some weeks later we referred to ourselves as the seven deadly sins because it seemed we couldn't do anything right."

They were part of the generation coming to age just post–World War II and, as women, beginning to understand the inherent changes that the period of war had spawned at home. If nuns, pre-war, were little different from married women who stayed at home, post-war coming-of-age nuns were subject to the same forces that had been percolating for some years just beneath the societal surface. The 1950s may have been regarded as the decade of the quiet generation, but women who had held things together at home during the war and who had provided a significant portion of the defense industry workforce began to change the calculus for American women. Chittister's final profession was in 1957. Betty Friedan's *Feminine Mystique* would hit the bookstores in 1963, kicking off what is widely regarded as the second wave of U.S. feminism. The status quo, so dependent on a certain feminine docility and accepted notions of domestic bliss, was unraveling.

When Friedan's book appeared, Chittister was a "young professed," having made her final vows just six years previously. She says she never read that work or others of that era, adding that her ideas about women in the church derived from a growing understanding of scripture and church history and the writing of historic and contemporary contemplatives.

Perhaps ironically, in hindsight, the major influence on her as a teenager and novice in the order was the male contemplative Thomas Merton, the Trappist monk whose writings were absolutely captivating for certain segments of the Catholic community. Merton himself was a sign of the transitions going on, a monk in an order known for its solitude and silence who possessed one of the most distinctive and challenging, as well as one of the most widely heard, voices in contemporary Catholicism. He made his solemn vows in the Cistercian order in 1947 and the next year his autobiography, *Seven Storey Mountain,* was published. This was followed the next year by *Seeds of Contemplation,* a kind of primer on contemplative life and an intimate look into the life of a thoroughly modern young man who had opted to live out the remainder of his days in one of the most ascetic Roman Catholic orders.

Merton brought a certain credibility to the art of contemplative journal writing because, as one reviewer put it, "the zealous Trappist ...was, only seven or eight years ago, a man like the rest of men, neither better perhaps nor worse. He was no withdrawn ascetic, no hairshirted prophet born out of his time, but a sophisticated worldling who lived, loved, drank, and collected hot records just about like a good many other college students in the final decade of the pre-Hiroshima age."[12] Unlike many of those other college students, Merton would consider it the role of the contemplative life to engage enormous moral questions about events like Hiroshima and, later, ongoing issues of war and peace in the nuclear age.

Chittister began reading Merton during her first year in high school. She eagerly read *Seven Storey Mountain* and committed to memory whole sections of *Seeds of Contemplation*. "His journals and reflections hit me right over the head. I began to question whether I was looking at life around me with that kind of depth or awareness or appreciation." When she entered the order, she set herself the task of writing a journal entry every day. Late in the evening, just before ten o'clock bedtime, she would sit at her desk in the novitiate and write a reflection on the day, on what she had experienced and thought, a kind of written extension of the silent *examen* she had performed earlier in chapel. The reflections were kept in a notebook with a black and white mottled cover and with pages that were divided into two. She disciplined herself by keeping her daily reflections to half a page.

The novice mistress at the time, Sr. Aurelia Carroll, had spent years as a very effective first-grade teacher and had recently been placed in charge of novices. She was of the old school in a community where some, even in leadership, were beginning to question the "why" of existing methods and to relax some of the traditional restrictions. Sr. Aurelia would have none of it, especially regarding her new charges. She was extremely rigid in applying the rules and exemplified a type of authority that demanded obedience without question. The training she provided was based not on an understanding of human growth and development, but rather on a centuries-old tradition of discipline, with an emphasis on rules and strict adherence to the daily schedule.

Chittister describes the period as "that acme of spiritual culture where the moral, the amoral, and the immoral had become totally confused. If I had done an examination of conscience in January of 1953, I could have said that in the morning I spilled food, in the afternoon I got angry that the coif machine didn't work, and later I killed sister so-and-so

---

12. *The Saturday Review*, April 16, 1949.

because I had had enough of her, and I would have confessed all of these in the same manner because they would all have been mortal sins to us. Things that were useless, meaningless, and totally amoral had become big things. So we were told, 'Sister, we do not walk that way. Sister, we do not sit on the side of our beds.' And here's this kid, reading Thomas Merton on the one hand and on the other living in a culture that was so far away from reflection that it might as well have been another planet. I saw things with two eyes, the inner eye and the human eye, and I was trying to reconcile these two. I wrote in this journal every night."

In hindsight she realizes that "the novice mistress was dealing with a major transition in her life and we were dealing with a major transition in our lives, and I've got this other factor, polio, and I'm trying to figure out what it means." The novice mistress and the young sisters-to-be were living a situation designed for conflict. "After weeks of hearing scoldings for walking too fast or being too loud, for breaking silence" and other such things, Chittister took to her journal one night and ended the entry with words she remembers to this day: "I didn't come to this community for any novice mistress, and I'm not leaving because of one."

The following day she "broke out into a mortal sweat" when she discovered the journal was missing. Though she heard nothing about it at the time, she suspected the novice mistress had taken the book. The mere fact that someone else could have been reading her private thoughts and reflections was enough to discourage her. She stopped keeping a journal.

Four years later, on the evening before her final profession, someone came to the scholasticate and said, "Sr. Aurelia would like to see you downstairs in the basement."

She went down to find her former novice mistress standing at the door of the boiler room. The nun indicated that Chittister should go in. "She didn't speak to me, she just nodded toward the door." She motioned for Chittister to open the lid of an incinerator. A fire was raging inside. The nun pulled the journal from the sleeve of her habit. "She handed me my own journal and said, 'Burn that. You don't want to do anything like that again.' And I did—and I watched it go up in flames."

Chittister returned to the scholasticate. "I wasn't rebellious or angry. I was deeply sad. She had kept it for all those years. I don't know why she did it. I don't know why. What I saw going up in flames was my life as a writer."

Her writing aspirations were resurrected, however, five years later when, having just graduated from Mercyhurst, Chittister received notice from the prioress, Sr. Alice Schierberl, that she was to apply for admission to the prestigious Iowa Writers Workshop at the University of Iowa to study for a master's degree in fine arts.

The news came at a point when she had resigned herself to the fact that an undergraduate degree in English would be as close as she would get to creative writing. She had concluded, she wrote, that religious life had been constructed "almost entirely around the functional rather than the creative. We were educated to do what needed to be done." Teaching English "was second best, but it was better than nothing. It was the closest I could get to literature, to real writing."[13] Then came the word from Schierberl, whom Chittister described as "a woman given to strong and uncommon ideas."[14] "I remember that my hands shook as I signed the final registration papers, enclosed the writing sample, and sealed the large manila envelope."

Her acceptance letter arrived in January and she was to begin classes that June. "All this time, it finally seemed, the superiors of the community had known what I really wanted, where I really belonged, and it was going to happen. It was going to happen. Here. Monastery or no monastery. To me." She described the moment later, writing in a gush of metaphor and image, "The future felt like gold and silver, looked like bright fuchsia and yellow sunflowers, smelled soft as lavender and warm as rye. I had never been happier in my life."[15]

May came around in a hurry and her thoughts turned to the reality of pursuing her dream when, out of nowhere, she received another call from Schierberl. The woman who had told her to apply for graduate school now told her that she would not be going. The only reason Schierberl gave was that it "would be better for my humility to go to our summer camp as third cook than to go to school." The prioress told her she wasn't yet ready for a master's degree.

It was a crushing and life-altering event. Schierberl, who was elected to only one term as prioress, was a brilliant and cultured woman who initiated stunningly modern changes in the community, upending old disciplines and in many ways placing the community on a more outward looking and compassionate course than had been the long custom. But those who knew her always speak first of her brilliance and then of her "dark side." She was a woman subject to wild mood swings and Chittister was not the only example of someone having had a door of opportunity opened by Schierberl only to have it slammed shut at the last minute.

Chittister used that event in her early years in the order as a core theme running through her book *Scarred by Struggle, Transformed by*

---

13. *Scarred by Struggle*, 5.
14. Ibid.
15. Ibid., 6.

Hope, a thickly layered exploration of the spirituality necessary to both deal with and benefit from struggle, which she terms "an unsparing lesson but a necessary gift."

"What we struggle against, what we struggle for, what we struggle with, all test and hone us. It is the resistance itself that seasons us." Struggle itself isn't a life choice, it is a fact of life. The choice is not about accepting it, but "whether to crumble under it or to brave it."[16]

She uses spiritual traditions—her own and those of others—to critique a wider civil culture that has become obsessed with avoiding pain and struggle and blind to the freedom of the kind of spiritual detachment, or "holy indifference," that has been a staple of religious wisdom for centuries.

Hope for her is not retreat into fantasy or an escape from reality; hope is "not some kind of delusional optimism to be resorted to because we simply cannot face the hard facts that threaten to swamp our hearts." Hope, instead, "rides on the decision either to believe that God stands on this dark road waiting to walk with us toward new light again or to despair of the fact that God who is faithful is eternally faithful and will sustain us in our darkness one more time."

Instead of embarking on her hoped-for life as a fiction writer, Chittister was assigned for the summer as an assistant cook at the order's Camp Glinodo, a name made up by one of the sisters using the beginning letters of the Benedictine motto in Latin. She often spent long periods in the off hours pondering her future while sitting on the bank of Seven Mile Creek, which runs through the property. She writes that she kept the pain of that moment mostly to herself. "I simply went on going on. But, suddenly, without warning, in the very next moment, I would find myself swimming in a sea of black, my arms and legs heavy and lifeless, tears in my eyes."

She discovered, in the day-after-day battle with herself, that struggle, like sanctity, is not a discrete event but a process to be lived through. One comes out of the struggle a different person. In her case, one of the differences was the realization that she had entered the monastery for purposes larger than a writing career. "Still desperate to write, to work with words, to find an outlet for the ideas that plagued me from morning to night, I began to find fiction in reality rather than reality in fiction. I began to become aware of the human stories in front of me that really counted. I began to be sensitive to the effects of the world around me on actual people around me."[17]

---

16. Ibid., 105.
17. Ibid., 85.

That final realization would not take hold for a number of years. In the meantime, she followed a more traditional path in the order. The following summer was the first of five she would spend on the campus of the University of Notre Dame in South Bend, Indiana, where she would graduate in 1968 with a master's degree in communication arts.

During the academic year, she continued to teach at Venango Christian High School, each summer returning to South Bend. Academically, the period was less than fulfilling. She took courses in television and film and recalls that they were unimpressive. They contained almost no theory and little else that she considered academically challenging. She described some of the courses as "like giving a second grader a piece of composition paper and having the child pick from colored crayons and then draw circles or triangles or squares in some order. It was terrible; it was fun; it was playschool. I came home to Mother Mary Margaret Kraus and I said that I would like to quit Notre Dame. She said, 'Why?' I said, 'Because I'm not learning anything.'"

It apparently was an easy decision for the prioress. "Just get the credits and come home," Mother Mary Margaret Kraus told her.

At that time Notre Dame did, however, offer other opportunities for a young woman who had spent most of her life in the confined circumstances of small Pennsylvania towns and a monastic community. South Bend may not have been a hotbed of campus radicalism, but the impulse of change was everywhere during the heart of the 1960s, even at Notre Dame and even during the summers when much of the usual student body was elsewhere and the campus was filled with nuns and priests taking courses, along with regular students at the university. Everywhere authority was being questioned, the debate over the U.S. role in Vietnam was escalating, the sexual revolution was in full swing, Vatican II had begun to roil the calm waters of universal Catholicism, and religious life as the American church had known it was beginning to change forever. The year of her graduation was the year of the assassinations of Rev. Martin Luther King Jr. and Robert Kennedy, of the summer riots in cities, of the violent clashes between anti-war protesters and police outside the Democratic National Convention in Chicago.

While she was a student on campus, Chittister became friends with some members of the Order of St. Basil the Great from Canada, who were like big brothers to her. One, especially, advised her as to which parties and gatherings to avoid. There were pizza and beer parties, however, that she attended and where the conversations went long into the night. Folk and protest music was in the air and sing-alongs (often called hootenannies in that era) were a regular part of campus life.

The young contemplative from Erie thought it only natural to take quiet strolls around St. Mary's Lake and St. Joseph's Lake that border the northwest edge of the campus. She realized, however, that evening was probably not the time to take advantage of the walking paths around the lakes after she stumbled over the prone bodies of students engaged in activities other than meditation.

In five years, she earned the credits she needed for the degree. It was August, and she anticipated a bit of a break back in Erie before gearing up again for the school year. But soon after she returned home, Tobin and Antoun asked her to attend a three-day conference that was being conducted by a professor from Penn State University at Edinboro, about forty-five miles north of Oil City, near the Ohio border with Pennsylvania.

She tried to beg off the assignment, but the two administrators felt a special obligation to have someone represent the school because the meeting was for high school educators who used in their honors English classes textbooks provided by the state. Chittister taught those classes at Venango and used those books.

"So I whittled them down and they agreed to what I proposed." She said she would go, "be present to the right people at the right time, and say 'thank you.'" She realized that "somebody had to go and say how important it was to our kids."

She showed up for the second day of the conference and walked into a lecture given by Dr. Gerald M. Phillips, who taught speech communication at Penn State, and, as she says, she was "quite taken with it."

She describes what happened when the lecture ended. "He breaks everybody into groups, which was quite rare in those days, actually, to deal with this material." Chittister remembers she could find no way to slip out unnoticed. "I find myself in a group, discussing what I don't want to discuss, getting involved in what I don't want to be in, and at the end of the group discussion, the group says to me, 'You do the feedback.'"

The event was, in many ways, pure Chittister. She may have been unwilling to go, but went for the sake of the high school and, in a broader sense, the Catholic community, to convey appreciation. She may have been a reluctant participant in the small group discussion, but once there, she was all in. Questions and people get her attention; she loves an academic challenge; and the only child knows how to handle being the center of attention.

In this case, the question put to the group was along the lines of, "What questions or issues did the lecture raise for you?"

"When I went into the small group they were having a little difficulty trying to figure out the task. They didn't seem to have questions." She did. She began by noting that she had not heard in the lecture any discussion of the nature of communication.

And so she began to do what she has done so well for years since. She went to the heart of the matter with her questions: "What is communication? What does it depend on? Perception or structure? Does it depend on known vocabulary or a perceived vocabulary? Does it have foundations of accuracy? Can it be proven or certified? Can you or I know if you've really understood me or not?"

Forty-five years later, she still remembers the precise example she used with the group to illustrate the point: "Open the gob and stick out the golliger." Which, of course, began a discussion of what she meant with her made-up words.

"Communication theorists are the persons who write the scripts that psychotherapists use later," she said in one of our interviews. How we communicate affects all we do, she added, our interactions with each other, how we communicate in our organizations, with personnel, and with the wider world.

She gave her feedback to the wider group, said her goodbyes, and headed for the exits to wait for her ride—Sr. Maureen Tobin was driving —but first she stopped at a vending machine to buy something to drink. Benedictines in that era weren't allowed to carry much money around, but she found twenty cents in her pocket and dumped it into the machine. As she was doing that, she heard a voice behind her ask, "So when are you coming down to grad school?"

"I paid no attention because it had nothing to do with me. There was a tap on my shoulder. I turned around and it was the little round Jewish professor who had delivered the lecture. He said, 'When are you coming down to grad school?'

"I said, 'Pardon me?'

"He said, 'You, when are you coming down to campus?'

"I said, 'I'm not. You must have me confused with somebody else.'

"He said, 'I'm not confused at all. I want you down there. When are you coming?'

"I said, 'No, I can't go to graduate school. I just finished a graduate program a week ago. I just got my master's degree.'"

The conversation went on a little longer, with Chittister explaining that she came from a very small community with meager resources and one that had only high schools, thus no need for doctorates. She told him that the order had no substitute teachers, that she had a contract for the coming year, and that it would be impossible to begin a doctoral program.

Phillips persisted: "If I get you the schedule and I get you the money, then when are you coming down to graduate school?"

She explained again and then finally excused herself, convinced that she had had the last word.

On the drive back to Oil City, she told Tobin about the conversation, and Tobin encouraged her to consider it. Some weeks later, Chittister was in her classroom doing some last-minute work before the start of a faculty workshop at the beginning of the new school year when she was summoned to Tobin's office. When she arrived she was greeted by Tobin, headmaster Antoun, and Phillips from Penn State.

"What are you doing here?" she asked the professor.

"I'm giving your workshop," he said.

"Dr. Phillips tells us that he had a discussion with you," Tobin said.

Chittister said, "Dr. Phillips talked to me about going to Penn State and I made it very clear why I cannot go and have no need to go."

Antoun said they needed to talk more about it and asked Chittister to sit down. He told her that Phillips wanted the high school to set up a schedule so she could teach all of her classes on a single day, which would allow her the other four days to take classes at Penn State. The plan they devised would have her teach all of her high school classes on Friday, get the rest of her community and preparation work done on the weekend, and travel to Penn State Sunday afternoons, returning each Thursday.

"I looked at them and said, 'No, thank you very much. I can't believe that you're interested, but I don't need to do that. I don't want to do that." Antoun responded, "We can't close this conversation here. It's too important a conversation."

After the workshop, Tobin sat with Chittister and continued to make the case for going to Penn State. In a later meeting with Chittister, Antoun said, "Of course this can be worked out. Under no conditions should you not have this opportunity."

Chittister went to Erie to consult with the prioress, her last line of defense against taking on a PhD program. She went through her list of objections, only to hear, "Oh, but my dear, it would be a wonderful thing for you. I think you should explore it. Go on exploring it," she said, "until it's not possible."

She made an appointment with Dr. Stanley Paulson who was, at the time, head of the speech department at Penn State. Going down in the car she told Tobin, who was driving, that she had a list of things written down "and if he says 'no' to any of them, that's my sign that I'm not supposed to be there."

Tobin asked, "Joan don't you think that's a little ridiculous?"

"No," said Chittister, "I think it's honest."

So she sat in the office with Paulson and went through her list of "seven or eight" things, including the fact that she had no money and that she had to have classes on specific days.

"And he sat there and said, 'Yeah, yeah, yeah.' We get right down to the end, and he says, 'So you'll be coming down in January, right? We have time. We'll get all this taken care of.'"

He did, including arranging for funding. The order didn't have to pay a cent toward her degree. And she began the grueling schedule: taking the bus back to Oil City on Thursday afternoon following four days of her own classes, teaching all day Friday, running the print shop at the school on Saturday, engaging in community activities and preparation on Sunday and getting back on the bus Sunday afternoon for the return trip to State College, where Penn State is located. She managed to finish her coursework and dissertation, including its defense, while teaching high school, in the unusually brief span of little more than two years. She was the first member of the Benedictine community in Erie to earn a doctorate.

Penn State provided a foundation in social science research and insights into organizational dynamics and human behavior that would serve her the rest of her life.

Toward the end of that initial meeting with Paulson, he picked up the phone to notify the person who would be her advisor. She presumed it would be Phillips.

But she was assigned to Dr. Carroll C. Arnold, who had been trained in the humanities and had a thorough grounding in classical Roman and Greek rhetoric. A founder of the journal *Philosophy and Rhetoric*, he is credited with increasing the connection between the social science study of speech and the humanities.

Chittister was profoundly inspired and influenced by Arnold, who exposed her to "a full philosophy" of "the nature of speech and what it was supposed to do, how it was supposed to do it, when it was wrong, and how you could see it. He was just exhilarating."

And so it was, she says, that "my life begins slowly...to turn." Again.

PART II

Joan Chittister as prioress.

FIVE

ON THE PATH TOWARD CHANGE

"Let no one hope to find in contemplation
an escape from conflict, from anguish or from doubt."
—Thomas Merton, *New Seeds of Contemplation*

The doctoral program would set Joan Chittister up to move off in new directions she had not anticipated and into leadership positions during a time of unprecedented stress and tension experienced both in the wider church and within her community.

Life's anxieties, however, were not confined to matters of the church and the monastery. At the end of 1970, midway through her second year at Penn State and just months before she would be elected to her first leadership position in the Benedictines, she went to spend Christmas with her parents, who were living in a small home just outside of Erie that they had purchased some years before.

She was helping her mother prepare dinner and waiting for Dutch, who had been visiting a brother, another heavy drinker. Hours past mealtime had ticked by when they received a call. Dutch was in the hospital. He had been driving home in an ice storm following an afternoon of drinking when he lost control of his car, which spun across East 38th Street and crashed into a utility pole.

Joan and Loretta arrived at St. Vincent's Hospital sometime after 9 PM. Dutch's first words were, "I'm sorry I'm late, Loretta." In the telling of the story today, Chittister laughs at the drama. "The whole thing's been a comedy affair. There's nothing else to say. It's just been up and down, up and down, up and down."

Dutch was in the intensive care unit for several days and eventually was released to go home, but he never fully recovered. He died a little more than a month later, on February 3, 1971. Joan and Loretta were with him. In making the funeral arrangements, they were asked, "What parish?" Loretta answered, "St. Peter's Cathedral."

"I said, 'Mom, just a minute. We can't have daddy buried from St. Peter's Cathedral. He did not belong to that parish. He's not Catholic, and we can't bury him from St. Peter's.'

"She said, 'Oh, they'll do it. You call them. You just call Father at the cathedral and you tell him.'"

The pastor at the time knew Joan and Loretta and expressed his condolences when he heard Dutch had died.

"Save your sympathy," she told the pastor, "because we have bigger problems than death." She told him of the complications, that Dutch had been baptized a Presbyterian, that he hadn't darkened the doorway of any church for fifty years or so, and that her mother was insisting he be buried from the cathedral. "I know it's not possible, Father," she said. "I'll handle this, but she's watching me make this call from the doorway, so I have to make it and talk to somebody."

"When do you want the funeral, Sister?" the priest responded.

A few days later, Dutch's casket was rolled down the center aisle of the Cathedral of St. Peter. Most of those in attendance were Protestants, Dutch's family. If there is such a thing as ecclesial payback, this was Loretta's moment, thought Joan. "There's not a Catholic in the crowd except my mother and me and the nuns, and we're walking down the aisle behind the casket, and I'm saying, 'Daddy, I'll explain this to you later. Just try not to sit up. Whatever you do don't get excited about this one.' It's the funniest story in my life.'"

A year later, Chittister and Tobin were back in Erie for the holidays. They had taken on new responsibilities, helping to take care of the five children of Maureen's brother, Jim, whose wife, Mary Alice, had died in April the year before at age thirty-five. The children at the time ranged from their early teens to about six, and the two nuns would drive the seventy miles from Oil City to Erie as often as possible to help out.

Their connection with the family would extend for years and become more regular when Tobin and Chittister moved back to Erie in 1974, and especially after Tobin's brother had to undergo a series of brain operations that increasingly impaired his ability to function.

In a 2014 interview, two of the children, John and Tom, recalled both the loss of that period of their lives as well as their fond memories of "being raised by nuns." Quite a few members of the community pitched in at times, taking the children to ballgames and to young people's theater productions, swimming at the order's Camp Glinodo, and fishing in Lake Erie. Chittister and Tobin even took the gang of youngsters to Washington one year when Chittister had to attend a conference. The two brothers, during the interview at an Erie breakfast spot, pulled out photos of the group in front of the White House. The nuns would often show up on Friday afternoon with a list of chores and do the housecleaning and meal preparation. Chittister, as the outsider, also acted as the heavy when family meetings were necessary to make sure schedules were kept and household tasks were done. And she even played the disciplinarian once when she met one of the older boys, late for a family meeting, at the door and smelled beer on his breath. "Let's just say we had a serious one-on-one and it never happened again," recalls Chittister.

One moment has remained with Chittister for life and even finds its way occasionally into her public presentations. In the days immediately following Mary Alice's death, she was helping one of the younger boys at bedtime and the youngster pointed to a crucifix and said, "Well, by this time, Mom is in God's stomach."

The teacher in her waited a few seconds and then corrected: "You mean Mommy is in God's arms."

Then she asked why he had said his mommy was in God's stomach.

"Because," he answered, "Sister told us God is all around us, and that's the only place I could think of that God could be all around you all at one time." In that moment, says Chittister, she discovered an image that she'd use the rest of her life. "Of course we all live in the womb of God together, created there, developed there, swimming there, our contact with the rest of the universe there. And I can't look at any of these kids without thinking of that—what a beautiful story."

Tragic as the situation was, the experience provided Chittister with exposure to a kind of family life she had never known. At the same time, it offered a concrete example of the expansion of the idea of religious life that was occurring at the time. Both nuns made the point that not long before 1972 they would not have been able to become involved in helping the family. It was possible only because the doors of the monastery had recently opened to the wider world. Chittister recalled an incident during her years in Oil City when a widow, the mother of a junior in their high school, died suddenly. "The student came home from school one day. Her mother was there and she dropped dead in the kitchen right in front of her." The student called the only person she could think of, a sister at the convent, who told the young woman she would be right over. As the nun turned to get her shawl, the superior told her she wasn't permitted to go. The sister made it known she was leaving. The superior then said she could call Mother Superior in Erie to make certain it was all right. The nun said that if that made her feel better, she could do that, "but by the time you get an answer I'll be at the house."

Chittister was present for this exchange. "I stood and watched her," said Chittister. "I had never seen that kind of insubordination. She made a gospel judgment on the spot. No doubt whatsoever it was one of the biggest lessons of my life. I felt that big," she said, spreading her thumb and forefinger about an inch apart, "because I didn't go with her."

A very similar incident occurred later, only this time it involved a widower raising seven children. When he quite suddenly died, Chittister got a call from one of the children and didn't hesitate. She was the first one on the scene to comfort the family.

The two nuns made an extra effort to keep Christmas special in the life of the Tobin children, so they spent every spare moment of their holiday period, between community commitments and liturgies, helping with preparations, decorating, wrapping gifts, and preparing food. On Christmas day in 1971, they were on hand for the celebration and meal. They didn't get to Loretta's house until late in the afternoon.

It was a year to the day following Dutch's accident and little more than ten months since his death. "I knew it was going to be different when we got to the house—both bad and good. I didn't know how much she might have been able to do herself. I hadn't gone to the house to decorate or cook." Chittister, otherwise busy with the community and the Tobin children, had been staying with a small community that included Srs. Christine Vladimiroff and Pat McGreevy at a house in Erie that Maureen had inherited from her parents.

The arrangement was not unusual at the time, because even with the new monastery there wasn't enough room for everyone to be under one roof. Small communities outside the monastery were, in effect, a necessity because of space considerations.

When Chittister and Tobin arrived at Loretta's the house was quiet. There were few if any decorations. Loretta had not prepared any of the usual holiday fare, including a candy that was a special favorite of Joan's. "One thing I noticed was that she never once said anything about my father. She never mentioned his name. She never mentioned a word. Even I thought that was strange."

In the middle of the night, Chittister was awakened by eerie sounds and followed them into the living room of the tiny home where she discovered her mother on the floor, her knees pulled to her chest, gasping for air. Chittister called for Tobin to drive them to the hospital. She wrapped her mother in a blanket and picked her up and carried her to the car. They raced to the hospital and Loretta was taken into the emergency room and then admitted. At some point soon after Loretta arrived at the hospital, she went into a coma. She stayed in the hospital for nearly a month, and Tobin drove Chittister the seventy miles from Oil City to the hospital and back daily.

One day toward the end of the hospital stay, Chittister walked into the room containing four beds that were separated by curtains. Her mother's bed was surrounded by doctors and other medical personnel. She had opened her eyes and her first words were, "I don't know who the hell you guys are, but I am going to tell you, I didn't order you and I'm not paying for you."

Someone with oxygen canisters came into the room and she threw him out. "I was so embarrassed I thought I was going to die," Chittister said. It was as if her mother's personality had been put on steroids. "Everything she did was embarrassing."

Out in the hall, the doctors told Chittister, "Your mother does not have a patch of lung larger than a dime that's healthy." They told her she would never again walk or clothe herself. She would not be able to live alone and care for herself.

"She couldn't go home. What was I going to do with her?" Most arrangements were financially out of reach. The only thing she had to live on was a meager social security payment. Dutch had died before reaching the age at which he would have been paid full benefits, and Loretta received only a portion of that. "Mother Mary Margaret Kraus heard about this. She found me and talked to me. All I knew was how much it costs to put someone in a home. And she said to me, 'Bring your mother here.'"

Joan objected. A lay person had never lived at the monastery. "I don't want to put you in this position," she said. "What's the community going to think of it?"

Mary Margaret responded: "How are they going to feel if she's not here and you're worried? That's not going to be a problem. Bring your mother here."

Loretta was moved to the monastery. Everyone thought she would be there forever. Three weeks later, Chittister visited from Oil City and found Loretta waiting at the doorway of her room, fully dressed. She declared, "I want to go home now. I'm ready." Chittister convinced her to wait the few days until she could see the doctor.

On the day of the appointment, Loretta sat on an examining table, declaring she was fine and demanding that the doctor tell her daughter that she was going home. The doctor said he couldn't in good conscience do that. "You can't live alone. You can't walk down this corridor alone. You don't have enough lung power to make it."

With that, Loretta slid off the table, walked across the room, opened the door, and proceeded on down the corridor and back. The doctor was forced to give in. Joan and Maureen also conceded and agreed to take her to her home. On the way, Loretta convinced Maureen to stop at a favorite grocery. Chittister refused to go in and help her. She thought her mother, confronted with a dose of daily reality, would find out she was unable to fend for herself. Loretta was in the store for some time and came out with two full grocery carts pushed by a boy who helped her place the groceries in the car. She tipped the young man, got back in the car and said, "Okay, let's go."

Loretta went on living on her own, in one fashion or another, often in government subsidized housing after she sold her home, for nearly a quarter of a century. During that time she experienced a slow but steady descent into the ravages of Alzheimer's disease and spent the last three years of her life at the monastery.

A more private bit of turbulence in the early 1970s threatened Chittister's smooth trajectory from graduate school to an increasingly significant role in the Benedictine universe. At some point amid the blur of going to graduate school, teaching high school, and learning what it was to be a nun, she experienced a brief period of inner restlessness that grew out of a question.

She is not certain why or exactly when in the progression of that period of her life the thought occurred, but she began to question whether she should leave the order to get married and have a family. She wasn't involved with anyone, nor did she have any individual in mind. "There was no particular man and there never has been, there just hasn't been," but that fact was not enough to dismiss the possibility. The question emerged, and it intruded in a way that she couldn't ignore.

She said during our interviews that she had dated a few boys in high school, that she "never missed a dance," and she told the story of having to inform the last boy she dated that she would be entering the convent at the end of the summer. However, she never became seriously romantically involved with anyone. Still, she says, at some point in her early thirties, having already been in the order for more than fourteen years, "I began to realize that the clock was ticking, and I said to myself, 'If you want a family, if you want children, you've got to move and you've got to move quickly.' But I don't do anything quickly."

She told herself that she had to "look at this thing very closely." She was already studying at Penn State acquiring "a working knowledge of the effect of symbols, customs, and institutions. I knew the stuff that made life go together, and I can remember putting myself through a series of imaginings," a process she said she has used over the years in sessions counseling other people.

She decided that for two weeks she would function as if she were getting ready to leave the community to get married. "That's all I would think of, and I did it. It was really successful, and I liked the picture that I saw. I could really imagine being with a guy I loved, someone who was a good man, and the things that we could do together, the joy we'd have in life and everything that went with that."

Two weeks went by and she was becoming quite enamored of the picture of domestic happiness and fulfillment she was increasingly engaged in, at least in her imagination. She said to herself, "Joan, this is a good thing for you to do. If you close this door and don't think this through, you're going to regret it. Given the way you feel, I think you have to rethink this whole thing. During the next two weeks, I went to the same image and I put children in it. The minute I put children in it, it disappeared. The man I loved. The children? I could not see myself as a mother."

That realization, she said, "was coming right out of the center of my soul. By that time I'd had a good education. I was a thinker. I had wanted to be a writer since the age of fourteen. I knew I was called to that, it was in me, that concentration, that laser beam on life and those issues. That was what I was about, and I could be about it with a man, but I could not be about it with that same intensity with our children. I said, 'You're not called to this, Joan. There is no way.'" She said she wasn't certain what she might have done if the moment of her original decision regarding entering the order had come twenty years later "with an array of other choices . . . but it's very possible that I would not have been married" because of her childhood experience. "I had no proof that marriage was successful." The only proof she had from personal experience was that women could be brutalized and children terrified.

The exercise of imagining marriage, however, "proved to me that it could happen pretty easily." But it remained in her imagination, and the exercise gave way to a reality that became the best evidence that she had reasoned and decided properly: she stayed.

She is comfortable with celibacy, though she isn't certain it is a gift that simply comes with a vocation to religious life. "I don't know how you impose it. I understand that there is a question around the priesthood. Now if you do have the gift, that's wonderful. I think I have a gift. I'm very comfortable with it . . . It's as genuine as the day is long." Though it was easy to imagine falling in love and getting married, she said, "This is right for me. Not without struggle, as you already know in several instances. Just staying teaching grade school tested everything." But the closeness, the intimacy among members of a monastic community, the sense of being committed to and part of an extended family suited her. In no small way the support of that family allowed her to become a national and international influence in areas of spirituality, peace, feminism, and reform in the church.

Other than leaving, imagining another state in life sufficiently to rule it out was perhaps the only option available to a professed member of a religious order. The exercise seemed to provide a satisfactory answer for Chittister. While her visualizations on the matter were entirely private, it might appear in retrospect that other people in her growing sphere of activities were just waiting for the final answer. Her peers, both within her order and beyond, wasted no time, as she completed her schooling, steering her directly into the center of the unrest and exploration that were already under way in some quarters and that would result in dramatic changes in the lives of women religious.

In fact, she was pulled into the vortex even before she had officially finished her doctorate. During her years at Penn State, while teaching high school and riding the bus several hours to and from her graduate classes, she was also becoming known in Benedictine circles for her understanding of social and institutional change.

The insights grew directly out of the work she was doing at Penn State, a deep immersion into theories of change, coursework replete with psychological and philosophical content. She became interested "in perception, and in the nature of perception and the effects of perception of messages on groups, on attitudes, on formation."

Oil City and the campus of Penn State University are 125 miles apart. Chittister was making the trip twice a week by bus. Regularly along the route she passed a big rock that bore the legend: "Where will you spend eternity?" She would look at it and say to herself, "On an Edwards Lakes to Sea bus," referring to the company that operated the line.

"I started in January of 1969 and I graduated in September of 1971, and I worked like a dog in case those numbers don't tell you anything. Most people were spending five to seven years getting a doctorate. I did it in two-and-a-quarter, with the dissertation ["The Perception of Prose and Filmic Fiction"] written, wrapped up, stamped, accepted, and sent off to get some sort of prize. My advisor, Carroll Arnold, was fantastic."

So was Tobin, who often typed her papers, served as her chauffeur, and helped keep her organized while she was juggling the classes she taught, community work, and graduate school. Another sister helped out by devising a program in which students typed up answers to questionnaires Chittister had distributed to other students at the high school as part of her research.

The time she spent in the doctoral program changed her life. "Here I was in a totally nonsectarian institution where what counted was ideas and what was provable and what wasn't. What was philosophy and how did you think, and what did that have to do with good communication?" It included "all manner of study of ancient rhetoric—Cicero, and especially Aristotle."

She spent only about a year actually on campus, but that experience had a powerful influence on her. "It was the first time in my life when 'Catholic' didn't define everything and everybody that I knew. Though her professors "very much respected my Catholicism and my religion," they "never talked religion" even though she was still wearing the modified habit at the time and was quite identifiably a nun. "Like everybody in my generation," she says, the nuns of her era "had been formed in absolutes and everything had an answer." In that culture, "the institution is the basis of all truth and the past is the criterion for all goodness." Add religious life to the mix, and "when community custom became the basis for the definition of perfection, you were on a pretty rigid path even if you never thought of yourself as rigid."

Carroll, her "beloved advisor," had a final lesson for her when all the coursework and dissertation work were done. He told her that beyond the theory and stored up knowledge remained one unanswered question: "'What does this mean to me and thee?' And I have been answering that question in my life ever since I walked out of Penn State."

The doctorate was something she didn't need. She called it "all a fluke. I should never have been at Penn State, and I never would have been there under the aegis of the Benedictine Sisters of Erie because we didn't have a college, we didn't need doctorates to satisfy the requirements of the state. I got thrown into the middle of this. It was a total fluke. And I came out changed."

If she left that experience a changed person, she was also learning all the while about how and why change occurs for individuals and institutions. "Every time they went to a blackboard and put anything up or gave us any kind of an assignment or told us to read a particular book, it was as if I were reading the history of women religious all over the world, and especially in the United States, and definitely of the Erie Benedictines."

Her community at the time "was embroiled in polarization." Its members couldn't find common ground or a way of proceeding with the change that was already upon them. The thinking among some was that "change had to be unholy." Others had "an intuition" and seemed to "know that this change had to happen because the old system was dying. It wasn't engaging any more. People weren't giving their lives to it any more. They were leaving. They came and they left. And then, in the end, they didn't come." During the late 1960s and early 1970s, however, few had the tools to understand what seemed to many to be chaos and a kind of inexplicable dissolution.

Sometime during the winter of her year at Penn State, Chittister was told that another sister taking classes elsewhere at the university wanted to talk to her. "I can't tell you who she was because I don't remember. I didn't want to have the conversation because I really was a bear about my work." She was intent on completing the degree as quickly as possible, so she didn't allow herself many distractions. But she agreed to see the other sister, and they met for lunch. Chittister was thinking "when lunch is over, the conversation is over" and that would be the end of it.

They met, and Chittister realized during the course of conversation that the other woman was deeply pained by what her religious community was experiencing. "There was nothing hysterical about her at all, but her heart was hurt. Her community was polarized. There were no answers; there were bitter questions. The peace of the place had disappeared. We had all known it."

As the conversation continued, Chittister moved from polite acknowledgment of the other's anguish to responses that came out of her own experience of community life and out of her work at Penn State. They continued talking through the lunch hour, on into the afternoon, and finally they realized that the restaurant was beginning to set tables for dinner.

The other nun told Chittister that the conversation had meant a lot, that she was leaving feeling wonderful. Chittister realized through the encounter that she had come upon new ways to understand and to articulate what was occurring with the changes in both the church and religious life. She realized that she understood the pain that the other nun was experiencing but also that it was possible to work through it and come out understanding religious life in new ways.

The other nun sat back and looked at Chittister for a moment and then said, "Would you ever come to my community and say the same things?" It was an unusual request for that era—nuns didn't go around talking to nuns in other communities. "If you got invited would you come and would you say to the community what you said this afternoon?"

The request appealed to the teacher in Chittister—this was the kind of material she wanted to handle, the level of discussion in which she wanted to engage.

When the invitation arrived shortly after their discussion, she accepted and structured a workshop titled "Self Understanding in a Time of Change." She dealt with the theory of institutional change and the history of institutional change in the Roman Catholic Church and in the American sisterhood. She discussed personal, psychological, and philosophical reactions to change.

"And the invitations never stopped coming." The news spread mostly word of mouth among the various orders and she soon found herself traveling throughout the East Coast giving workshops that often began on Friday night and ended sometime on Sunday.

"There are always two roads in my life—the order and everybody else." For decades she has continued to live in and between those two realities, often with one informing the other. At the outset, however, what she had learned outside the community and her work to explain to others their complex circumstances in rapidly changing institutions ultimately was self-revealing.

"For the first time in my life I could see my own life objectively. I could step back, I had the distance—like an out of body experience—to look at my own community and religious life in general and say, 'If an outside expert came in and placed on us a template for change and development, what would it look like?'"

This was also the first time in her life, she said, that she would have had the maturity to look at her existence in religious life objectively. Such an examination would have been impossible in an earlier period. "The environment wouldn't raise or wouldn't allow such questions."

By the late 1960s, however, the environment not only tolerated such questions, it invited them in formal settings. Women religious throughout the country were taking seriously the instructions of the Vatican II document, "Decree on the Appropriate Renewal of the Religious Life." The document set out two "simultaneous processes" for renewal:

- A continuous return to the sources of all Christian life and to the original inspiration behind a given community
- An adjustment of the community to the changed conditions of the times

The document went on to discuss the need for "suitable adaptations" in the "manner of living, praying and working" within communities. It recommended collegial approaches to seeking the approval of community members for the anticipated changes, and it strongly urged that the training of members of religious orders be comprehensive, suitable to their ministries, and that it include study for appropriate degrees.[1] The orders were advised to carefully examine the intent of their founders and rediscover the roots of their charisms and ministry and determine how they could be applied to the needs of the day. The renewal was to be not only structural and organizational but also interior. The members of religious orders were being called to incorporate new attitudes and dispositions about their lives and work.

The erratic Sr. Alice Scheiberl, during her single term as prioress, recognized even before the council that certain adaptations needed to occur to meet the demands of contemporary society. While she instituted some mildly consultative processes, the changes were mostly prioress driven and subject to her whims alone. As was clear in Chittister's case, Scheiberl's generosity could be withdrawn in an instant without warning or rationale. In hindsight she seemed to embody the tensions of the transitions between

---

1. Walter M. Abbott, SJ, ed., *The Documents of Vatican II* (New York: Crossroad Publishing Co., 1989), 466ff.

the rule-bound past and a more relational and less rigid future. She promulgated instructions, for instance, about what could be said to family about the community, how one should sit and speak, what the sisters should and should not do during recreation hours, how they were to relate to one another. At the same time, she pushed sisters to become educated and far more adventuresome than they might have previously imagined. Some members of the community, while acknowledging her "dark side," also said they owed a great debt to Scheiberl for encouraging them to move well beyond their own expectations. Toward the end of her life, Scheiberl often spoke with regret about how she had treated people as prioress. For all of her idiosyncrasies, she was among the first to break old molds. She resigned her post early because of health reasons, but a path toward change seemed unalterably established.

In the world of U.S. Benedictines, the impulse for change was certainly encouraged by the Vatican II decree on the renewal of religious life, and its earliest formal phase was instituted by the order in the general chapters of renewal held in 1968–69. Chittister was elected as one of the delegates from the Erie community.

She attended the two meetings as well as the 1971 general chapter of the Federation of St. Scholastica, one of four federations in the United States. She went in to that assembly in June, having just turned thirty-five in April. Her major concern at the time the defense of her dissertation that was to take place at Penn State in two weeks. She came out of the assembly as president of the federation. She was just old enough, canonically, to hold a leadership position in the order.

Chittister had come to the attention of the wider Benedictine community because of the workshops she had been conducting. Her academic discipline combined with her ability to articulate what was occurring in religious life made her a good fit for leadership at the time. Life was becoming increasingly demanding and hectic.

When she looks back, she considers that "it wasn't all that astonishing" that she was elected, because of the work she had been doing. What was astonishing was her age. It was highly unusual for the order to elect someone so young to a position of leadership.

"I walked out of the general chapter in Florida as president, and I distinctly remember noticing that everybody else had left. They had come in from all over the country, and many in cars. They had driven because it was cheaper at that time. And I got in the back seat of the car that we came in. I put my head back, and they say that I said, 'Now maybe I can have a dog.'" There would be dogs, and pet birds, and ultimately, based on those pets, even a book about humans' relationship with animals. The pets, however, would also become a community project. They would never have her undivided attention. With the invitations to do workshops and her early election to leadership, she was just beginning a life that would be lived in large measure on the road for much of the next four decades.

"A president has certain canonical authority in a community," she explained, "and the single greatest authority is the obligation to have regular visitations." A strength of Benedictinism—that it is strong, local, and independent—is also a weakness. Communities, should they become too isolated, can become distorted places with strange practices and bad teachings. It was to protect against such distortions that Benedictines first were confederated in the thirteenth century.

Chittister's role as president was to make regular visitations to see how communities were doing. With her training as a social psychologist, she understood that "articulation of present values is as important as the articulation of past history." She helped the fifty or so prioresses throughout the United States write statements of contemporary Benedictine values. One of the statements was titled "Upon this Tradition." Another was done on the liturgy of the hours as a central dimension of Benedictine life. A third, focused on work, helped Benedictines who found themselves in the midst of structural change to reassert the values for which they were changing.

"I have a personal organizational theory," said Chittister. "I will not live long enough to test it . . . but I have a theory that when organizations are in a state of renewal, when structures are in flux, ideas should be stable, and when ideas are in flux, structures should be stable.

"What did you have in the 1960s? Both structures and ideas were free-floating. So why wouldn't you have total disaster? Why wouldn't this thing just fall into its own basement? So I said to myself, 'The structures are going to be in flux for a long time because this is an experimentation period, and it's like the Fourth of July fireworks.' It was breaking every place I could see."

She hoped that by defining basic values and throwing them into the night sky, people would recognize them as true, grab onto them, and say, "This is what we are still about, but in this culture, slightly differently." The documents seemed to give life and direction, said Chittister. "They became part of their formation programs, and those documents are still around."

Chittister had not arrived easily or willingly at that first level of leadership. It had taken some persuasion to get her to make the presentation that helped shine the spotlight on her and her work. And it had taken a manipulation of nature to convince her to run for office.

"Here I was at Penn State finishing my doctorate, just finishing my dissertation, and a general chapter came up. I didn't want to go to the general chapter, and I definitely didn't want to do anything there. I wasn't that dumb."

In 1970 a delegation of Benedictines had approached her to deliver a talk during a pre-chapter meeting. She was then asked to give a talk at the general chapter, a meeting of all of the prioresses in the federation, about how individuals and groups change. She told them "no" several times. But, she says, "they just stayed at me and stayed at me that year, and I finally gave in. I went to the general chapter."

She gave the paper in 1971 during the general chapter meeting at St. Leo Benedictine Abbey in Central Florida. It was well received, Chittister recalled. Two days after she gave the paper, the group took nominations for the presidency. Chittister was nominated.

Discussing her reaction, she says, "Here's the embarrassing but painfully true part of the story" that everyone eventually learned.

When she was first asked if she'd accept the nomination, she privately thought the idea "crazy" but said she'd have to think about it. "Then guilt set in and I said, 'I can't say no to these people. They've been so good to me. What they've done for me, how they've carried me.' So the next morning I said, 'Okay, put the name on.'

"That night I wilted, went down to the office, and said, 'Take that name off.' The next day there was pressure from people, and the name went back on. Now we're at three. The next morning it came off."

The young Chittister sought the counsel of an older monk named Matthew Benko, a Benedictine from St. Vincent Archabbey in Latrobe, Pennsylvania, the canonist advisor to the chapter and a figure who helped the Erie Benedictines navigate the complexities of the renewal years. Chittister remembers him as a gentle man, a "wisdom figure" who had a calming effect. "He had a crew cut, and he used to stand up and rub his head and he'd say, 'Sisters, Sisters, what you have to remember is this: Just tell us what you want and we'll write the law that says you ought to do it. He taught us so much."

He approached Chittister and said, "Joan, I think we should have a talk."

The two of them went for a walk. "We walked the monastery grounds, and I went through one of those tortured stories." She explained why she thought she wasn't the right person for the job, why she wasn't the right fit, why it wasn't really who she was.

"Well," he asked, "do you think you don't know anything about religious life?"

"No, no, I know plenty about religious life," she answered. "I know where religious life should go. I know where we are going. It's plain as it can be. It's just a matter of getting there peacefully and trying to do it well."

"That sounds right," he said.

To her, however, it still felt wrong. "Matthew, I'm just telling you inside of me it's wrong. I want to help the sisters. I want to help religious life. I'll do anything I can. But be president of the federation? No!" She asked what he would have done.

"He said, 'What I think you ought to do.'

"And I said, 'What's that?'

"He said, 'Why don't you let them decide? If they don't want you, if they think you can't do it, they won't vote for you. That's what chapters do. And just because they put your name in, no matter what they're saying to you now, when they go in there and vote it will be a different thing.'"

She said that his suggestion sounded both simple and right. "If I were you," he said, "I'd get my name back on that list and just let them decide." If she did that, he said, they wouldn't be able to say later that they should have elected her but she wouldn't allow it.

She didn't do anything immediately. She didn't reject Matthew's counsel, she thought about it and mulled it over. And then her impetuous side took over.

One of the exercises conducted during the chapter sessions involved planting flower seeds in little plastic containers, the kind banana splits are served in. The nuns referred to them as banana boats. As the story will make clear, Chittister apparently had never grown anything in her life. She had no idea how seeds and soils acted or how long it took for seeds to germinate and grow. And so she announced at her table in what she describes as "one of those major, loud Chittisterisms," that if their table's plant bloomed within the two days left before voting began, she would accept the nomination.

Less than an hour before the close of nominations she was making her way to breakfast down a long slope and arrived at a patio where all of the little plastic containers from all of the tables were lined up in the sun. Not one had "so much as a weed in it except one." Someone behind her told her to look up, that one of the containers had a flower in it. "They ran over and picked it up and said, 'It's table 8' or something like that. I remember feeling very sick to my stomach. I remember standing there saying to myself, 'You fool. You fool. Why did you say something like that out loud?'"

She went to the office once more and placed her name back on the ballot. Later that day, it was final. She had been elected president of the federation.

Not long after, during a visit to the Benedictine house in Chicago, the prioress asked Joan to "tell us about the banana boat." Somebody else said, "Tell us about the flower." It was all over the federation. She said, "Boy, somebody needs to tell me. I learned my lesson. I'm never saying anything like that again."

The prioress started to laugh and laugh, and finally said, "It was the best thing we ever did. It was the smartest thing we ever did."

What was the smartest thing they did, Chittister asked.

"Putting that flower in the banana boat," the prioress answered.

Chittister said, "What?!"

The prioress responded, "You didn't know that?"

To this day Chittister insists that she didn't know they'd pulled a fast one on her. "What do I know about agriculture? Never said I did, and I don't." She laughs in retrospect that her leadership career got its start because of a fraudulent "sign."

There was nothing fake or lighthearted, however, about the tensions that ran through religious communities, the Benedictines included, during that era of turmoil and reform. Chittister was already accomplished at explaining what was happening, and her travels to other houses as president of the federation gave her deeper insight into what was going on. But she wasn't out blazing revolutionary trails.

"At that time, every single house was in turmoil, every single house was polarized by the whole notion of change, habits changing, structures changing." She was wearing a modified habit at the time, but had resisted even that change. "Yes, I resisted the change of the habit. I resisted just about everything."

The conflicts were personal as well as institutional. Sr. Christine Vladimiroff, for instance, who was not quite four years younger than Joan and who later became a major figure in the confrontation between Chittister and the Vatican, was, of the two nuns, much farther down the road of renewal and change in those early years. In fact, the tension between the two, as much a clash of personality and leadership style as it was of genuine disagreement, was never entirely resolved. At the same time, the relationship illustrates the bonds of sisterhood within the Erie community that can transcend even deep personal disagreement. That element will be explored in more detail in a subsequent chapter.

To the topic at hand, however, Vladimiroff—who died in 2014—explained during an extensive interview in 2012 that the tension that had grown out of renewal activity in the 1960s, not infrequently over matters that might seem inconsequential today, could have had serious consequences. At some point she, as was the case with others, made a decision to do whatever was necessary to keep the community together. She recalled a chapter meeting where the realization dawned that in order to stay together members of the community who disagreed would have to make compromises. Some would have to slow down; others would have to speed up.

She recalled another moment during that period when the realization was even more dramatic. She was approached by "a very venerable sister" who had been principal of the high school when Vladimiroff was a student and had also been a subprioress at one time. "I'll never forget this. She said, 'I think we're going to split and I think we should make a community together,' I thought, 'Hell, I'm not doing that.' I loved this sister and she had been one of my mentors since I was a young person, let alone a sister, and I thought, 'We can't do that.'" It took a great deal of work as a community, some of it with outside help in mediating the differences and seeing the way clear, to reach accord regarding the steps along the path of renewal. The path included such seemingly obvious conversations as: 'If I want to take the veil off, why can't you let me take the veil off and you keep yours on and not let it be something that breaks or frays the bond of charity between us? It's a veil.' But we weren't used to communicating that clearly with each other."

When they first met, Chittister was in her early twenties and Vladimiroff was nineteen. It was 1959 and they and others shared a house in Oil City, where they were both teaching. Asked if there was a moment when she realized that Chittister was giving expression to some ideas that weren't normally heard in a lot of Benedictine communities, Vladimiroff replied: "I think I would have been impressed that she was bright." But she quickly followed with a comment establishing that, during the Vatican II period, "I was probably part of the young leadership. In terms of renewal, I would say that we were not always on the same page together." When pressed to explain further, she said, "Well, I guess I would have been for moving faster and more radically than she was at that time."

Chittister agrees and recalls that the tension was more about attitude than content. Christine, she says, was among a group of younger members of the community who were "highly intuitive. There was no doubt that they had a good sense of vision," but she remembers their approach to change to be one of presumption. "If you asked them, 'Why would you do that?' they sneered. If they didn't sneer, they just said, 'Well, anybody would know. It's obvious!'"

It wasn't obvious to Chittister at the time nor did such an answer fit with her need for cogent and persuasive argument. "It was more personal than it was theological or theoretical. Obviously, I could handle the theological and theoretical. I could not handle that kind of an attitude. It was so negative and so demeaning. In other words, if you don't see it our way, you're stupid. And maybe so, possibly true. But there's another way to tell people they're stupid that isn't as destructive. So the community split down the middle. This community wanted to split."

At the time Joan was "on the side of the habits." At the very beginning of renewal talk, she argued for retaining the habit because she thought the alternative would adversely affect relationships with lay people. "And you had fifteen hundred years that somehow or other you had to explain to yourself." How was it that, through all of that history, it was never touched, "but now all of the sudden it could be just discarded at all times, in all places, at one time"?

She was also concerned because she watched the effect on older sisters in the community. "It was terrible for them. It was terrible. I really felt that you could do it, but you could do it in pieces, not at once. Why would you have to do all of it at once?" Whatever the questions—and the eventual answers—she admitted years later that "these personal conflicts and the sense of domination or being demeaning, I couldn't get beyond the personality." Despite their differences, in later years Chittister, during the last two of her three terms as prioress, would appoint Vladimiroff to her council, a kind of leadership team that includes both elected and appointed members. She said she valued Vladimiroff's intelligence, vision, and intuition.

Chittister eventually got beyond the habit question and her turning point on this issue occurred in one of those imagining tasks that she occasionally assigns to herself. "I got to the point where I said to myself, 'Joan, are you or are you not a Benedictine in a bathtub? Are you a Benedictine when you have nothing on? Does it take clothes? When you're in the bathtub do you see yourself as Benedictine or not? Do you stop being a Benedictine?' You see, that line of questions unlocked everything for me. It took me right to essence. It skipped over all this other stuff. It led me to a question that held the answer I was looking for: What do clothes have to do with philosophy or meaning, the philosophy of identity, the sense of commitment?"

Finally, the community set a date after which the sisters did not have to wear any kind of habit—the Christmas holidays of 1971. They left school the day before Christmas holidays in full habit and returned on January 2 in ordinary clothing. Chittister and Tobin were in the high school office that day as usual when a young man walked in to pay his tuition. Tobin took the money and asked about his family and the holidays. The youngster gave curt answers, looking at the floor most of the time, not at Tobin or at Chittister, and as quickly as he could after answering her questions turned and walked out of the office.

"What's got into him?" Tobin asked.

Chittister said there was nothing wrong with the student, that the problem was them.

"What do you mean?" Tobin asked.

"I said, 'Maureen, he's never seen you without a veil on before. There, dear sister, in fifteen hundred years, all we've managed to do is make a hairline obscene. The kid couldn't look at you."

Slowly, some of the visible, traditional markers of religious life, many of which could be traced to a time when they were either a normal part of a culture or instituted to meet some need, fell away. For many religious orders, Chittister became the interpreter of the times and the forces at work.

But she has apologized, she said, to members of her own order, and she has repeatedly explained to the community and the general public that she did not lead the renewal effort. If anything, she may have led the thinking about renewal and fashioned ways to explain what was happening. "I was not one of the people who could leap so easily and lightly from the eighteenth century, let alone the sixth, to the twentieth. I had to do a thought, a piece, at a time."

Having found some answers for herself, she also discovered that she was relatively good at teaching others. "That's what I do. I simply explain what happened in the church."

In the workshops, which by the late 1970s she was giving throughout the country almost non-stop, she was explaining to people "what freezes in us when the institutional structures around us begin to break down and there's nothing to hold onto." She would show graphs of the rise and fall of religious communities as well as other great institutions and traditions. The question always returned to "but what happens to the people who were formed in them and are standing there when the roof falls in a hundred years later? What do they do and how do they get through it and how can we get through this?"

She didn't need to stake herself to one side or the other in the debates she knew were occurring in the communities she visited because "I had been there, because God had allowed me to be there." When a sister in one of the communities came through the door angry, she knew the anger was fear. "These people just wanted it stopped. 'You're the president of the federation, stop this!'" She knew what they were experiencing because she had experienced it herself, once going so far as to announce to her mother and stepfather during a home visit that she was leaving the order. It was sometime during the turmoil of the 1960s, before she had been elected to any office, and the scene she describes is one of unusual familial intimacy, one of the moments that allowed her to understand Dutch in ways other than his alcoholism.

"There were no outbursts or anything. Both parents took it very well. My mother said, 'Why are you leaving, Joan? All you've ever wanted was to be was a sister. Why would you change your mind now?'

"I said, 'I didn't change my mind. I didn't leave religious life. Religious life is leaving me. It's got the community torn apart. We're just not happy anymore.'"

Her mother was fixing Sunday dinner. "I don't know what Dad was doing. He was usually smoking a cigarette someplace. A game was going to be on and we were accustomed to watching or listening to games together, so I went in to turn on the television." Dutch came in and sat down. He spoke quietly, telling her that this would always be her home. "When you walk in that door, this place belongs to you. You can come and go anytime you want and you can stay as long as you want." He and her mother were happy she was home, he said, he just wanted to ask her one question: "Who's going to take care of the older sisters if you all leave?"

"I don't know," Joan answered. "I guess they'll take care of themselves. They always have."

He pressed on, reminding her that the sisters had done a lot for her. "You've always loved them, haven't you?" he asked.

"I thought to myself, 'This is the guy who would have killed to stop me from going into the convent.' Then I answered, 'Yes.'"

"He said, 'Well it's a tough one, don't you think?'"

"'Yes,' I said."

"All of a sudden," she added, "my mother appeared from the kitchen. She had got an apron on. I can still see it. She'd obviously been doing dishes. She still had the dishrag in her hand. She came in and perched herself on the corner of his chair and said, 'Joan, you know things change. They never stay what you think they are when you start. They change.'"

"I said, 'I know that, Mom.'"

"She said, 'You don't think that our marriage is today what it was when it started, do you? You don't think this has been all the same, do you?'"

"Silently, I thought, 'Jesus, I lived it. Well, yes and no.' I said, 'Well, no.'"

Chittister says the conversation turned her to thinking about the "continuing responsibility to people who are carrying you through life. You have to keep helping them make it what it becomes."

She was surprised by her parents' reaction, especially her father's. There wasn't a hint of the old enmity toward the sisters or a sign that he was happy she might leave the order. "He had really come to love the sisters. He saw them carry me all the way through the polio thing. They both knew I was happy doing what I was doing, and I think they saw good things happening. I walked out of that house and said to myself, 'You have a lot of thinking to do.'"

SIX

THE STRUGGLE TO RENEW

F or the two decades between 1971 and 1990, when she was between the ages of thirty-five and fifty-four, Chittister was elected
by her immediate peers and others to positions that gave her an
unparalleled view of religious life at all levels and connected her with
religious leaders here and abroad. The positions brought her into contact with Vatican authorities and deep into the heart of the tensions involved with questions of governance and authority during what were
arguably some of the most turbulent years in the modern history of
women's religious orders in the United States.

In 1974, three years after she was elected president of the Federation of St. Scholastica, Chittister was elected president of the Conference of American Benedictine Prioresses, an office she held until 1990,
even though she was not a prioress at the time. Canonically, presidents
of federations and prioresses are of the same status.

In 1976, she was elected president of the Leadership Conference of
Women Religious (LCWR), an umbrella organization that represented
almost all of the women's religious orders at that time. Two years later,
she was elected prioress of the Benedictine Sisters of Erie. She was re-
elected prioress two more times, serving a total of three four-year
terms, a period of leadership that ended in 1990.

She was also a U.S. councilor-delegate to the Rome-based International Union of Superiors General (IUSG) from 1982 to 1986.

It was during this period that she began to find her voice as a writer,
applying her background as a social scientist and her experience as a
member of a religious order to begin formalizing her analysis of religious life and the changes under way. The year before she became prioress of the Benedictines in Erie, Paulist Press published *Climb Along*

the Cutting Edge: An Analysis of Change in Religious Life, a book she
helped organize and to which she contributed. Using data gathered from
participants in the renewal meetings, or chapters, held by the Federation
of St. Scholastica in 1968 and 1969, Chittister and four other Benedictine nuns—Stephanie Campbell, Mary Collins, Ernestine Johann, and
Johnette Putnam, compiled one of the first analyses, using survey instru-
ments, of religious life during this extraordinary period.[1]

"We began this work because history was slipping away from us,"
Chittister wrote in the preface of the book. "In the space of one decade,
convent life had undergone momentous change." Despite "volumes of
position papers, meeting minutes and constitutional amendments" that
evinced the work of renewal done since the close of the Second Vatican
Council, very few materials existed "to enable the next generation to
narrate the train of events which led to renewal or to describe the personal pressures which surrounded it."[2]

What resulted was a volume thick with data, history, and articulation of the tensions that, to that point, had accompanied renewal efforts.
In light of Chittister's later work, one small note in the preface is significant. The writers acknowledge, in response to "reader-reactors" who
helped shape the work, that feminism was one of the elements underlying the renewal of women's orders in the United States. However, the
writers state, the matter of women's rights was never a point of debate
during the chapter meetings "nor used to substantiate a position. For
that reason, this explanation is not given in the text though the writers
acknowledge the likelihood of the woman issue as a residual influence
on community renewal programs as early as 1966." The writers also

---

1. In addition to Chittister, whose credentials have been amply listed earlier, this was an accomplished group of women. Stephanie Campbell was an
elected delegate to the 1968–69 renewal chapter, author of the St. Walburga
Convent community history, "Chosen for Peace," and, at the time, principal of
Martin Spalding High School in Severn, MD. Mary Collins had earned a doctorate in liturgical theology from The Catholic University of America and had
been first councilor of the Federation of St. Scholastica, delegate to the 1971
and 1974 chapters, and had worked on renewal of the Benedictine community
at Mount St. Scholastica in Atchison, KS. Ernestine Johann was prioress of St.
Benedict's Convent in Bristow, VA, had a master's in theology, and had been active in renewal efforts at the local and federation level for some years and as an
officer of the LCWR. Johnette Putnam had been prioress of St. Scholastica Priory in Covington, LA, and a participant in renewal chapters from 1968
through 1974. She succeeded Chittister as president of the Federation of St.
Scholastica (1978–90). She was active in the civil rights movement in her state
and had been a long-time member of the federation council.
2. Joan Chittister, *Climb Along the Cutting Edge: An Analysis of Change
in Religious Life* (Mahwah, NJ: Paulist Press, 1977), xiii.

note that "most of the consultants to whom the sisters turned for direction or approval were men."

Indeed, the text throughout contains references, particularly in quotes from respondents, regarding the incongruity of consulting men in this business of renewal of women's orders. The work itself stands as an unusual effort by and on behalf of women religious, a rare record of women examining their lives as religious and deeply investigating the purpose of religious life in the modern world.

The results of the sociological study established, at least in the Benedictine world as experienced in the Federation of St. Scholastica, that certain elements of renewal had taken a strong hold in the space of a decade following the final session of Vatican II. The work is substantial and covers an impressive range of issues involved in the changes under way in the post–Vatican II period. Two areas of inquiry, however, might serve to give a sense of what the compilers of the work found early on. The areas considered here contain telling indications of both the why of renewal and of things to come.

In a section on Attitudes toward Pre–Vatican II Religious Life, the study found that two-thirds of Benedictine women who responded were quite satisfied with life in the previous era. They found that the structures of that period gave meaning to their lives.[3] If life then was ordered to the last detail and predictable, it was also "purposeful and clear."

"Women who lived the life well were enriched by its tranquility, and people who observed the life were convinced of its good intentions and sincerity. Nothing was ever much disturbed; turmoil was foreign and order was pre-eminent." In addition, the sisters, as different as they appeared from the prevailing culture, "nevertheless felt accepted and dignified, committed and fulfilled." So why, the writers ask, would a group so satisfied risk the change? The answer perhaps captures the ambivalence that attends change that is not forced but is agreed upon by a group, as was the case with the members of the Benedictine federation. While two-thirds of the respondents found their former lives satisfying and fulfilling in many ways, two-thirds were also "just as strong in their association of negative qualities with pre–Vatican II religious life. It is true that the group in large part agreed that the religious life of the past was peaceful, stable, and secure. It is also true that they considered it *closed, introverted, restrictive,* and *static.* They said it was *impersonal.*" (Italics in the original.)

A section subtitled Ministry is more indicative of the outside, pragmatic forces that may have been pushing sisters, Benedictines and others across the country, to examine the work they were doing and the structures

---

3. Ibid., 170–71.

that ordered their lives.[4] Responses from the sisters acknowledged the need they perceived to move beyond traditional roles into more specialized ministries that demanded more education and time away from the monastery or convent. They also recognized that their numbers even then were dwindling. The exodus of nuns and priests was well under way, and the sisters felt the pressure of fewer people taking on increasing demands. It affected the small matters of life: Who cleans, cooks, looks after the details of everyday life? Where is the time for sustaining the contemplative life, for quiet, for refreshing body and soul?

Those questions, however, were also entwined with larger issues having to do with the corporate work of the community. At the time, the work usually involved running and staffing large parochial institutions, such as diocesan schools and the orders' own schools, which needed slots filled by members of the community. Much of the predictability of religious life relied on the maintenance of such ministries. "The theological rationale was that an essential part of the religious vocation was to be 'sent,' to be disposable." But times were changing, and at least two new realities were altering the traditional patterns. First, even areas of traditional ministries were becoming more specialized, which meant that slots were becoming more difficult to fill, and second, many nuns acquiring specialized education and training were moving "outside the community school systems to use their specialties in new areas and among the poor."[5]

What also became clear a bit later in the history of the Erie Benedictines was that as the number of nuns dwindled and the costs of maintaining old structures kept rising, the economics of some traditional ministries no longer worked for communities. This is an element briefly touched on in *Climb Along the Cutting Edge*. The trend became more evident over time and continues to be the case even into the twenty-first century, for example, in areas of the Northeast and Upper Midwest. Downsizing in the form of parish and school closings and mergers has become a central part of pastoral planning in many major cities. The parochial model that had served so many waves of immigrants arriving in the United States and that had boomed from the 1940s through the mid-1960s was becoming unsustainable.[6]

---

4. Ibid., 232–33.

5. Ibid., 233.

6. I covered the demographic shifts among people and clergy within the United States and the effects of those shifts on that old model of church rather extensively in a reported series for *National Catholic Reporter*, eventually expanded into the book, *The Emerging Catholic Church: A Community's Search for Itself* (Maryknoll, NY: Orbis Books, 2011). I also reported on a similar dynamic in the Australian church in a series that appeared in *National Catholic Reporter*, March and April 2014.

The writers note that such changes, "whatever the motives, affect the traditional ministries in numbers as well as in costs and cause tension among the community members themselves." The sisters' perception of motives, however, was not incidental or unimportant. Quoting from responses, the writers record that some viewed the moves to individual ministries as "a sign of waning commitment, an 'unrealistic and selfish response'" placing personal prerogatives above "the needs of the people of God or demands for personnel."

Other respondents took a more favorable view of such changes, suggesting they indicated an extension of community life and involvement in "larger needs of the Church [which] are often ignored." Yet others felt that lack of personnel was causing particular motherhouses to reconsider their ministries and whether these ministries could be maintained.

Agreement existed among all respondents, the writers conclude, "that the number of personnel has declined, the cost of maintaining older institutions has risen, the desire to maintain traditional commitments is in question, and the call to new ministries has increased. Each of these factors—some a direct result of the renewal period, others an outgrowth of culture—is apparently a pressure point for a number of communities in the Federation of St. Scholastica."

The Erie Benedictines were not spared the upheaval of reassessment and tough decisions. By the time Chittister was elected prioress, a great deal of ground had been plowed and seeded. Sr. Mary Margaret Kraus, prioress from 1964 to 1978, was, it can be said with the certainty of hindsight, a brilliant choice to guide the community through that period of deep introspection and turmoil. Expressions of warmth and gratitude for her wisdom and leadership came often and without solicitation during many of my interviews with community members who lived through that period. She seems to have been able to intellectually and pragmatically provide a bridge from the early impulses of reform that found erratic expression in the term of Alice Schierberl to the more established direction of renewal that found a solid stride during Chittister's tenure.

The renewal process was long and tedious, stretching over years and general and renewal chapter meetings beginning in 1966, one year after the Second Vatican Council ended, and extending into the 1970s. The extraordinary general chapter, for instance, was called by Mother Mary Susan Servier, president of the Federation of St. Scholastica, who had received permission to hold the chapter by the Sacred Congregation for Religious in Rome "only after several disappointing delays."

During the sessions, the nuns were warned that the process could take a long time. The intent at the first extraordinary chapter, for instance, was to rewrite the constitutions under which the order had been living since 1922.[7] The new constitutions of the Federation of St. Scholastica were finally approved by the Vatican in 1988.[8]

Subsequent renewal chapters of 1967 and 1968, held over two years because of the enormity of the task, involved exhaustive preparations by individual communities and their representatives who would make presentations at the chapter gatherings. Committees and subcommittees prepared papers and suggestions, based on the documents of Vatican II, on changes in everything from lifestyle to ministry, liturgy and worship to attire. In the end, that last item, particularly whether to abandon the veil, was the most contentious and took the longest time to resolve.

Kraus established structures that would greatly increase participation in decision-making, and specific times were established for experimentation with renewal ideas. Still, despite the work that went on and the new openness to receiving ideas from all quarters, dissatisfaction ran deep among some members of the community. Sr. Stephanie Campbell writes, "there were elements of dissent, dissatisfaction and divergence evident, as expressed by Mary Margaret [Kraus] in her letter to the community following the January 1968 pre-chapter meeting in Atchison. While she acknowledged the disapproval of some with the method for preparing experiments to be carried out...she assured the sisters that all had been approved by Mother Mary Susan and by the two Benedictine canonists present at the pre-chapter sessions."[9]

One of the unforeseen bumps in the road to renewal was the appointment in September 1966 of John Whealon as the new bishop of Erie.[10] This appointment, as the order's history diplomatically describes it, "served to inject a new and unwelcome dimension into the relationship of bishop and community." Whealon, who had been an auxiliary bishop in Cleveland, was installed in Erie in the spring of 1967, and it appears that his relationship with the Erie Benedictines was almost immediately strained.

Two of the great agonies Mary Margaret Kraus dealt with as prioress were the division in the community between, roughly, those for and against reform, and the number of sisters leaving the order. One of the spoken recollections gathered in *Vision of Change, Voices of Challenge*, captures the pathos of that moment:

---

7. Sr. Stephanie Campbell, *Vision of Change, Voices of Challenge: The History of Renewal in the Benedictine Sisters of Erie, 1858–1990* (Xlibris, 2015), 27.

8. Ibid., 81.

9. Ibid., 83.

10. The depictions here of Whealon's interaction with the community at this stage of renewal are taken from *Vision of Change*, 84–90.

When a community discussion arose over what constituted a "true Benedictine," unsigned notes appeared on the bulletin board at 345 [9th Street, also known then as Pax Priory, one of the small-group convents in Erie, apart from the main monastery], with conflicting views. When one note appeared it was removed and replaced by someone with another opinion. Margaret Ann was so disturbed by this ongoing dialogue that she went to ask how she could leave the community. At this, Mary Margaret broke down and cried; so many sisters were unhappy. Later she and Mary Margaret talked; she stayed.

And another recollection recounts:

Mary Margaret suffered deeply over the sisters who were leaving in record numbers. "I don't understand it. I never doubted my vocation," she would say. "But these times were unsettling, full of inner conflict, unanswered questions."

She had to contend not only with the stresses within the community but also in her dealings with the new bishop. The first communication between Whealon and Kraus was over his interviews with women who were then seeking a dispensation from their commitment to the Benedictines. He said that while some had valid reasons, others did not. There is no indication in the written history that Whealon attempted to stop anyone from leaving or that he or the prioress would have had any authority or power to do so. But the situation led him to voice his concern "about sisters out late at night 'to the wonderment of people'" and about "elaborate coiffures." He viewed some nuns' hair styles "a total contradiction in terms for a religious," and he believed that the sisters' hair "must be done with simplicity, naturalness, and without any artifices." Whealon's interjection into such matters, Campbell notes, came during an "unusual period of experimentation on many levels in religious life and certainly not limited to Erie. The question of self-determination by a canonical local chapter of sisters was under scrutiny."

His criticisms went well beyond the appearance of the local nuns. The renewal chapter of 1968 had resulted in "well-formulated position papers" for the congregational council and advance copies were "dutifully sent" to the bishop. "His response was a nine-page letter refuting the total content on the grounds that much of it had only an indirect connection with the teachings of the Vatican Council, some had no connection at all, and some matters were actually opposed to Council teachings."

Whealon wanted the sisters to eliminate use of such words as "mature," "freedom," and "responsibility" because they were "subjective."

He termed portions of the papers "unspiritual" and "Pelagian in nature, devoid of religious reasoning" of the council.

The bishop had "great difficulty with [the] idea of experimentation of sisters living in an apartment: [the] ideal of Christian living is to be in the house and not out of the house." This critique came at a time when the order was about to go ahead with an experiment allowing women to live in small households and be involved in ministries other than the traditional teaching role. It is worth noting here that the controversy over whether nuns could live apart from the monastery was, at least partially, based on the incorrect assumption that all nuns prior to Vatican II lived in a monastery and seemed partly related to episcopal control over how nuns lived. As was clear in the case of the Erie Benedictines, and as the bishop certainly was aware, the order had always had mission houses where groups of nuns teaching in diocesan high schools lived, and the spread of the order itself from one location to another often required moving out of a monastery to develop new communities. The expansion Whealon opposed had to do with the ministry and living arrangements that were chosen, not dictated by the order or the bishop. The move to other ministries, strange at the time, would become a normal part of community life in years to come, particularly when working in education was abandoned as a major community ministry. In the 1960s, however, it must have appeared random and rebellious, especially to a bishop who himself was hearing such complaints from members of the community.

Whealon advised the sisters to re-read the Vatican Council documents and quote more from the actual text and to include quotes from the Rule of Benedict. "He concluded," wrote Campbell, "Look not so much at the 20th century as you look at the perennial teachings of Jesus."

He formally asked that the community halt "any further escalation of your Renewal Program." Kraus posted the bishop's letter at the motherhouse and sent copies to the missions. She also invited Whealon to speak during the community's June retreat. He accepted, and the event apparently went well, although Whealon again registered his displeasure with the permission given to some sisters "to live in an apartment. I adjudge this to be of dubious legality and to be inadvisable from the viewpoint of Benedictine spirit and of proper experimentation," he wrote.

He told Kraus he had "asked his chancellor to study the canonical issues involved and to write to the apostolic delegate [the pope's representative in the United States, today called a "papal nuncio,"] for a ruling."

"It will be no surprise to yourself or to the community," he wrote to Kraus, "if I should refuse to permit the Benedictine Sisters to establish a new religious house . . . If you should indeed have the authority and should proceed, let it be known that this is against the wishes and judgment of the Bishop of this Diocese."

In a foreshadowing perhaps of the way the community would conduct itself decades later during a confrontation with a Vatican congregation, Kraus had done her homework on the matter. She had consulted two canonists who had attended the chapter meeting where the decision had been made and both had agreed that the statute cited by the bishop "did not apply here, as it was not a question of a new 'house' in the sense of a new religious group coming into the diocese." (The reference was to canon 497 in the 1917 version of the Code of Canon Law, revised in 1983.)

For practical reasons, Kraus could not back out of the arrangement, since an apartment had been leased, furniture had been purchased, and the move was pending. She wrote to the chancellor saying that the sisters living in the apartment would live by the same rules as those living in a mission house of the diocese.

Whealon, however, would not drop the matter and asked Kraus to write to the apostolic delegate's secretary to seek an opinion on the question regarding church law: "Does the Bishop have the authority to prevent the rights delegated to Superiors and General Chapters by the Sacred Congregation of Religious?" The secretary responded that he had no authority in the matter and suggested that Kraus write to the apostolic delegate directly. Campbell's history contains no explanation for why the secretary didn't simply show the apostolic delegate the original letter, but she notes that the same day Kraus received the reply from the secretary she wrote to the apostolic delegate himself with four essential questions:

- Does the canon apply in this case since it [the new housing arrangement] is experimental?
- Do religious communities have the right to carry out the proposals of their general chapters?
- Is this not an internal matter?
- If so, does the bishop have the right to forbid the action?

The apostolic delegate's office responded that Kraus, as superior, had the authority to absent women from the monastery "for a just cause" and "on that basis" the experiment was permissible. The correspondence also noted that the bishop retained authority over the sisters' involvement in diocesan ministries.

Two months later, "Bishop Whealon acknowledged receipt of all the position papers from the Erie Community which had been accepted by

the General Chapter," even describing the papers as "a laudable approach to *aggiornamento*," a term used at the Vatican Council and
roughly translated as "to revise" or "update." Whealon served only two
years as bishop of Erie before being named archbishop of Hartford,
Connecticut, where he remained until his death in 1991.

Srs. Miriam Mashank, Patricia McGreevy, and Christine Vladimiroff, all of whom would play important leadership roles in the community in the years ahead, moved into an apartment to work in parish
ministry at St. Luke's Church in Erie while continuing to teach at the
order's St. Benedict Academy.

At some point in the late 1960s, Chittister experienced a moment
similar to that described by Vladimiroff when a former teacher and
mentor suggested the two join others who were in favor of quicker
progress and start a new community.

In her 2005 memoir, *The Way We Were: A Story of Conversion
and Renewal,* Chittister writes that by 1969 the two factions of the
community were contemplating a split. She, as a member of the federation council, had been given a petition from some in the community to
negotiate a split on behalf of those who wanted to slow down the reform. At that point, she said, she was somewhere in the middle of the
two extremes, understanding the sentiment of the more traditional sisters but increasingly leaning toward reform and renewal, especially as
she continued giving presentations about change.

"I remember standing backlit in a doorway, almost unable to see the
face of the sister who delivered it, and saying into the darkness, 'I believe that most splits do not do anything but destroy both groups. What
will happen to those we leave behind? No, I will not do this.' Then, I
tore up the papers." She described that period in the community as a
"dark and dangerous" time "... when the very future of the community
was at stake from pressures both outside and inside the group."[11]

In that same memoir she recalls three events that may have done
more than any others to "bring a new perspective to the way the Erie
Benedictines saw religious life and their own role in it."[12] The first involved a visit to the community by Marist Brother Ronald Fogarty, an
Australian who at the time was in the United States doing postdoctoral
work in clinical psychology at the University of Chicago. He used his
counseling skills and insight into human change to work with religious
communities around the world on renewal issues. At Erie, in the darkened cafeteria of St. Benedict Academy, he opened a session by showing

---

11. Chittister, *The Way We Were,* 153.
12. Ibid., 154–58.

slide after slide of monasteries around the world. At the point where the community was becoming restless and wondering where he was going with all of this, he turned on the lights and said, "Do you know what all those monasteries have in common?" People shifted in their chairs. Silence. He answered his own question: "They were all great abbeys at one time. They are all dead or dying now."

Wrote Chittister: "The myth of immutability disappeared before our eyes."

Fogarty would return to the community three times. In turn he spoke of the nature of change, the process of consensus, and human development. She recalls, however, that "more than teach, he listened. He lectured for hours every day, yes. But then listened between conferences. During meals, through half the night working with one individual after another, he got to know them. He listened to their fears, their anger, their frustrations, their desires to be a community again."

He became both loved and trusted.

By the end of his first visit in 1969, "the community had voted to allow all the major elements of constitutional change—veils, blouses, open placement, vacation schedule changes and personal budgets." Chittister recorded that "no one had to abide by any of them" but that the group knew "most of the community would."

The day after Fogarty closed the workshop, a sister made her final profession. She had been debating whether to wear the veil or not, and the workshop had helped her make the decision. "We are walking together into the future and the future is going to be different," she told the community. She didn't wear the veil.

During the ceremony, unknown to anyone, Chittister slipped her ring from her right hand, where it had been since the time of her profession, to her left hand, "a sign of commitment to the Erie Benedictines born anew in this day and age. In fact, we were all beginning again."

The second event that smoothed the path to renewal for the Erie Benedictines was the move at the beginning of 1970 to Mount St. Benedict, a low-slung complex newly constructed on a portion of 120 acres of land purchased by the order in 1906. The new monastery was seven miles east of the one they were leaving, well out of the city and surrounded by wooded tracts. The move, which came at the end of years of planning, fundraising, borrowing, and community decision-making, occurred in the nick of time. The order had been informed in January 1970 that the insurance company would not renew the policy on the old convent because it was in such poor condition.

Abandoned with the old building were "old rules about space, old memories of another kind of life. In its place came a new way of being women together in large beautiful spaces and private rooms and on great open grounds."[13]

Women were able to choose their rooms, some for the first time in their lives. A wall of windows allowed sunlight to pour into a large, airy refectory and adjoining common area. For the first time, every member of the community could have meals at the same time. The sisters were able to sit at meals where they wished, not by rank as in the past. Gone were the dark parlors and cramped spaces of the old convent.

The new facility opened up space for visitors and was more inviting to those outside the community. The Benedictine gift for hospitality, a central tenet of Benedict's rule, was allowed to expand and mature over the years in this new space.

"There was a new way of keeping silence in the new building as well," wrote Chittister. "With the residence halls separate from the gathering spaces in the monastery, rather than times of silence, the community gravitated toward a respect for places of silence."[14]

Quite a few community stories are tied to the move from downtown Erie to what came to be called the Mount, but one particularly stands out as an example of inventive moxie and a certain Pauline pragmatism in the sense of doing what needs to be done to build up the kingdom, or at the least, a new monastery.

While community leaders were meeting with a new lay board to devise plans to raise funds for the new monastery, some community members took it upon themselves to work up their own scheme. In 1966, a group of Benedictines (including three graduates of the Eastman School of Music), most of whom were teachers in the diocese of Erie school system, formed a singing group.[15] The intent was to work up a ninety-minute show in which they would perform and tell their story. Kraus granted permission. Sr. Mary Lou Kownacki wrote the script, the trained musicians chose the music, and Sr. Miriam Mashank marketed the production. According to a 2002 retrospective on the event in the *Erie Times-News*:

> Calling themselves "Sisters '66," 53 sisters, five postulants and two high school students jumped on a bus every weekend during the fall and winter of 1966 and gave concerts in all the Catholic

---

13. Ibid., 156.

14. Ibid., 156–57.

15. This description comes from an October 6, 2002, story in the *Erie Times-News*, an account in *Vision of Change*, and a conversation in April 2014 with Sr. Miriam Mashank, one of the organizers of the group.

Diocese of Erie schools where they taught. They sold out performances in Erie, Oil City, Sharon, Clarion, and points beyond.

One of those points beyond was the biggest of the big time of that era, the *Ed Sullivan Show*. The sisters thought that getting on the show would really boost their profile and revenues. Someone in Erie knew the show's program director. Mashank immediately sent off some "showcards mounted on wood too large to be easily discarded and sent them to his CBS office in New York."[16]

Someone in the office got back to her and instructed her to call near the end of the summer and then again after Labor Day. Not satisfied with such a vague reply, Mashank and Sr. Jean Lavin, who directed the group, put on their full habits (the community by this point had already transferred to modified habits) and boarded the plane for New York and a visit, without invitation, to the CBS offices. Mashank remembers that as they were walking toward CBS, they thought they'd look more official if they carried briefcases, so they popped into a store, bought two inexpensive bags, and headed to the office. When they arrived, they were stopped by a receptionist who told them they couldn't see Jack Babb, the program director, without an appointment. At that moment, however, there was a commotion elsewhere in the lobby and when the receptionist looked away, the nuns slipped into an elevator and headed for Babb's office. He reluctantly agreed to see them. They came away with no guarantees, but Babb said he'd try to make one of their performances to evaluate the act.

Mashank was nothing if not persistent, and she kept calling Babb's office as the performance dates dwindled week by week. Babb finally showed up somewhere in the Erie area for the final performance of the season. He watched the show and afterwards told Mashank, "You're in."

And that's how forty-four nuns from Erie (in full traditional habit by request) happened to be on stage for the *Ed Sullivan Show* on Sunday, January 15, 1967. They performed a richly harmonized version of Kumbaya and were warmly received by audience and Sullivan, who, in a rare appearance at a rehearsal, showed up the day before to hear and meet the nuns.

It was an unusual display of star power considering that Sisters '66, which soon disbanded and was never heard from again, shared the stage that evening with Mick Jagger and the Rolling Stones, singer Petula Clark, comedian Alan King, and the Muppets in their first TV appearance.

---

16. *Vision of Change*, 152.

The nuns received an offer for a recording contract and other offers to do a concert tour. But these were Benedictine sisters from Erie, teachers, members of a community, and they turned it all down. They had accomplished their purpose—depicting their lives as sisters in song and raising money for the new monastery. They were able to hand over a hefty donation after expenses of $4,100—for music, instruments, printing, props, telephone, postage, and rental of a U-Haul and some of the auditoriums—was subtracted from total proceeds of $60,000.

The third element Chittister notes in the journey of renewal was a moment of unspoken reconciliation following a horrible tragedy. In 1971, Srs. Mary Bernard Niebling and Ellen Niebling and their parents were killed in a car crash in Michigan on their way to a sibling's wedding.

Mary Bernard was forty-two, Ellen was thirty-five; the elder wore a modified habit, the younger, contemporary clothes. They were both "universally loved by the community" and in their own ways represented the major divisions in the community.

The funeral for all four was held at the Mount and people thronged to the ceremony from the city of Erie. For Chittister, the scene provided a visual for "the whole process of social change." Among the mourners were very different kinds of people who had been affected by the lives of the two sisters. "It wasn't the dress or the work or the theology that mattered here. It was the people, their lives, the witness of goodness and kindness and whole-hearted giving of self that mattered," she wrote.

The scene—sisters, some with veils and modified habits, some without, bearing the caskets and tending to the mourners—symbolized to Chittister the attainment of a new level of awareness in the community. "The sudden confluence of factors—organizational, physical, emotional, and psychological—changed the direction of the group from hopeless division to a common hope that just as, over the years, the community had survived epidemics of tuberculosis and influenza, poverty and near economic collapse, they would survive change together too," she wrote.[17]

---

17. Ibid., 157–58.

SEVEN

PRIORESS

A bit of irony clings to Chittister's assessment of the period of renewal that began in the 1960s and stretched through the 1980s. Where others might see religious orders slipping into a sameness with the prevailing culture, she viewed renewal as an emergence from institutional anonymity to a new way of being a religious community that required greater individual maturity.

In the case of the Erie Benedictines, conditions conspired so that the transition, in a way more concretely than other communities might have experienced, meant actually leaving their old life behind. In addition to the habits that disappeared, two thirds of the original motherhouse, in such bad shape that it couldn't be insured, was leveled. The entire community was relocated.

The old icons were vanishing, and to outsiders it might have appeared as if the sisters were becoming indistinguishable in many ways from others in the culture. To critics of renewal, the very identity of religious life was being obliterated. Yet inside that life, Chittister writes, "We thought of ourselves as adults now. We were treating one another as adults. Our public presence had changed. We weren't invisible anymore. We weren't anonymous, interchangeable parts anymore. We were individual people who had chosen to live a life of prayer, service, and community as followers of Jesus."

Somewhere in the transition, she writes in *The Way We Were*, "we stopped talking about 'what we needed to change next.' Instead we began to question what we were doing now." The first disposition is all about breaking out of the cocoon. The second "owns being the butterfly, being something new, being something that is ready to fly."[1]

She characterized the transition as moving from renewal, a recognition of what has to change, to revitalization, changing what needs to be changed. During the years when the community was wrestling with renewal issues, Chittister, as we've seen, was going through her own metamorphosis. She considered quitting religious life over the divisions in the community but decided to stay; wondered if the teenage postulant turned woman might consider marriage, but realized her deepest calling was with the Erie Benedictines; was recruited for a doctorate not knowing to what purpose only to discover it a fitting preparation for religious leadership at that moment in history.

For years she had been teaching others to understand the changes under way in religious life. She had built a reputation as a speaker and teacher, as a social scientist able to name and articulate what others were experiencing. Under evolving rules of leadership through Kraus's years as prioress, Chittister served twice on her council, a kind of inner circle of advisors. The first was as an appointed councilor, the second as an elected "first councilor." She was seeing the shifts in the landscape of religious life from both a high altitude across a vast canvas and from so close up and in such detail that at times it was difficult to see the larger picture. By the time she was elected prioress in 1978, she had a good understanding of both the sociology functioning in the culture of religious life and the personal pain people had experienced.

What the sociologist knew going into her first term as prioress was that she had been elected to lead a community facing the death of much that had defined it in the past. "The world has seen many groups, vital at one time that ceased to exist at another. The Pony Express ended with the railroad. The Erie Canal disappeared when the highway system emerged. Single-sex clubs and schools ceased to be common coinage with the rise of the women's movement. But that is not defeat. To have a system die at the top of its history may be the most complimentary thing that can be said about it. It succeeded. There was nothing more the system could do in the society it was in—except begin again to serve a new one in a new way."[2]

The problem, of course, was that if religious life as the church had known it in the United States had achieved the apex of its history, no one knew precisely what the "new way" entailed. The equivalent of a

---

1. Joan Chittister, *The Way We Were: A Story of Conversion and Renewal* (Maryknoll, NY: Orbis Books, 2005), 159.
2. Ibid., 161.

railroad or a highway system wasn't immediately evident. The ten years of implementation and study between the 1968 renewal chapter and Chittister's election in 1978 gave the community a broad grounding in new types of acting and coming to decisions and a new space in which to begin the new way. "In those ten years, of course, both ideas and structures were in flux," Chittister said during one of our interviews. "If you imagine the community as bees in a bottle, that's exactly what you have. All this stuff is going on, but in every single sister, the other thing that's going on is some confusion."

Prior to the election in which she was chosen, she attended a community meeting that, as was common practice, broke into small groups for discussion. The community was looking for a new prioress and speaking about goals for a new administration. "So here we find ourselves," said Chittister, "very aware that we have been deeply polarized, but also are now at 100 loose ends. If there are 130 of us, it's 130 loose ends, at least to the outside eye and to people who have lived in this very structured life."

The term "structured" doesn't begin to do justice to the life this community had so recently left behind. Many of the details of that life have already been described in previous sections, but it is worthwhile going a bit deeper into the rigidity and tedium of daily life in order to better understand just how "at loose ends" members of the community likely felt.

Within the memory of most of those attending the community meeting in 1978 was a time when "religious life alone guaranteed a woman any real degree of internal autonomy and personal expression, limited as it was."[3]

That calculus was changing. Granted, it took far more than the promise of a college education and satisfying career for women to enter and remain in religious life in any period in history. But in the 1960s and '70s, women in the wider culture had unprecedented options and increasingly were making life decisions that were different from those made by their mothers and grandmothers. College degrees and professional careers were becoming common pursuits for women, and those changed realities in the wider culture were influencing changes inside the enclosures of religious orders. Greater choices for women in the general culture meant a drain of membership as well as fewer considering a vocation to religious life.

Many in that meeting room in 1978 recalled as young sisters having to "speak fault" regularly for such imperfections as spilling food,

---

3. Joan Chittister, *The Fire in These Ashes: A Spirituality of Contemporary Religious Life* (Kansas City: Sheed and Ward, 1995), 6.

losing pins, speaking at the wrong time, walking or sitting improperly, wasting soap. They remembered windows in the novitiate papered over to prevent novices from losing "custody of the eyes" by glancing at the streetscape outside. Well-educated women who managed finances and personnel and ran major institutions—schools, hospitals and the like—inside their religious community's enclosures were made to kneel before mother superior to ask "permission" to meet the needs of everyday life and perform the most mundane activities. They were required to ask for toothpaste and soap. They had to ask permission to stay up beyond the mandated bedtime to study or prepare coursework. They needed permission to go on a Saturday to their school classrooms to do extra preparation for work they already were required to do. As their time in the order progressed into the period of renewal, it became increasingly difficult if not impossible to explain the "why" of such things to new generations of women interested in religious life.

In a 2012 interview eighty-five-year-old Sr. Mary Daniel, an accomplished musician who had entered the Erie Benedictines as a senior in high school in 1945, spoke of those rituals as a fond memory. She gave me a written summary of a typical day for members of the community in the mid-1940s, from rising at 5:30 for meditation at 6, Lauds and Prime at 6:30, Eucharist at 7, and the beginning of the school day at 7:50 or 8:30, depending on where one taught.

Novices washed the serving dishes and pots and pans and were permitted to talk and sing as they worked. "Candidates, novices, and scholastics each had a bed, a wash stand, and a chair, with a white sheet surrounding the area where they slept" in a large dormitory-like space. "Each one's habit was hung on a hanger near the foot of the bed on the pipes that held the sheeting. We rose in the morning when the assigned person rang a big cow bell for rising."

All was quiet at mealtime as someone read the readings for the day. The reader stopped when the prioress rang a bell and then the reader "knelt next to the prioress to speak fault for her errors in reading and went to her table to eat. The prioress then said, 'Praised be Jesus and Mary' to which all responded, 'Now and forever, Amen.'"

Sr. Mary Daniel said she loved the quiet and the routine. She missed keeping silence as in the old monastery. She never became fond of the informality and what seemed randomness of the later years, though she loved teaching music, had several quite successful students, and was still spending her days practicing in a ground-floor room that accommodated two pianos and a harp.

In 1978, the order tottered between those who saw the old way of doing things, even in its excesses, as distinctive, a manner of pursuing perfection and holiness that set it apart from other walks of life, and those who saw such rigid routines as having far more to do with the maintenance of a docile workforce and suppressing the Spirit than with the pursuit of holiness.

Was the community heading down a path of liberation or of laziness? Was this newfound freedom going to lead to the "new way" of serving or were they simply becoming like everyone else?

If religious life was no longer to be "a life within a life, a subculture defined outside the mainstream by its own property, its own clothing, its own lifestyle and its own customs," what was it to be? If it were to no longer be "insulated, isolated and limiting," what were its new boundaries, and who defined them, and how?[4]

It would be more than fifteen years before Chittister would begin publishing the books about religious life that made her thought and analysis more widely known among not only religious orders but also the Catholic population in general. In those works, primarily *The Way We Were* and *The Fire in These Ashes* (the book she terms her "manifesto on religious life"), Chittister would use her own experience combined with the much broader view to which she had access to construct a whole and compelling narrative about the direction of religious life. As she sat at the small-group table in 1978, however, she was one of the bees in the bottle trying to figure out how to get out of the bottle and what to do once liberated.

At the table was a nun known as quiet and soft spoken, someone, said Chittister in an interview, from whom little was ever heard. Unexpectedly, that nun posed the question at the heart of the matter: Why are we here? As Chittister recalled, the woman continued: "To teach? I can teach anywhere and I can get paid for it, and I can do what I want with that money." Chittister just listened as the conversation went around the table, the sisters variously saying what they might want in the future, and she remembered saying to herself, "They don't get it."

"Remember, I'd been teaching this stuff since 1969, but I'd been teaching on a larger canvas, on a bigger slate—everywhere. I'm going into every possible kind of community and the same themes are dropping down everywhere. Now, then, this one says, 'What are we here for? I could teach anywhere,' and I say to myself, 'Oh, man, what does, what will, hold us together?' What will give us a sense of common purpose? What would tell us that we need one another to do the good things we want to do as people who see that the Christian mission is self-giving?"

That's the moment, she said, when she came up with the idea of the "corporate commitment," some overarching concern that would serve

---

4. Descriptions quoted are from *The Way We Were*, 9.

as a kind of glue for the community, a commitment decided on by the community that might even change from year to year given the perceived needs of the times.

She was elected that year to her first of three terms as prioress aware that the community "was in a real state of breakdown. We had come through renewal with the saint [a reference to Kraus], we are sitting with younger women who have no idea what they're doing there now. Nobody is saying to them 'If you march down the hall in order, that's holiness.' No, everybody's saying to them, 'Well, you know, you should be doing something that you're gifted doing.' But why?"

It was another office she didn't want or seek. In fact, she had written a letter to the community telling them just that. The year before, she had finished her term as president of the Leadership Conference of Women Religious (LCWR). She was just completing her third term as president of the federation "and then I was going to be free. To do what, I don't know. I didn't have an ambition." She had been running on several tracks for some years and was looking forward to a break, some time to figure out next steps.

Her wishes didn't matter. The community figured out the next step for her. Her election occurred on the first ballot. "It was just very clear. You could hardly argue with the clarity of it," she said.

The feeling among community members, according to Sr. Stephanie Campbell, was that "Joan had given enough time to these other Benedictine groups (the federation and the Conference of Prioresses); it was time for her to devote her leadership skills at home."[5]

Before accepting the nomination, however, Chittister advised the community that she "would feel bound to continue her travels when invited to speak" but would arrange her calendar so that she would never be away more than four months in any given year.

Sometime either before or just after her election as prioress, she had a dream. She rarely remembers her dreams, she says, but there have been several that have been significant, even "life changing," and this was one of them. At the same time, she added, "these are hard things to tell."

In the dream she was in a small boat and driving it up a hill. (This is perhaps as good a place as any to note that in real life she loves boats and would often motor around the bay and Lake Erie.)

In the dream, she was attempting to drive the boat over the hill to a lake beyond. "I wanted out of this pond and into that lake. I could

5. Sr. Stephanie Campbell, *Vision of Change, Voices of Challenge: The History of Renewal in the Benedictine Sisters of Erie, 1858–1990* (Xlibris, 2015), 202.

laugh about it now, but I'll tell you that night that I had that dream I felt strangled, like I was being hanged. I knew. Something inside me told me that I was supposed to be somewhere else. I was landlocked in a small pond and I knew the lake was out there and that we had to get there. We had to get into that lake."

In hindsight, she speaks confidently of its meaning. "Well, little Erie cannot exist by itself. Somehow or other I had to get this community risen above its locale . . . it had to join the larger world, and I had to see that we joined it no matter what I had to do. I had to break through or this community was going to die very quickly."

In the dream, she guns the boat's engine and it gets to the top of the hill, she can see the lake beyond, but the boat keeps sliding back down. "The dream ends. I don't get to the lake." She woke up frazzled and said to herself. "I can't do it. I can't do it. It's a little town and we're all from it. Or we're from even smaller towns. What do we do? We've never done anything but teach."

She knew that the community's main ministry was coming to an end, that the academy, the community's primary identity, was not sustainable. As in the journey of renewal itself, the dream pointed to something new but didn't provide clear directions for getting there. "I felt very strongly that the Erie Benedictines had to have a broader vision. They had to be seen more broadly than they had been seen for one hundred years teaching."

There wasn't any major breakthrough that Chittister can point to that changed things. It was more a host of points that formed an arc along which the community traveled to its new destination. "I'm not sure we are on a larger map, but we have a larger vision now. Everybody in the community has a much wider vision than we did when I was younger. Even than when I was elected. When I was elected it was all Vatican II theology. I always felt the theology was for something—I wasn't quite sure what—but we were a long way from it. We were still too close to the internecine renewal wars, and we had to move beyond that. I knew it."

When she went to the microphone to accept the community's vote that she be the next prioress, she took some notes with her that made several simple, direct points. "I can't be your mother," she said. In fact, she banished the title and would be known only as Sister. "I can be your friend, and I can be your sister in this community. But I'm not here to give orders, and I hope that I can help you. I see a lot that religious communities have to do and I know we can do it together. We can do this."[6]

---

6. As related to me in an interview.

One of the lines she read was this: "Sr. Mary Margaret Kraus enabled this community to grow up. Now we have to ask ourselves what we grew up for."[7]

In her heart, she writes, she knew "that religious life as we had known it, however much we had lived it well, was dead." The question remaining, she would tell women religious, was "What do we want to be caught dead doing?"

Her answer to the question was, "I, for one, wanted to die following Jesus the contemplative—the contemplative Jesus—from Galilee to Jerusalem doing good: healing the sick, raising the dead, contending with the legalists' interpretation of the Law, empowering women as he did the Samaritan woman to 'go into the town and tell them who and what you have seen' . . . and on whose account thousands believed that day."[8]

She wrote about all this with more than twenty years of hindsight. By then, she had the benefit of evidence: the visible success of the Erie Benedictines in transforming themselves as a religious community and the community's impressive imprint on the wider culture. The boat, indeed, had made it over the hill and into the lake beyond. Much of the change occurred through Chittister's writing and lectures. What she produced, however, would have lacked depth and authenticity had it not been written out of lived experience. The community around her was also developing its spirituality in new ways. And the daily prayers (with gender neutral language), the daily practice of *lectio divina* (a contemplative reading of scripture), the explorations of meditation and the meaning of contemplative life amid the din of daily activities, all of that was nourished and enriched by the community's work. Not only was the community transforming itself, it was transforming countless lives it came in contact with, and often those lives were the poorest, the most marginalized, the most broken. The monastery had opened its doors to the world. The new place of education had neither partitions nor grade levels. The teachers were learning new skills that weren't to be found in a PhD program.

Back in 1978, privately, Chittister's's head was spinning as she tried to figure out how to begin. "Somebody had to decide, now that all of this was done, how you make any sense of it. How do you bring a community to any kind of new cohesion when you don't know what the cohesion is about? No, I didn't want to be elected at all."

---

7. *The Way We Were*, 169.
8. Ibid., 170.

She remembers that the next day, as she drove from where she had briefly been staying in town out to the Mount, which would now become her residence, she focused on some inane counting exercise. It sounds a bit hyperbolic, but she says she did it "to keep from going mad, to make sure that I could count consecutively, that I could hold myself together, that I didn't cry. If I knew the next number, I'd probably know what to do when I got myself in a mess."

Perhaps her anxiety was magnified by her understanding of what would become of the academy, something she said that even before she was elected she knew had to be dealt with. She was convinced that amid all of the deconstruction of life as the community had known it, one of the most iconic representations of their community life in Erie would have to be jettisoned. At her first council meeting she announced to her closest advisors that "the major problem facing this community is that academy. We cannot afford the academy. That academy is going to take us under."

She didn't move quickly to close it. She knew that the community's identity was intimately tied to the school and all that it had meant. Generations of young women had been educated there and moved on to college and careers; dozens had been influenced by the lives and examples of the nuns they encountered—in the same way she and so many of her peers had been influenced—to join the order. Preparing the community and building consensus around the idea that the academy had to close would take time. Meanwhile, there was much else to be done.

Chittister started a community publication called "The Leaven," a title taken from a line in the Rule of Benedict: "teaching should be instilled like a leaven of divine justice." Leaven, she explained, is supposed to "produce fermentation, to enliven, to excite, to agitate or to lighten something subtly."

"The Leaven," she hoped, would be more than a newsletter and somewhat less than an essay. "Sometimes it will tell you what has me excited; sometimes it will simply raise questions; sometimes I'll talk a little about things I'm concerned about; sometimes it will carry facts or explanations. But always, I hope, it will make all of us think about our lives together."[9]

Each issue contained her travel schedule, and the first issue listed the members of her council. They included Maureen Tobin as her first councilor and personal assistant. Kraus was to serve as consultant to the council.

---

9. Ibid.

A number of the public ministries that would eventually supplant the academy as the identity of the Erie Benedictines began to take shape during Chittister's term. In her recollection, the transitions often began fairly informally. "I tried to do two things," she said in an interview. "I think I opened up a lot of thinking and I supported anybody. I really supported newness. I was looking for life." The approach, she said, was her training in social change "operating long and hard here."

"I took the position that what anybody really wants to do they will do. It can be done. So, if a sister came in with an idea, I didn't play any of those permission games. I didn't do anything like that." Instead she would say that an idea sounded interesting and then she would ask, "Can you tell me anything about it?"

Often the sister, after explaining for a while, would acknowledge that she wouldn't have a salary.

"Oh, let's not worry about the salary right now," Chittister would say. "The money will come. If we're doing the right stuff, the money's going to come. This sounds like the right stuff to me. You love it, and I can see that. I'll tell you what—you go do it for a year and then we'll talk about it."

She purposely did not say try it for only a year. She said try it for a year "and then let's sit down, see how you feel about it, see how it's going, see what your plans are. We're not going to put any end time on this. We're just going to do some checks."

When people found out about this new approach—that they didn't have to work on things on the side or go through a rigorous permission process—"all sorts of things just started to happen." And all sorts of people, from local reporters to other religious congregations, began to notice and to come around to see what was going on.

The transition to new ministries didn't occur overnight, but on Chittister's watch the Erie Benedictines, once the educators of girls from the city's working class and underclass, began transforming the wider community in new ways and for a period that would extend far beyond her twelve years as prioress. A soup kitchen, an education center for hundreds of preschoolers, a place for older kids to hang out after school and receive both food and help with homework have become permanent parts of the East Side landscape. State-funded but Benedictine-administered and -run education programs give hundreds of immigrants a start at life in their new country, including job training and placement. Some years after her term was up an old garage and tire center was transformed into an "art house" where hundreds of youngsters, mostly from low-income families, are introduced to everything from arts and crafts to literacy and music. The sisters went and begged for much of the landscaping that has transformed the outside of the low-slung building into a series of attractive gardens that also serve as settings for outdoor sculptures and meditative space.[10]

The ministries that today are making over whole sections of one of Erie's poorest neighborhoods and hundreds of lives each year grew as much out of a new sense of spirituality and what it meant to live a Benedictine life as they did out of a practical need to find new things to do. Giving up the academy also meant giving up salaries, so the community had to find new revenue sources. Giving up a long-time ministry with all of the accompanying predictability in terms of lifestyle and unanimity did not, for Chittister, mean abandoning the contemplative life.

In one entry in "The Leaven," Chittister makes the point that "a community must be contemplative if it is to be authentically monastic," and she then lists five ways in which that can be achieved:

1. Make time every day for quiet/solitude.
2. Keep halls quiet so people can find real rest and sanctuary in their rooms. Create a reflective atmosphere.
3. Read, especially in areas important to the spiritual life, areas you don't understand or have questions about.
4. Pray reflectively; go into the psalms and readings of the day.
5. Share insights/reflections with other sisters.

She would regularly close with handwritten messages and in one such note, she wrote: "To be closed to growth, to new zeal, to love, is to die long before our time. That is the great monastic lesson."

In an Advent entry she gives instructions on praying, asking the sisters to try praying with "a blank mind" in an attitude of waiting to "see what comes... knowing that whatever it is, it probably will not look like anything you were hoping to get. The baby did not look like God. The manger did not look like the kingdom. The place did not look promising, but in those things lay our salvation."

Chittister thought of herself as a teacher, a role that found expression in the workshops and talks she continued to give throughout the country, but she also took that role seriously within the community. Each year she was in office she incorporated regular conferences, given

---

10. In this section on Chittister's years as prioress, I clearly note in the text when the information came via one of my interviews with her. Material about those years emerged at various points during interviews over many months. The rest of the information comes primarily from Campbell's treatment of Chittister's tenure in *Vision of Change, Voices of Challenge,* 201ff.

by her and others from outside the community, on aspects of community life and the community's interaction with the wider world.

As Sr. Christine Vladimiroff remembered, "In her meetings with LCWR or the federation, she'd come across speakers whom we could invite to come to Erie to give retreats or whatever." Eventually this created an ongoing formation program that showed the community's commitment to spending time and money on educating its members theologically and in other matters—the environment, politics, spirituality, social trends, and personal development. The topics were wide ranging and ecumenical, with the community inviting speakers from other Christian traditions as well as from other faiths.

If all of that fed the intellectual and spiritual life of the community, it also benefited Chittister's writing. For instance, during the first two years she was prioress, she conducted eight conferences on the Rule of Benedict, parsing the ancient passages for their contemporary relevance, especially to a group of women at the end of the twentieth century. Those sessions and the research she did for them were later fleshed out in two books, *Wisdom Distilled from the Daily: Living the Rule Today* (Harper and Row, 1990), and *The Rule of Benedict: Insights for the Ages* (Crossroad, 1992).

An overarching theme—the corporate commitment that Chittister envisioned during the small-group discussions prior to her election—took shape during her first year as prioress. It was initially explained in "The Leaven" of August 1978 when Chittister wrote that the community "will identify for the first time a justice issue or issues which we will give our efforts to, both corporately and individually, for the coming year." Finding that issue would go a long way toward answering, Chittister hoped, the question: "Where was our unity without the common ministry of teaching?"[11]

Mary Lou Kownacki, cited by Campbell, best explains the origins of the corporate commitment in her book, *Peace Is Our Calling*.[12] Describing the corporate commitment as "Chittister's brainchild," she said it "emerged after working through renewal for 15 years with religious communities across the United States." Before Vatican II, she says, religious orders were identified by their corporate ministries. Sisters would describe what they did "in terms of institutional ministry: 'Our order teaches' or 'Our order cares for the sick.'" But the move to individual ministries, in which sisters had the freedom to develop their gifts, to

---

11. *Vision of Change*, 233.
12. Ibid., 233–34.

reach neglected segments of society, and to respond to new needs, had an obvious downside. The corporate identity could be lost.

"A corporate commitment is a vision or a project or a goal that members of the community commit themselves to promoting no matter where they are or in how many diverse ministries they might be engaged." Kownacki explained that unlike prior institutional commitments that drained a community's resources and required facilities and personnel, corporate commitments could range from working for solutions to world hunger to advocating for the elderly or minorities.

The process of arriving at a corporate commitment began with a weekend of workshops in which Chittister asked community members to come up with what they thought were the five most important issues facing the church and/or society at that moment. With five possibilities, the community understood that none would get an overwhelming majority. The community agreed that whatever issue got the most votes would be the corporate commitment. Over the course of the weekend the community arrived at the five possibilities: housing (or lack of affordable housing), poverty, peace, women, and food.

When she received the community's votes, Chittister tallied them and realized she didn't have much of a mandate. The community had members involved deeply in each of the issues. Chittister explained that "in the 1800s the community had decided that the education of Catholic children was an important gift to the United States of America and the American church, and we have done it ever since. Now, what does this community say? In looking at these five issues, what would you say is the most important thing this country or church needs now, but which also is closest to the charisms of this community?"

Tobin and Sr. Mary Grace Hanes, who had been elected recording secretary of the community, were seated on either side of Chittister as the votes were counted. Chittister recalled that Hanes, especially, wanted to delay the decision because she thought the issue had not been resolved. Peacemaking was the choice, but only by one vote.

Chittister went with the original agreement. She asked that the ballots be gotten rid of and announced that "the first corporate commitment of the Benedictine Sisters of Erie" was peacemaking and opposing nuclear weapons.

Almost everyone seemed on board. The next step was for community members to make personal commitments to highlight the corporate activity in their daily work, to designate what they would do and how they would participate in the commitment. At a future meeting called for the blessing of ministries, they would present their signed intentions to the prioress in a community ceremony.

The commitment to peace activity was not exactly new to the Erie Benedictines. Kownacki, introduced to peacemaking and non-violence through the writing of Gandhi, Merton, and Fr. Daniel Berrigan, the Jesuit peace activist and resister, received permission in 1972 to open Pax Center in Erie at the monastery. Although the local paper, the *Erie Times-News*, has been generous in its coverage of the Erie Benedictines and often quite supportive editorially to its public ventures and positions on issues, the initial activity of the Pax Center generated a lot of adverse public reaction.

One of the earliest steps taken was to invite actress and anti–Vietnam War activist Jane Fonda to town. Campbell describes the action as "explosive," but the publicity it and other activities generated eventually moved public sentiment to a more sympathetic point. The center attracted so much attention that it soon outgrew its small quarters at the Mount. It was relocated to the facility on 9th Street in Erie and the Pax community and its number of volunteers grew. "After eight years, the original focus on peace work and the Vietnam War was enlarged by providing temporary shelter for women, a soup kitchen, a resource center and a Third World craft shop."[13]

The group published *Erie Christian Witness* monthly, and it was mailed to interested readers around the country. Campbell notes that a wonderful benefit, unanticipated when Pax Center opened, was that twelve women who lived at the center at different times joined the Erie Benedictine community.

Not everyone in the community agreed with the new activism that grew out of the Pax Center. When some of the sisters involved, including Kownacki, joined demonstrations large and small, placed the Benedictine community amid such movements as Mobilization for Survival, and were occasionally arrested, others voiced concern about the level of political activism. Some wondered whether enrollment in and support for the academy might be affected.

During Chittister's years as prioress the community became even more aligned with peacemaking efforts and linked with Pax Christi USA, a branch of the international Catholic peace organization. Headquartered at the time in Chicago and on the verge of bankruptcy, the organization came to Erie in 1984, when Kownacki was named national coordinator by the group's national council. The following year, Kownacki received the 1985 *Pacem in Terris* award from Georgetown University.

The corporate commitment today incudes commitments to be a healing presence and prophetic witness for peace by working for sus-

---

13. Ibid., 171–74.

tainability and justice, especially for women and children. "We have a lot going on," Chittister said in an interview, "and we maintain the commitment to peace and justice."

If the community, by Chittister's time as prioress, had developed fairly established ways to arrive at consensus, the new prioress also displayed a tolerance for dissent. As previously noted, participating in demonstrations against war, for instance, was not unanimously embraced by the community. Chittister recalls one sister, especially, who was livid at the decision. "What kind of religious activity is this? Why aren't we going back to the schools?" That first year, the only commitment the distressed sister could make was, "I'll pray."

She was not looking for unanimity. By holding a vote, it was implicit that people could disagree. "Okay," thought Chittister. "That's what we told everybody: maybe all you can do is say a Hail Mary a day. That's enough. That's part of the community commitment." Some years later, the same sister wrote that she promised that year to talk to her brother, a retired Air Force officer, about her opposition to nuclear weapons and preparation for nuclear war. Chittister remembers saying to herself, "Now that's prophecy. Now that's the prophet in the city square, and we have come to it."

Kownacki tells of another example, this one also dealing with a collision of patriotism, militarism, and monastic life, in which Chittister showed a creative flair in dealing with a disagreement that could have become a major point of division. It involved a flagpole that someone had donated in the early 1980s to be placed in front of the monastery. Mary Lou at the time had "a strong feeling that monasticism was always prophet to the church and the state and that there was no place for symbols of the state in a monastery."

She was still involved in Pax Center, which by then had become a "quasi Catholic Worker community" with a soup kitchen, education sessions, and housing. The main work at the time was mobilizing against the nuclear weapons buildup. Kownacki wrote to the council, "adamant that we should not accept the flagpole. There were other sisters," she said, "just as adamant that we should have some manifestation that we were citizens of the United States. It was getting a little heated, so Sr. Joan called a community meeting."

The rule for the meeting was that anyone could come to the microphone for two or three minutes to say why she was either for or against accepting the gift. No one was allowed to respond. This would not be a discussion, but a session to hear one another. "We were to listen to everybody with the ear of our hearts," said Kownacki.

"I gave my spiel—very charged and zealous about what our place in church and state was," said Kownacki. And then she listened to others. "What I learned was that sisters who wanted to accept the gift were really reacting to and speaking from the experience of World War II and what it meant and how important it was to them to fly the flag." Wrapped up in their notions of the flag were memories of family members—mostly brothers—who had served in World War II. "These sisters had prayed every night for them to come home, and their mothers were weeping for them to come home, and they wept for them to come home. And some didn't come home. It was an eye opener for me. We were really speaking from two different visions, and from two different heart centers, and I learned a lot that day."

The community came to a compromise—sometimes it flew the American flag, sometimes the UN flag, depending on the holiday and other circumstances, the details of which Kownacki and others no longer recall.

It is not much of an assumption to say that others intensely involved in the peace movement and holding such principled convictions might not be brought to such a compromise. But Kownacki credits two things in her life with allowing her to temper her view in that circumstance. The first was the rather robust debates that she remembers occurred regularly in her home around the dinner table. Her father was wont to introduce a subject and then, for the sake of argument, take the role of devil's advocate to prompt his children to think beyond their assumptions.

The other was Benedictine life. "You don't do *lectio* just to say you've done it," she said. "The idea is to change your heart. You're supposed to whittle away so you have a compassionate heart and can look at people with compassion," which she describes as "just respect for another person's viewpoint."

Her sisters in the community, she said, were not speaking out of a wish to do violence. "We all want peace. Do they think it can be arrived at in different ways than I do? Yes. I always have to leave that open. I trust their goodness of heart and that they really believe this."

Taking on U.S. militarism—the spending on the military, the development of new and more dangerous weapons systems—exacted a cost from the community. In *The Way We Were*, Chittister recalls intending to resign as prioress so the community could choose someone new precisely because the corporate commitment was causing a backlash. Fundraising was drying up and benefactors and old friends of the monastery were leaving. She went into the chapel that weekend for a liturgy and it was packed with people she didn't know. She deliberately left Mass early so she could greet those leaving. "Most of them were young couples. Some of them had driven for miles to attend Mass at the Mount." She asked what had brought them here. "We heard about you," one young man told her. "We want to be part of a community that thinks like this about these things." She wrote: "The chapel was never empty again."[14]

Heady issues of spirituality, community, and new ways to live monastic life took a great deal of the community's time and energy. But for the prioress, there was always the monastic equivalent of making sure the trains run on time. The Erie Benedictines were never a rich order, and the need for funding to keep the whole enterprise running was a constant worry. The concern over money grew with the new monastery and more women taking on individual ministries and living in small communities in town and apart from the monastery. While it was in operation, the academy was a perennial drain on the community's resources.

"We were broke, and I said, 'Drill a gas well. Go ahead,'" said Chittister.

It wasn't quite that simple. The community had become aware, because of developers' interest, that there might be gas beneath the land along East Lake Road where the new monastery was located. "They wanted you to lease them your land for a hundred years and they would pay something like 8 percent. At any rate, it occurred to me that we have 120 acres and I sat down with a piece of paper and an engineer and plotted where we could put four gas wells."

But Chittister wasn't happy with the premise "that they're going to tie up our land for a hundred years for eight percent of what?" So she began to explore with local engineers, academics, and others the possibility of the order drilling its own well. The estimate for the venture came in at $100,000, much more than the community could afford. Even though she wasn't happy with the idea of leasing the land, Chittister concluded that she might be denying the community an ongoing resource, so she called a special meeting to place the matter for a vote. Leasing the land was approved. Weeks went by and Chittister didn't move on the matter. Tobin, now community treasurer, kept at her. "When are you going to call those people about that gas well? They told you they're going to be in this area and they'll have the drilling equipment. When are you going to let them know they can come?"

"I don't feel good about it," Chittister said. Tobin reminded her that she had a community vote.

Chittister said that it wasn't an overwhelming majority vote, it wasn't a two-thirds vote of the community. It was almost two-thirds, Tobin argued. "But it's not two-thirds, and I don't feel good about this," Chittister

---

14. *The Way We Were*, 237.

said. "I have not liked this idea from the beginning. I like it less right now when I'm faced with the right to do it." The hub at the center of the wheel, to use Chittister's description of Benedictine leadership, was resisting the direction in which the spokes were trying to go.

For weeks, Tobin had also been pushing Chittister to make a decision about what to do with a small amount of stock someone had given them. Chittister finally told her to call a financial consultant for the community to find out what it was worth. A few days later Tobin showed up with the report. "You better sit down," she said. "Why, what's wrong with the stock?" asked Chittister.

There was nothing wrong with the stock, Tobin said; it was worth $100,000.

Chittister told Tobin to make arrangements with the drilling firm and "tell them I want them in here, and I want a gas well now." There was paperwork to sign, and she was scheduled to leave for France and England, so the whole process had to be completed in a hurry.

Chittister was in Paris when Tobin called saying that the firm had arrived, was to begin drilling the next day, and had explained what would be involved in the process. Chittister had been under the impression that the company would drill until it found something. Tobin said, "No, they drill until they think they find something, then you have to tell them again if you want them to go on for the rest of it [at added expense]. If you don't, they cap the well, take the money, and leave. If you do, they'll go another certain number of feet."

Chittister said no one had told her that was the way it worked. "I'm about to lose $100,000. I said, 'Well, I didn't have it to begin with so, okay. All right. Well, good luck. I'm sorry I'm not with you. I know it's a lot of tension in the community, and I feel bad about it, but I can't get home by that time anyway.'" Tobin said the community was doing well and that they would tell the drillers to begin.

That night, Chittister had another of the few dreams she's ever remembered. "All of a sudden I'm sitting in front of a large piece of paper, and it looks like somebody is drawing a pond and there are all these figures and ripples around it." She's trying to get closer to the pond and realizes she's standing over it and "all of a sudden something shoots up out of the ground, and it's all there and the pond disappears." She called to someone. "What's that' And someone answered: 'It's oil!'" And then she woke up. It was about 4:30 in the morning. Tobin called later in the day with most of the community hovering near the phone. "They found gas!" she said.

Chittister told her that there was also oil. Tobin said they weren't yet certain. Chittister was. She told Tobin that she was to tell the engineers and the drillers that there would be oil. As it turned out, there was gas enough to supply more than 50 percent of the monastery's heating needs for decades, and the nuns sold the oil. For years, barrels were picked up each week from the monastery driveway.

The Erie Benedictines were temporarily connected to the wider world with news of the drilling that was carried by the *Wall Street Journal*, the *New York Times*, the *Chicago Tribune*, the *Los Angeles Times*, and other news outlets. The well was named Josepha after Sr. Josepha Miller, the prioress who had purchased the land in 1906.

Not long after the gas well began producing, Chittister took a walk along the lakeshore at the order's Camp Glinodo, a short distance from Mount Benedict, in a very strong wind, and in that moment began wondering about the possibility of installing a windmill. Two years of research and fundraising followed, and on December 5, 1982, "Ignatia," the windmill, was formally dedicated and immediately began to produce more than 90 percent of the electricity required by the several buildings and homes at the campsite.

But the windmill, which was placed atop a 120-foot tower, soon created a giant headache for the community. Because of the high winds coming off Lake Erie, its blades began to splinter and shear off, blowing onto neighbor's properties and creating a hazard for those who lived nearby. The windmill eventually was airlifted by helicopter to a location in the woods behind the monastery, where it produced electricity at the same rate and was distant enough from any other properties to pose no threat.

The gas well and windmill were high-profile items in a long list of "green" innovations the Benedictine community's Energy Committee put in place during Chittister's tenure. The committee looked at every potential for saving energy, from weather-stripping and thermostat controls to studies of air conditioning in the community's chapel to installation of solar panels that would heat the pool at Camp Glinodo and generate heat for a greenhouse. Ten years earlier, when the sisters were leaving behind the old life, the spaces that defined it, and the inherent disciplines that went with that space, they weren't certain how the new life would take shape. Concern for the earth, for how they lived, for their relationships with the wider community and, indeed, the entirety of creation were beginning to shape their new life for them.

Chittister, meanwhile, continued to make connections between the Erie community and national and international organizations. Her travel expanded as she gained recognition as a religious leader as well as a writer and lecturer.

Campbell records that in the two decades between 1977 and 1998, Chittister spoke in fifteen countries and wrote eighteen books and five pamphlets. She received honorary doctorates during that time from eight colleges and universities, was an elected fellow to the University of Cambridge for a year as writer-in-residence, and was named the 1996 Von Hügel lecturer there. Her travels—as a leader of women religious, as a speaker, and at times as a member of international delegations— took her five times to Rome, twice to Russia, Australia, Belgium, and Canada, four times to the Philippines and Ireland, and once to China, Hungary, New Zealand, Egypt, Israel, Colombia, and Haiti.

The most nagging and divisive question for the community during the twelve years of Chittister's time as prioress was the matter of what to do with St. Benedict Academy, which had started as a school housed in a small convent in 1869. It moved in 1890 to a four-story, late Victorian building of sandstone and brick at 345 E. 9th Street, which stands today and houses the St. Benedict Child Development Center, the order's development office, the offices of Benetvision, the office of Emmaus Ministries, and the Office of Alliance for International Monasticism.

The academy became a boarding school in 1928 and a four-year high school in 1929. The newest version of the academy had been constructed a block away on 10th Street in 1955.[15] By the mid- to late-1970s, it was clear that the school was in financial trouble. A lay board worked for years with the civic community in Erie, the Benedictines, and others interested in saving the institution. The board noted at the time, however, that sisters were no longer entering the community exclusively to teach and that staffing was becoming a growing problem.

Vladimiroff became principal of the school in 1974 and stayed through 1981. She cut the deficit and built up a bit of a reserve. But even she realized that the school's future was limited. "The high school was a big venture. It took us many, many years to talk through, and then in 1988 it was pretty clear that it had to go. That was a big question for the community," she continued, "because we'd been here from 1869, and there were some sisters who had taught nowhere else but here. So to try to say, 'Yes, but we're going to close,' that was a big decision during Joan's time because in some people's eyes, that was how people knew us, by St. Benedict Academy."

From her first year as prioress, Joan had begun preparing the community for what she had seen as inevitable. She brought in Basilian Fr. Frank Bredeweg, a financial expert, for the October 1978 community meeting to talk about the financial situation at the academy. "He made a presentation on the present and future projections of the school population and teachers' salaries; it was not an encouraging picture."[16]

---

15. *Vision of Change*, 307.
16. Ibid., 305.

Prior to the gathering, Chittister wrote in "The Leaven" of the importance of the upcoming meeting. "I'm asking you to include in your daily liturgies the petition that God will send us the understanding to see the situation clearly; the courage to proceed faithfully; and the fortitude to follow, both individually and together, whatever decision we choose."[17]

Bredeweg's immediate recommendation was for a substantial increase in tuition. Vladimiroff held meetings with parents of students, explaining the need for the increase. Even though tuition at St. Benedict Academy would remain the lowest of the city's four Catholic secondary schools, its students were still from the lower economic strata of the city and for many the increase would be formidable. According to Campbell's account, only a few students didn't return for the next school year.

Maintaining a balanced budget proved increasingly difficult, and only so many cuts in staff and programs could be made before the quality of education at the academy would seriously suffer. When the announcement of closing finally came, the Benedictines received support from other orders in the city who worked with academy parents to provide alternatives.

Every year for ten years after that first meeting with Bredeweg, the community reviewed the situation. Chittister was clearly leading the community toward closing the school, and the community must have either agreed or sensed the inevitability of it because she was twice re-elected prioress during that time.

"I did take a strong position that you cannot barter your future to pay for your past and that what we needed to do, and what we did do, was determine the amount of debt we could dare" accumulate, she says. "I had seen too many communities refuse to give up schools that should have been closed fifteen years before." Communities poured their resources into dying ventures and had nothing left with which to develop new directions.

Chittister saw in Erie what she had seen elsewhere—that the number of students was dropping each year and the costs were rising, as were the subsidies required from the community.

"I just simply took the position, 'Sisters, do you want a future? Just ask yourself if you want a future, and is the name of the future a ministry or is the name of the future the Benedictine Sisters of Erie?" Eventually the answer was clear: ministries come and go; the community was the constant amid change.

"That's a big thing in the Benedictine mind—if it's really a Benedictine mind—that sustained us," she said in an interview. "We couldn't have handled a debt of over $100,000, so every year we studied it."

---

17. Ibid., 306.

She brought in experts to help trim the academy budget but the point was reached where no further trimming was possible.

Eventually some of the most ardent supporters of the academy, women who had spent their entire careers there, who had seen the academy as essential to the mission, began to think otherwise. "In ten years' time, they cried in that room, but they were the first people to say, 'We've done everything we can and it has to go.'"

Campbell quotes from a journal entry written by Chittister a few days after announcement of the impending closing:

"We can't support a declining institution. And here's why: money—mortgage—loss of government funds—declining birth rates—rising lay teachers' salaries—exhausted efforts at fund-raising—need for new programs—availability of other Catholic schools in area...And I gave the message over and over: to the school board, to the principals, to the faculty, to the students, and come home feeling drained and numb...January 19, 1988—the end of 119 years of a simple ministry. Strangely, though we were sad, we were not beaten."

She said "goodbye to an era" and asked herself if the order would survive the loss. "Why not? Like Exodus, we've survived so much already. What's a little more sand, one way or another?"[18]

When the closing was finally announced "this community went to chapel with our arms around one another and a lot of tears," Chittister told me. "We didn't divide over the academy; we didn't. We held together on love and trust. That's about all I can say."

The last graduation was that spring, with commencement exercises held on June 6 at St. Peter Cathedral. Chittister delivered the commencement address.

———————————

Joan had come in promising to be not a mother but a sister and a friend, and there were times when the monastery inhabitants engaged in the kind of zany activities one might expect among sisters and friends.

One time, during a federation meeting on women's issues in the South, a Benedictine sister from Alabama came up to Chittister during a coffee break and wondered if she could ask a personal question. "Could you tell me why you're wearing two different kinds of shoes?"

For several days that had included flights and presentations and other conference activities, Chittister had not noticed. And she had to fly directly to Boston to give a major address. Panicked, she called Tobin,

———————————

18. Ibid., 307–8.

who was to meet her in Boston, asking if she could bring a matching shoe. "I only had two pairs of shoes, so either one would do," she recalls. "When I finally returned to the Mount, I was heading to my room in the monastery. I obviously am not really observant at times about physical things, but I'm sensing something overhead. It's like one of those 'what wrong with this picture' things, and I finally stop and look up. And I see something hanging from the ceiling. It's fifty pairs of little shoes—all cut out of catalogues," she says, roaring at the memory.

She went to her room laughing and thinking, "I'll get them. I'm gonna get 'em good" and there some of her sisters had spread out a Montessori school exercise for little kids all about matching things like salt and pepper and clothing and shoes, with their proper places. And, a note said that if she got them all right she would win a prize.

Some weeks later she was giving one of a series of First Sunday conferences on the Rule of Benedict. "They had a cue word—they knew I was going to say a certain thing—I can't any longer remember what it was—but the moment I said it they all got up in linked pairs. They all were wearing different shoes."

One time when Chittister was away, a group of about fifteen sisters, members of her staff, decided to play a prank by writing fictitious thank-you notes for favors she had supposedly granted—things like restaurant gift certificates, tickets to the symphony, a week's trip home. When Chittister returned she said nothing about it, and the plotters thought their joke had flopped. But when they received their next monthly stipends — personal spending money, which at the time amounted to $45 a month and today is $100 a month—the envelopes contained notes saying that an amount of money had been withheld to pay for the "favors" she had granted. The envelopes also contained copies of a *Washington Post* cross-word puzzle and a note saying that if they completed the puzzle, they could claim the rest of their money. One of the sisters, who received the *Post* regularly, retrieved the issue with the answers and shared it with the other nuns, who huddled together and made quick work of it. "I couldn't get ahead of them," Chittister laughed.

She loves to laugh, loves good food, and has become a somewhat accomplished cook, according to the sisters with whom she shares a house. As prioress, she had the reputation for not only encouraging parties at the Mount, but joining in. Often at community parties she'd break out her accordion and play for sing-alongs.[19]

Occasionally, the community could dish out some sisterly advice. When Chittister decided to expand her musical prowess to the recorder,

---

19. Ibid., 385.

she took to practicing for long stretches in her office, which happened to be under Sr. Dorothy Szczypinski's bedroom. "When Joan was learning 'We Three Kings of Orient Are,'" writes Campbell, "she practiced it so much and so often" that Szczypinski began jokingly dropping signs out of her window so Joan could see them.

They said: "If you're humble enough to ask, I'm sure the community would pay for lessons." "Not bad, but try again and this time, get the high C." And, "Haven't those kings gotten here yet?"

Chittister loves to fish and she would motor around the bay and Lake Erie and generally accomplished that without incident. She and a few of her friends, however, howl with laughter telling of her boating misadventures, especially one day when she was taking several groups of nuns and visitors, including Auxiliary Bishop Thomas Gumbleton of Detroit, for rides in a sixteen-foot motor boat. Chittister purchased the vessel, an upgrade for the community, with money given to her as gifts for her silver jubilee. Regularly she and a group of sisters would go out fishing and return to Camp Glinodo, where the fish were cleaned and frozen until the end of summer when the community would have a fish fry. The boat was christened "The Abbey." Chittister laughs as she explains, "We named it that so that if anyone called, they could say, 'Sorry, sister is busy in The Abbey.'"

During a day-long picnic with friends and visitors, she was providing boat rides. She likes to go fast, and after loading the boat with passengers, she gunned the engine and raced across the bay. Twice she was stopped by the Coast Guard and given tickets for speeding in "no wake" zones. A third time, she was stopped for a routine safety check, "and they didn't like my flare! I got three tickets on the water in one afternoon!"

On another day in another boat with a group of nuns, she had to call the Coast Guard when their anchor got snagged and they began to take on water. The Coast Guard arrived in a few minutes. One of the rescuers asked, "Who's the captain?" Chittister answered, "Well, we don't have a captain."

"That's not what your hat says," was the response.

"I was wearing this old Greek sailor cap with 'Captain' sewn right across the front," says Chittister. "Well," she responded, "I guess I'm the captain."

"Right," said the Coast Guard. "The rest of you come on board. You stay with the boat."

"So off they went," says Chittister, "and they were given cookies and punch. They waved to me as I stood in our boat and got towed nearly the entire length of the bay."

The last boat tale someone remembered in an evening of storytelling at St. Scholastica Priory in April 2014 was strikingly more somber. As part of a normal routine, Chittister and a few others would stop to fill the boat's fuel tank with gas before lowering it into the lake from their trailer. One nun was particularly expert at backing the boat into the water. This day she was also endlessly fussing and muttering about the bill for gas, which was much higher than the usual cost. Most of the others wanted to ignore the matter and get on with a day of fishing. But suddenly Chittister, concerned that they might have been overcharged, began shouting for everyone to get out of the boat.

She realized in that instant—and just a moment before she was prepared to start the engine—that the attendant at the station had somehow mistakenly filled the boat's hull instead of the tank. They avoided a potential catastrophe and spent the rest of the day draining the fuel out of the hull and repeatedly washing it with laundry detergent and rinsing it out.

By 2014, the boats were long gone. Chittister maintains that she never received a traffic ticket on land, but her sisters are quick to add (and she doesn't dispute the claim) that she has no sense of direction and once, not realizing that a shopping center road had ended, drove right off the edge of the development into a small ravine. Her good friend, theologian Gail Freyne of Australia, was with her and swears she yelled "Thelma!" as Joan drove them over the edge. Though she has called Erie home since childhood and will give a visitor a tour of its sights worthy of the Chamber of Commerce, waxing especially poetic at the beauty of Presque Isle, the bay, and the lake, she often still gets lost. The stories are legendary of Chittister calling back to her house just minutes away to get directions to somewhere else in the city.

She was a prioress of a different sort, building on an ancient tradition but refusing to be a captive of a practice for its own sake. Having women determine for themselves how religious life should be lived, and why, was essential to Chittister in her attempt to guide the community to a new understanding of itself. There were small things, unnoticed by the outside world but of sizeable consequence within the community. Early on in her tenure as prioress she decided to alter the way that the traditional "First Sunday" was conducted. Historically, the community had adoration of the Blessed Sacrament and a conference. The change occurred when Chittister, on one First Sunday, got out of her pew and told the community that she would be giving monthly conferences, "something that had traditionally been done by the priest celebrant but never by a prioress. It was a step in claiming our womanhood, our education, our experience, and our right to explore and shape our own part of a Benedictine heritage."[20]

---

20. *The Way We Were*, 182ff.

The conference format was changed from a list of agenda items, usually recommendations or plans to be voted on, to lectures "for the sake of understanding where we'd come from, who we were, and what was happening to us." These lectures were intended to lead not to conclusions but to "discussion of the ideas they provoked in our own lives."

She would reteach the Rule, which too often, she said, had been the rationale for changing nothing at all. In the same way religious orders had gone back to their roots to reinterpret the founder's vision for the twentieth century and beyond, she returned to Benedict's words "with an eye to distinguishing between the Rule's values and the social system of the time in which they were embedded." Over time, she writes, those two elements "had often become hopelessly conflated." The spiritual essence of the rule could be separated out from long black habits, veils, coifs, and enclosed cloisters and reapplied.

Hospitality, for instance, could expand to extending an invitation to the surrounding community and beyond to join in liturgies and special feast celebrations and to spend time with the sisters in the monastery. It could include the construction of hermitages in woods behind the monastery where people from outside the community could spend time in quiet retreat and meditation, choosing whether to join the community for meals, prayer, and liturgy during their stay.

It could also extend to an artist in search of a place to work, and that's how Benedictine Brother Thomas Bezanson came under the aegis of the community. Chittister met Brother Thomas in 1979 while a "canonical visitor" at Weston Priory in Vermont. Bezanson was a native of Nova Scotia who had joined the monks at Weston Priory in 1959. At some point in his development as a serious and accomplished ceramicist, the demands of his art began to clash with the demands of monastic life as practiced at Weston. Chittister said he once told her, "There was a time when I thought I was a monk who was also a potter, but I found out that I was a potter who was also a monk."

His first attempt to leave the community in the 1980s, an extremely difficult decision that Chittister said he struggled with for a long time, lasted only a few months. He had originally hoped to go to Erie. Chittister had offered him a place at Camp Glinodo, which was no longer a children's camp. But he decided to try another location closer to the Vermont priory. When that didn't work, he called Chittister again, asking if he could accept her earlier offer. In the meantime, however, she had opened the house to a mother with two disabled children.

A different building at Glinodo was considered, but it would have been too expensive to renovate for his purposes. Chittister hit on a solution: a large building on 10th Street, near the rest of the inner-city

Benedictine complex, that she had convinced the mayor of Erie to sell to the community for a dollar in exchange for the promise of upgrading the building's exterior appearance and remodeling the inside. Pax Christi had moved its offices from Chicago Into the building in 1984. Thomas arrived in 1985—with a multi-ton kiln in tow. A doorway had to be cut wider so the kiln would fit, and a hole had to be cut in the roof of the building in order to vent the kiln. The apparatus also required a huge propane gas tank to heat the kiln to the extreme temperatures needed to fire the pieces Thomas created.

In a bold, some might say reckless, exercise of the maxim "act first, ask permission later," the community did all of the alterations and had the equipment installed knowing that ordinances existed prohibiting probably most of what they were doing. "I went every year and blessed it with holy water," said Chittister, and then trusted in another bit of wisdom from her grandmother having to do with a belief that the right angels will always be there in a time of need. The community never got to the second part of the "act first" adage; the sisters never asked permission from anyone, and the city, in the more than twenty years that Brother Thomas worked in that space, never came asking any questions or wishing to inspect. The building today houses a mailroom for Benetvision, as well as part of the ministry to refugees. One section is used for storing maintenance material for the inner-city properties.

Brother Thomas produced world-class ceramic art of breathtaking shapes and stunning glazes, including pieces that have been acquired by such distinguished institutions as the Museum of Fine Arts in Boston, the Smithsonian Institution, Windsor Castle, the Metropolitan Museum of Art, and the Vatican. He ultimately exhibited widely and found enthusiastic sponsors in Bernie and Sue Pucker of the Pucker Gallery in Boston. A gallery catalogue of his art contains an essay about his work that is headlined with one of his quotes: "We are not material beings on a spiritual journey, but spiritual beings on a material journey."

In an email exchange, Bernie Pucker wrote: "Joan essentially saved his art and his ability to create."[21] Indeed, Chittister said she valued the conversations she and Thomas had at times, for instance, when pots were being fired over long hours. The talks would range over such topics as art and philosophy, theology, spirituality, and monasticism. In an essay about Brother Thomas's work, she wrote about the close relationship of monasticism and art through the centuries. "Medieval monasteries were centers

---

21. Pucker also told me that Brother Thomas had befriended the Erie fire marshall who quietly approved the arrangement with the propane tank.

of the arts and patrons of the arts. Art, as a reflection of beauty, itself an attribute of God, came to be understood, in fact, as simply another expression of incarnation." In Western theology, she said, sacred images were seen as transcending nature. "They overcame the distractions of matter. They superseded the merely human...art gave both linkage and expression of the presence of God in time."

Again, in something new—this accommodation of a monk associated with a community of women religious—Chittister sees a fulfillment of very old themes. "Monasticism is the most piercing expression of the search for truth, the conscious investigation of the marrow of what it means to be fully human. The monastic gives life over to the search for the spirit in life that makes matter holy and the spiritual attainable. Monasticism is about more than living every day well. It is an exercise in living every day on a plane above itself, of seeing in the obvious more than the obvious, of finding even in the mundane the creative energy that drives creation to heights beyond itself. If, indeed, truth is beauty and beauty truth, then the monastic and the artist are one."

She said that Brother Thomas "moved out of one monastery so he could dedicate his life to pottery and then moved into another one for the same reason." In Erie, Thomas lived with the community at Pax Center on 9th Street, where he died in 2007. He had just turned seventy-eight.

The building where Thomas set up shop was not the only real estate deal Chittister pulled off that left people shaking their heads. The house where she has lived since 1990, St. Scholastica Priory, on 9th Street, the width of a driveway away from the former in-town monastery, had been owned by a woman who had a fondness for the community and let it be known that she wished the Benedictines to have the first opportunity to purchase the property when it became vacant and was put up for sale in 1985. The price, however, was beyond what the community could afford, so the house, in need of repair and in a location known for crime and drugs, remained vacant.

In the meantime, the community, on separate occasions, was willed two smaller homes that were not suitable for repurposing as priories apart from the monastery. So, in consultation with her council, Chittister put them up for sale and, in short order, they sold, each for $30,000, in 1988.

Chittister held a council meeting to discuss what to do with the $60,000 the community had suddenly acquired and the group, worried about the problems that could occur in a vacant home in a drug infested neighborhood and so near to the center where they operated programs for pre-school children, voted to go back to the seller of the house on 9th Street and make an offer. The plan was to offer the quite unreasonable sum of $30,000 for the house, with the intent of using the other $30,000 to fix it up and renovate a large third floor into two bedrooms.

The real estate agent, said Chittister, responded to the offer over the phone with "dead silence" and called it unrealistic. It was less than half the asking price. Chittister said she understood the amount was ridiculous, but that her council had asked her to make the offer and the only thing she was requesting was that the agent promise to deliver the offer to the owner.

The agent said she would. The next evening the agent called back and said she had delivered the offer. Chittister said, "Thank you," and was ready to hang up when the agent said, "Just a moment—and she has accepted it."

"And that's how we got the house."

The question Chittister asked herself upon her election—how to begin to make sense of all that had occurred in the previous fifteen years—was answered in the short term during her years as prioress with her renewed examination of the Rule of Benedict and an emphasis on the contemplative life and a monasticism that was not dependent on a routine built around a single ministry.

The longer-term answer had been taking shape even before the formal community and federation meetings dealing with renewal. Well before Chittister's time as prioress, as we've seen, prioresses encouraged more extensive education and tolerated the development of ministries such as peacemaking that had little to do with staffing schools and the academy. That direction achieved fuller expression toward the end of Chittister's tenure and particularly with the formal closing of the academy.

After it closed, St. Benedict Academy was vacant no longer than the normal summer vacation. By September 1988, the space "was fully occupied by new programs" and the building itself was renamed St. Benedict Education Center. The repurposed property was under the direction of Miriam Mashank, one of the organizers of the community singing group that had appeared on the *Ed Sullivan Show*. Her entrepreneurial and organizational skills were once more on display when she "turned her attention to a new area for which she felt an imperative need: promoting educational efforts for economically disadvantaged students."[22]

22. *Visions of Change, Voices of Challenge*, 309.

Immediately, the center began a job training program for thirty-six economically disadvantaged students. In another section of the building, community members were involved in developing a Head Start program for youngsters. In still another portion of the space a 13th Year program worked to further prepare high school students who were not yet academically ready for college or to enter the work force. An Office Services Program prepared others for work in office positions. Mashank's efforts attracted the attention of Erie businesses—and their funding—to sustain existing programs and introduce others.

"Employment preparations expanded to training in computer skills, employment search, a reading clinic, GED preparation"[23] and a food preparation class. Mashank's was the only program in Erie awarded a $550,000 state grant to provide case management and job training, placement, and other services.

Over the years, the programs and the program names have changed, but the activities at St. Benedict Education Center have remained much the same, often state-funded work with immigrants, the poor, the under-educated, the unemployed—all sorts of people on the margins of society trying to find a foothold and the path to some stability.

With its increasing work among the poorest of the poor in down-town Erie and its expanding engagement with environmental concerns, the community was slowly remaking its identity from a community defined by a single ministry to a community defined by its monastic life expressed in a range of ministries and work.

During one of my early visits to Erie while working on this book, I parked my car in front of 345 E. 9th Street, which houses St. Benedict Child Development Center and Benetvision, among other ministries. On the sidewalk a startling scene was developing. A young man was screaming and cursing, spewing obscenities directed, I thought at the time, at a much smaller woman. My initial instinct was that the woman was in trouble and that I should try to intervene, but it quickly became clear that she knew him and wasn't attempting to get away. She didn't yell or become aggressive even as his voice got louder and he became so angry that he smashed his cell phone to several pieces on the pavement.

I was surprised when she took the man by the arm and headed toward the door of 345 and up three flights of steps to the quiet, tastefully appointed offices of Benetvision.

The woman, I came to learn, was seventy-one-year-old Sr. Mary Miller, head of the community's Emmaus Ministries. She handed the young man off to Kownacki, a combination of realist, poet, and a cre-

---

23. Ibid., 310.

ative force behind Benetvision, who, in a measured but no-nonsense tone, laid down the rules for how whatever was disturbing the man would be talked about.

Later, the two smiled when explaining that the young man with a difficult domestic circumstance was long known to the community. It was my first exposure to the reality that when the monastery opens its doors to the world, the world can sometimes intrude on its own, messy terms. There are risks in practicing what Pope Francis has described as "the art of accompaniment," and dealing with those risks can require a type of competence that was never part of previous monastic practice. That, in itself, might be a true test today of the contemplative, monastic life.

More than a year later, in summer 2013, I sat with Mary Miller in the dining room of Emmaus Ministries' Soup Kitchen. Out back beyond the loading dock and parking lot, work on the Emmaus Grove—a garden recently expanded thanks to the generosity of a neighboring Protestant church and donations from foundations and the efforts of a host of volunteers—was in full swing. Many of the volunteers at the time were newly arrived immigrants from places like Bhutan, who were also taking courses at the nearby St. Benedict Education Center. The garden served at times as an informal language classroom.[24]

On one wall of the dining room was a series of pieces depicting Jesus on the road to Emmaus. The progression of the artwork is a fair depiction of the community's growing understanding of itself. The first piece is a standard illustration of a well-groomed, WASPish looking Jesus with two men. As the work progresses, one of the men is replaced by a woman, and in one of the images, Jesus is breaking bread with a couple, a man and a woman. It is the sort of touch one encounters frequently with this community, a kind of turning of the question or the point of view to pose a new question or to see things from a different perspective.

Miller spent her first twenty-five years of religious life on the opposite side of town as a member of the Sisters of St. Joseph, and switched orders in 1988, toward the end of Chittister's years as prioress. She is one of nearly two dozen from other communities who transferred directly into the Benedictine Sisters of Erie from other orders between 1978, Chittister's first year as prioress, and 2015. (Another nine who had left other communities for a time returned to religious life by joining

---

24. Much of the following account was first printed as a story in the Augus 30–September 12, 2013, issue of *National Catholic Reporter* in its Ministries section. Additional information came from interviews with Miller and others on July 23, 2013.

the Erie Benedictines during that period.)[25] For Miller, the attraction to the Erie Benedictines, however, had developed long before and had grown over the years. It began with her wish to be more involved in peace work. She had asked a superior in her order for permission to attend a demonstration in Washington to engage in civil disobedience with other sisters following the murder of four churchwomen in El Salvador in 1980. She said the response from her superior was "Well, my dear, we don't do that here." She went to Washington but had to walk away when other sisters were being arrested.

Back home she began "hanging around" the Benedictines' Pax Center more frequently "and peace and justice issues started getting more and more ingrained in my heart and soul," she says. She was spending more time with Chittister and Kownacki and reading the literature of the Christian peace movement. "I just knew I had to make the move."

The transition turned out to be a rather easy one in her case. Her superior was agreeable and Joan had already asked her if she wanted to run the soup kitchen. Just as she was preparing to make the move, she developed hepatitis. "I thought, 'My God, they're not going to take me,' and Joan said, 'Oh, all the better. You won't be able to do much; you'll be able to learn the rhythm of the life better if you can't work.' So, I moved into the monastery and learned the rhythm of the life."

Chittister's approach to monasticism and community was influential in Miller's decision to join. "You want to say it's her words, but it's not her words. Her words come out of a spirit that is unlike any other. Her words come out of—she's so passionate and she engages you. She's really with you in the now. What attracted me? I guess maybe, obviously, it's charisma, but it's her zeal for God that embraces you, and you catch fire. I mean, don't you see that? I mean, she loves God primarily and she loves everybody else she comes in contact with. I don't know how to describe zeal for God except I know it. You can experience it and hear it in her words, but you also see it in her eyes and experience it in her presence."

Miller was interrupted twice during the time that I was with her that day, once by a woman recently released from prison who was des-

---

25. In addition, twenty-one Benedictine Sisters of Holy Name Priory, Benet Lake, WI, transferred into the Benedictine Sisters of Erie when their community merged with Eric, according to information provided by the Erie Benedictines. Of the total of fifty-two women who came to Erie from other communities between 1978 and the beginning of 2015, some twenty had died during that period and a few had left.

perate for help with rent and was trying to find another sister, a member of the community, who had visited her in prison. The second took place as we were leaving the soup kitchen when a couple with a baby approached Miller. The woman had just lost her job and needed help to make a payment. "I don't want to lose my house," she said.

Depending on circumstances, said Miller, the ministry had access to small amounts of aid for emergencies. But emergencies can sometimes seem the order of the day in this section of a city that, like many other once-powerful centers of industry in Pennsylvania, have watched their manufacturing lifeblood drain out of them to other countries or to the U.S. South. Since the 1960s, the hulking factories and heavy industrial work have been overtaken by lightning quick technology employed elsewhere and by the rise of service industries. What remains are lots of poor people, marginalized minorities, and substantial new populations of just-arrived immigrants.

All around this section of the east side of Erie are indications the Benedictines are here: gardens, landscaping, renovated houses, well-kept buildings that welcome those in need of so many things, oases of calm and order. Chittister has written that the initiatives that have grown up are "as important now to the city...as St. Benedict Academy ever was. The only difference is that now its population is just as needy as the German immigrants before it—but neither German nor Catholic."

Work on the margins of society, among people of other faiths who may never sit in the pew of a Catholic church, doesn't produce the same measures of success, or a level of identifiable Catholic culture, as a private school full of Catholic girls who will memorize answers to catechism questions and go systematically through training for the sacraments. There's nothing on file to show that you've served hundreds of meals a week, saved hundreds of other kids from hunger in Sr. Gus's Kids' Café, a place where youngsters between the ages of six and seventeen can come after school for food and a safe, quiet place to play games, read, and do homework.

The café was created because one day a teacher who had volunteered to wash dishes at the soup kitchen told Miller that she had recently asked a third-grade student what she had had for dinner the night before. The student replied that she had eaten at school. "Yes," said the teacher, "but what did you eat last night?" The child responded, "I eat in school."

"So we opened a Kids' Café," said Miller, and it became much more than a place for something to eat. Still, as essential as it is to meet an immediate need, she is left wondering what the long-term effects might be. Too often, she said, "We lose them to the streets. You read in the paper about our older kids getting arrested for armed robbery or assault or stuff like that."

The bleak record can become overwhelming. One woman who worked there at one point told Miller, "I don't think we're doing any good."

Miller responded, "Were the children safe? Were they fed and did you love them? For a brief moment they'll know that there's another way to live and maybe when they're forty-five they'll remember it and choose something different. I don't know, but it can't solve their immense problems. They're living in a culture of drugs and violence and inattention and abandonment and everything else." So the Benedictines can provide a couple of hours of calm and order, food and attention, knowing it's never enough to remedy the effects of whatever trauma the kids face the other hours of the day.

There are no records for how many people were visited in prison, how many women may have been saved from domestic violence, how many economically deprived youngsters got to try their hand at all forms of art and music in the Neighborhood Art House. The results of accompanying the poor and the broken just can't be as easily documented as the achievements attained when running a private academy.

The certainty of accomplishment gives way to the uncertainty of just being present. No one quite knows what that might mean in the day-to-day routine. Sometimes, however, grace becomes apparent. Miller and Kownacki, whom Miller describes as a formidable behind-the-scenes force in the development of many of the community's ministries, live in a neighborhood called Trinity Square, notorious for violence, crime, and drugs.

Quoting the late Jesuit theologian and preacher Walter Burghardt, who said that contemplation "is taking a long, loving look at the real," Miller says, "I prefer close contact with the poor, with the real. And so I choose to live in a place where I look out the window and I can see both a beautiful poetry park and an abandoned house with garbage in the front and a family being evicted, and bedbugs crawling out of their couches." If that is important to her it is because of the potential for transformation among people most in need. So far she and others in her small community have raised money enough to acquire twelve houses. They've demolished four of them, renovated at least six, and established a community garden and a children's center and the poetry park.

The neighborhood is so named because of Trinity Church, a parish that serves as a kind of anchor. Miller and Kownacki and a few others convinced some friends to help them form a little nonprofit agency, the Trinity Square Foundation. Slowly the neighborhood, home to Puerto

Ricans, Iraqis, Burmese, Nepalese, African Americans, and Poles, among others, is being transformed. Pressure was brought to bear on a local nuisance bar—with constant calls to the police—and it was finally shut down. Redevelopment money from the state and generous donations from individuals helped purchase and rehab homes and build the park.

One night there was a knock at the door of Miller's home. Two women and three or four little children announced that they wanted to move into the house across the street that the Trinity Square Foundation was in the process of renovating. The two women were sisters and their families had been in a refugee camp in Thailand for twelve years. The husband of one of them had died of a snakebite in the camp. All of the children with the exception of the oldest girl had been born in the camps.

"They moved here and we love them; they're part of our family now," said Miller. The kids go to Catholic school and the sisters help pay tuition. Most of the adults are Catholic. "Katherine comes out of her house every morning, stands on the front step, faces the church, bows her head, blesses herself, and goes off to work at some lousy laundry, eight hours a day."

Sometimes it may seem as if the foundation is hardly making a dent, Miller says. And then there are little reminders that they might, indeed, be involved in a bit of transformation. "A couple of years ago, a little girl selling Girl Scout cookies came to the door of the Catholic Worker House that's also located in the neighborhood, and she told the sister who answered, "My mama says it's safe to come to this neighborhood now.""

At the soup kitchen one day, Miller was cleaning tables with a high school volunteer and she asked the teenager: "What do you think of this joint?"

Before the volunteer had a chance to answer, "a guy sitting in a corner of the dining room called out, 'Hey, Sis, this ain't a joint. It's a church.'" She approached him and asked why he had said that. "Because this is where I find God," he answered.

By July of 2013 when I visited many of the Benedictine ministries, little was evident of the anxiety that had been a part of the years of discovery, of venturing beyond the ministry which for so long had provided the community with identity and purpose. For all her fame and, some might say, notoriety, for all of the causes with which she has been associated, all the accolades she has received, it is safe to say that Chittister would name the corporate commitment near the top of any list of her achievements. Through all of the changes, the exploration and the development of new ministries, that commitment has remained the constant.

The community has integrated into its life a range of ecology and environmental issues, a concern for the earth that grew out of its members' spirituality, and a growing understanding of humans' relationship with all of creation. They continue to work on women's issues at many levels.

"Over the years, every three or four years," Chittister says, "we review and rescind or renew and reclaim a corporate commitment, but we know who we are and we know why we're doing what we're doing and that has been a real glue for us. When you look at those twelve years [that she was prioress], what's the narrative? The creation of a corporate commitment, the immersion in study of contemporary issues, the freeing of the individual sister to follow her own gifts."

As the new direction for the community began to take shape, Chittister says, "people would come and say, 'How did you get all of this started?' and I would say, 'I didn't start anything. I allow our sisters to start what needs to be done. But I can only hope for this: that when you come back in twenty years, the commitment of the prioress will still be a commitment to the development of the gifts of the sisters, because if we do that, we'll be a strong and a healthy community.' So that's about the whole thing."

Joan with her mother, Loretta, and her father, Daniel Dougherty.

Joan.

Grandma Cuneo, Joan, and (Dutch) Harold Chittister.

Original Motherhouse of
the Benedictine Sisters of
Erie on E. 9th St.

Joan (Sister Mary
Peter) in habit.

Joan at Venango Christian
High School, 1968.

*Joan and
Danny, 1974.*

On the accordion.

Joan's installation as Prioress, 1978.

With Pope John Paul II.

Good Friday pilgrimage in the mid-1980s.

With Native women in Chiapas, Mexico, 1998.

In New York City in 2005 with the International Peace Council.

With the Dalai Lama.

In Bhutan in 2013.

With Lady.

Mount St. Benedict Monastery today.

In China, 2007

Joan in the Monastery garden.

PART III

Speaking.

EIGHT

WOMEN

C hittister can't remember the precise year—it was sometime after completing her doctoral work at Penn State and while she was still teaching at Venango Christian High School—that she came across a slim volume, *Women and the Church*, by Dominican Sister A. M. McGrath.[1]

The cover described the work as "A modern woman's sensitive, objective analysis of woman's 'place' in the church and the world—past and present." Perhaps the words "sensitive" and "objective" were the publisher's way of preparing the reader for the jolt just ahead. The book presents an unblinking catalogue of the church's attitudes and statements about women through the ages; it escorts the reader through centuries of demeaning statements toward women from church fathers, popes, thinkers, and theologians, all stacked up in one compelling little volume.

McGrath's arguments are tightly wound and economically expressed. Her conclusions are severe, including the deduction, given women's exclusion from all decision-making and sacramental positions in the church, that their treatment was comparable to that of blacks subjected to segregation.

It is an unrelenting, unapologetic, and highly polemical Catholic feminist treatise. The pioneering Catholic feminist theologian Mary Daly had already published *The Church and the Second Sex*, a groundbreaking treatment of how Christian structures historically subjugated women. She

---

1. Sr. A. M. McGrath, *Women and the Church* (New York: Image Books, 1976). The book had originally been published in 1972 by the Thomas More Association under the title, *What a Modern Catholic Believes About Women*.

would follow in 1973, a year after the initial publication of McGrath's book, with *Beyond God the Father: Toward a Philosophy of Women's Liberation*. McGrath's offering seems to be one of the earliest, if not the first, such critique to come from the ranks of women religious. She was chair of the history department at Rosary College, an institution founded by the Sinsinawa (Wisconsin) Dominicans.[2]

The A.M. in her name stands for Albertus Magnus, the thirteenth-century Dominican saint and philosopher credited with recognizing and nurturing the genius of his student, Thomas Aquinas. The latter saint provided the material for the first footnote of McGrath's book where, in the introduction, she notes that women were excluded from the first sessions of Vatican II and permitted only as silent observers during the final two sessions. She laments that a "brilliant" female economist was not allowed to read her own paper for the council fathers. Church leaders required that it be read by a man. McGrath noted that the woman had addressed members of the World Council of Churches around the same time. "But a dictum of St. Thomas Aquinas barred her from sullying the air of St. Peter's: 'The voice of a woman is an invitation to lust and therefore must not be heard in the church.'"

McGrath begins her book with the scene of Pope Paul VI celebrating Mass for thousands of Catholics in Yankee Stadium and millions more watching on television during his 1965 visit to the United States.

"Visibly moved," she writes, "the Pope turned to deliver his allocution, his hands outstretched in a gesture of embracing love. 'Brothers and Sons!' he began, and again, 'Brothers and Sons!'

"In that twice-uttered greeting, there was no word, no gesture of love for the women who constituted, one would suppose, at least half of the congregation, half of the television audience. In six words, Paul VI had made bitterly clear 'women's place' in the Catholic Church."

McGrath called the papal snub an "insult" to women in the church, "all the more poignant," she said, because Paul VI would not have recognized it as such. She viewed it as another in the "series of indignities experienced by women during Vatican II," the last session of which was wrapping up the very month the pope was in New York.

Chittister can't remember how she acquired McGrath's book—whether someone gave her the volume or she merely happened upon it

---

2. The Sinsinawa Dominicans founded St. Clara College in 1901 in Sinsinawa, WI. The school was renamed Rosary College in 1922 when it moved to River Forest, IL. It was renamed Dominican University in 1997 to reflect its founding heritage.

on a table in the convent—but what followed is seared in her memory. She began reading and couldn't put it down. She devoured its 142 pages in one sitting. Chapter after chapter, she took in McGrath's densely packed evidence building the case that women had been devalued for millennia, their worth based primarily on "biological processes misunderstood."

Aquinas would again come in for criticism in McGrath's observation that the ancients viewed woman as "an ambulatory incubator," a reference to the saint's inadequate understanding of biology that underpinned his assertion regarding the inferiority of women. He believed, as did others of that era, that women contributed the fertile container, and little else, to the procreative process. "But the seed was the man's seed and the child was the man's child," she says, quoting Aquinas. "It was his ongoing spirit, his continuing life."

In the lines of Ecclesiastes—"No wickedness comes anywhere near the wickedness of a woman, may a sinner's lot be hers" (25:19), and "Sin began with a woman, and thanks to her we all must die" (25:24)—she sees the formulation of "the Eve syndrome, the projection on to women of cosmic guilt," so effectively used by "St. Paul, the Fathers, and the scholastics . . . in shaping the Church tradition."

In McGrath are early soundings of Chittister's much later conviction that the God encountered in the established Christian tradition is one imagined and formulated by men, for their purposes, and not a God modeled on the example of Jesus.

McGrath quotes the Lutheran theologian Dr. Conrad Bergendorff: "Christ nowhere distinguishes between men and women as children of God and objects of his redemptive ministry . . . Jesus Christ erased all lines of superiority and inferiority between men and women and placed all on the same level of grace." She includes a page of examples showing just how completely equal was Jesus' treatment of men and women.

Mary the sister of Martha, in taking "the better part" of direct contact with Jesus, stands in for what has been taken from women in the church since. McGrath argues that the scandal of Jesus' talking to the woman at the well is not that she is a Samaritan but that he is speaking to a woman, alone, in the full light of day, an act that defied cultural conventions of that era. As the woman runs off to announce to others her encounter with the good news, Jesus does not "prevent her from proclaiming the Gospel because she is a woman."

Mary, his mother, argues McGrath, is treated by God as a full adult capable of making her own decisions, not, as the law at the time would dictate, "a perpetual child whose decisions would have to be ratified by father or husband." If Mary is given a role ministering to

all humankind, she asks, "Is it too much to see here the full integra-
tion of all women into the ecclesia, the church of the New Covenant?"

One can imagine the young Chittister especially riveted by the chapter
headed "Historical Development," which contains a lively history of religious orders with a particular emphasis on the centuries of absolute control of women's institutes by men and papal insistence that women remain
in enclosures, restricted from moving outside the monastic setting. "They
were rules made by men to be observed by women, formed on the usual
androcentric premises that women were the guilty sex, weak and morally
frail, unintelligent, 'slow to understand,' 'dangerous in public affairs.'"
McGrath writes that a motto "dear to the hearts of the male clergy was always '*aut maritus, aut murus*' ('either a husband or a wall')."

She cites the thirteenth-century papal bull, *Periculoso*, of Boniface
VIII, mandating cloister for all religious women and even giving bishops
permission to call in civil force if necessary to put down resistance. She
says most orders, not having been established as cloistered, ignored the
papal order. The mandate, though, was reinforced during the reign of
Pius V, who, in 1566, decreed that all women who took solemn vows
were required to observe strict cloister, the violation of which would result in excommunication that could be lifted only by the pope himself.

McGrath argues as fervently for non-vowed women and is as critical of the church in that regard as she is of hierarchical control of
women's orders. "The church needs a new anthropology," she writes,
"a real and healthy theology of sex relationships in marriage and in society. And the church must recognize that this anthropology, this theology, can no longer be the result of male experience, male understandings, male insights alone. There are two halves to the human race."

On and on went this slim tract, arguing for women's rights in society, tracing the church's views of women which, in the late 1960s and
early 1970s, had begun to sound terribly out of tune with the reality
that Catholic women in the United States and elsewhere were increasingly experiencing in other spheres of life.

In the following excerpt, McGrath articulates the argument that
would resound through the decades to follow as women challenged the
church's prevailing views:

> Women's experience of themselves, of their world, of their rela-
> tionship to God is not consonant with clerical attitudes nor with
> the law of the church in their regard. Aristotle, Aquinas, Freud,
> and canon law to the contrary, normal women experience them-
> selves neither as incomplete, mutilated men, nor as perpetual chil-
> dren. They experience themselves as intelligent and free, as mature

human persons needing, and capable of, creative self-fulfillment on every human level. Standing in awe before the vastness of the universe, they yet recognize it as their home, to whose destiny they can contribute in proportion to their total personal gifts, not just by the exercise of one biological function. They experience themselves as loved by God, as fully redeemed by Christ, as communicating personally with the Deity in prayer and in graced action. It does not seem too much to ask that the Church repudiate the statements from the patristic age and after which see women as diminished and inferior human beings.

Of religious life, she says that sisters are only beginning to say openly what they have known for a long time: "conformity is not community. Marching two by two in silent, shrouded anonymity is not living, certainly it is not mirroring Christ in the world."

If self-giving and self-denial are at the core of Christianity and religious life, "there must first be a self to deny and a self to give." Community is essential to Christian life, but women religious need not dress the same and all do the same work to be a community. Rigid conformity, she writes, stifles leadership and tends to "put a premium on mediocrity." The experimentation then under way in religious communities, she writes, was intended "to encourage the growth of the person in Christ, to prevent the stifling of personal and apostolic gifts."

In the end, she calls on women in the church to lift their "voices and pens against any church decision, any church publication, any churchman who does not recognize the equal human dignity, equal personal worth, equal potential for spiritual and intellectual growth of women with men."

Chittister read the book well beyond the 10 PM lights-out directive. "The next morning, I'm due in the car to go at 7:30, and prayer is at 6, and I get up. I can't have had more than four or four-and-a-half hours of sleep. I'm so excited. I can feel my heart beat just thinking about it again. I've got this book in my hand, and I race into the car." At the high school, she headed directly for the office. She couldn't wait to share this source of new insights on women with the school's headmaster, Fr. Lawrence Antoun.

Beneath her excitement of the moment, competing emotions were at play regarding Antoun. Chittister was torn between her deep affection for him, whom she described as a kind of father figure, and her anger that he had been installed in the new high school, in her view, as a male figurehead. "My community had had a school in Oil City for a hundred years. We had staffed it, been principals of it, gotten accreditation for it, graduated our kids, and 88 or 90 percent of our kids went to college and stayed there. This was one of the premier high schools in the diocese." And then the diocese came along and decided to close the school and open a larger central high school.

When that happened, Tobin, who had a principal's certification, was no longer principal. Instead, the diocese created the position of headmaster, and appointed Antoun, "a guy with a twenty-nine-cent plastic collar who never finished a master's degree." In fact he was one of a number of priests the diocese decided to install as headmasters in Catholic high schools.

Tobin was the de facto principal, but Antoun filled the newly created top spot. Tobin was called his assistant. Chittister and Tobin had had numerous discussions about it. "I got so angry," says Chittister. I told Maureen, "'You should be principal.' Her credentials were covering our existence.

"Maureen said, 'Joan, don't do that, I don't want to be principal.'

"I said, 'Whether you want to be or not, Maureen, is not the question. You should have been asked.'

"She said, 'Forget it.'" Chittister, of course, wouldn't forget.

The rub was that she had a sincere fondness for Antoun. He was to her, in so many ways, the kind of father she had never had, the one who had encouraged her to go to Penn State, where new worlds of ideas were opened to her. If, in one breath, she could disparage him for lack of credentials and pulling rank with a cheap collar, in another breath she'd say: "I love this guy. He was the first genuine intellectual that I had ever seen outside the community, and he loved me like a father. I was very close to his sister, who was a Sister of St. Joseph." Chittister waited for him that day "because he was a great reader" and "because I knew that when he walked in, he would love this book."

Fr. Antoun finally showed up. "He's wearing this big, black overcoat and he's got a hat on. The hat's coming off like this, and he looks down at me. I'm sitting there like a kid on this little chair, and he says to me, 'Well, what are you doing here so early?'

"I answer, 'I'm waiting for you, Father.'

"He says, 'Really? What's up?'

"'I've got something to show you,' I say. 'I got this book last night and I read it all night long. You have to read it.'"

She handed it to him. He stopped and looked at it. "Why would I want something like that?" he asked. "I'm not going to read anything like that." And he tossed it back across the desk.

"Not in a mean way," Chittister recalled. "It was worse than mean. It was dismissive. It had no value, and I realized that every word that woman [McGrath] had said, every word my mother ever said, in that moment, became frighteningly true and clear."[3]

Perhaps this man she loved and respected, a father figure, someone she referred to as "my hope," had no idea how deeply the book had affected her, how fascinated she was with the history McGrath had laid out and the questions she had raised. One can only assume at this distance that he had no idea how deeply his dismissal of the book hurt Chittister. "It went through me like a knife. I couldn't believe it. By throwing that book, he threw our relationship, he threw my value, he threw my hope in the church right out the window. That may seem like too much to say. Even I think it's too much to say, but I can tell you that at the feeling level, it was truth. It wasn't too much to say."

Another event would solidify her conviction that McGrath's analysis was on target. Chittister was a homeroom teacher for juniors and had to compute all the grades for the National Honor Society. She handed them in to Antoun. On the morning of the National Honor Society assembly she went to her in-box in the faculty room to pick up the paper with the names on it. "I looked at it. My God! There had been a terrible mistake. I turned and ran down the hall to the principal's office." Chittister walked through the receptionist's area and into Antoun's office without being announced.

She told him there had been a terrible mistake and showed him the paper. The placements were all wrong. She had named five candidates for the National Honor Society, the top three of whom had been girls and the bottom two, boys. "They had been flipped. He had flipped them." The boys had been barely eligible, but on the sheet in her hand they topped the list.

"He said, 'Sr. Mary Peter, I did it and it's going to stay that way. These boys need this on their resumes to get into college."

She argued that the grades now were gifts and that what he was doing was wrong. "He said, 'Sr. Mary Peter, it's my problem, not yours. You put the paper on my desk. I'll have the assembly.'"

They remained friends, said Chittister, but her memory of those two events stayed with her.[4] Some twenty years later, she and Tobin were visiting Antoun's sister, Laureace, in the hospital. She was near the

---

3. Tobin, whose office was near the space where Chittister was sitting at the time, confirmed the encounter. She said she heard the entire exchange and knew that it was extremely upsetting to Chittister. She also confirmed the conversations she and Chittister had over Antoun being installed as headmaster.

4. Fr. Lawrence Antoun later became a monsignor. He died in 1986.

end of her life and both Tobin and Chittister recalled the conversation. Laureace asked Joan how she had become the person she was, how she had arrived at the questions and the convictions about church, about women, and about religious life that she had lectured on and begun writing about so extensively.

"Sr. Maureen was sitting next to me. We were at her bedside in the hospital," Chittister said. "I looked at Maureen kind of out of the side of my eye, and Maureen looked at me. She knew what I was going to say."

Chittister told Laureace that she had always had a sense of the questions, "at least subconsciously, out of other life experiences. But your brother radicalized me." Laureace was surprised. She told Chittister, "My brother loves you. He has such respect for you."

Chittister responded that Fr. Antoun had turned her into an ardent feminist "and for that I thank the church."

The encounter with him over the book and the young women who should have headed the National Honor Society list were life-changing for Chittister, moments that she called "step-over" points. "Women could think it, swallow it, try to talk people out of it, try to reason around it, make enough cookies so everybody's happy when you do it, but if you just stand up and say: 'No. No more. Enough. No more,' they don't know what to do. So get into a lot of trouble I have."

She said she was late to feminism, a claim that, on second thought, she said, "is both true and false. I discovered that what I had seen in my mother and been taught by my mother was what they were talking about," referring to those who formally wrote about feminism. "Then I realized that what those women were doing applied to us as well as to anybody else. I'd always been a 'feminist' before I had language for it.

"There was no cleavage there," she said, but because she was in a monastery from such a young age, "I was so completely cut off from any of the social movements that were going on around me that I kind of fell into it [feminism] myself, and there was a language there now to help me. So I was late to feminism only in the sense that I did not come to all of this through feminism. I came to all of this, ironically enough, through faith."

She admired women like Betty Friedan and Gloria Steinem for raising awareness of the issue of women's equality, but she had not read them. "I love them all but they didn't teach me anything. Jesus did. The New Testament did. The Old Testament did. The prophets did."

By the early 1980s, when she published *Women, Ministry and the Church,* she was challenging the church's conception of Jesus via the debate on women's ordination. In a claim that she would repeat and maintain, she wrote that the ordination of women "has not been the central issue in my personal life." She never sought ordination or felt called to it, as many women have, concentrating instead "more on what I thought were the pressing and the immediate woman issues; the right to equal educational opportunities, economic equality, civil rights, equality of status and position or, in the case of women religious, community self-determination."

But her attention turned to the ordination issue anew when the Vatican Congregation for the Doctrine of the Faith issued a statement in 1976, "The Role of Women in Modern Society and the Church." While acknowledging the earlier insights of the Second Vatican Council's pastoral constitution, *Gaudium et Spes*, about the growing role "women are now taking in public life" as well as its prominent condemnation of discrimination based on sex, the document reduces the argument about ordination to biology.

Priesthood is "of a sacramental nature" and the priest is the sign, "the supernatural effectiveness of which" comes from ordination. In order for the sign to be perceptible, a "natural resemblance" to Christ is required, says the document, quoting Aquinas: "Sacramental signs represent what they signify by natural resemblance." In the priest's fulfillment of his role in the Eucharist, "there would not be this 'natural resemblance' which must exist between Christ and his minister if the role of Christ were not taken by a man: In such a case it would be difficult to see in the minister the image of Christ. For Christ himself was and remains a man."

The document cites Paul's assertion that in Christ there are no distinctions between Jew and Greeks, slave and free, male and female. "Nevertheless," it continues, "the incarnation of the word took place according to the male sex; this is indeed a question of fact, and this fact, while not implying...natural superiority of man over woman, cannot be disassociated from the economy of salvation."

The consistent teaching of the church, the document restates, is that the priest acts not in his own name, but "represents Christ, who acts through him: 'the priest truly acts in the place of Christ.'" Indeed, in celebrating the Mass, which "the priest alone has the power to perform," the priest "acts not only through the effective power conferred on him by Christ, but *in persona Christi,* taking the role of Christ, to the point of being his very image, when he pronounces the words of consecration."

For Chittister, the document raised questions "about the effect of 'maleness' on the integrity of the faith itself." In the limiting literalism with which the Vatican approaches Jesus as symbol—any human seeking to represent Christ as sacramental minister has to be male because Jesus was male—Chittister sees wide-ranging and distressing implications. "If that is so, then many other things are not: that Christ is God, that both women and men are bound to be 'other Christs,' that sacraments are effective by virtue of the power of God, that grace makes new creations of us all."[5]

The thinking that fostered exclusion of women from priesthood across cultures, she writes, was based on "faulty understandings of biology, on social systems that depended for their existence on physical force, on false psychologies that promoted the education of men but not of women, on primitive blood taboos, on the incorrect identification of the man as life-giver."[6]

In those same cultures, women were also excluded from the ranks of teachers, doctors, politicians and the like, circumstances that changed in many areas over time.

The use of symbolism to explain an all-male priesthood also raises three fundamental questions for her:

- What is a symbol, a sign, an image, a representation?
- What is being symbolized in the priesthood and its supreme moment, the Mass?
- What is being communicated by this kind of sign?[7]

If the Mass is simply a reenactment of the Last Supper and "nothing invisible is being commemorated" during the liturgy, then a representation of the man Jesus will do. "If, however, as Church doctrine maintains, the Mass is the re-creation of God's saving plan for humanity, then more needs to be communicated than the simple act of the Last Supper."[8]

While males may accurately reflect Christ's humanity, she writes, "they are no more a symbol of his divinity than women who in their person also recall the humanity of his birth." While the disposition of the minister, in Catholic teaching, is not essential to the validity of the sacrament, "apparently maleness is. In the spiritual order of things, that is a difficult conclusion to draw."[9]

McGrath's book, *Women and the Church*, represented an early and forceful expression of Catholic feminism, an articulation, perhaps, of the "increased demands of the age" by women and evidence of "the

---

5. Joan Chittister, *Women, Ministry and the Church* (Mahwah, NJ. Paulist Press, 1983), 97.
6. Ibid., 98.
7. Ibid.
8. Ibid., 99.
9. Ibid., 100.

whole process of change now taking place," as put by a Vatican document on women's ordination.[10]

As the 1976 document from the Congregation for the Doctrine of the Faith, *Inter Insigniores*, made clear, the church was aware of the growing feminist movement, the questions about women's ordination it provoked, and the fact that the church increasingly looked at odds with itself as it insisted on the equal dignity and status of men and women but maintained just as adamantly that women could not be ordained.

The document first takes note of Pope John XXIII's remark, in his encyclical *Pacem in Terris,* promulgated in 1963, acknowledging "the part that women are now taking in public life," a development occurring most swiftly "among Christian nations."

The fact that Protestant denominations had begun admitting women "to the pastoral office" was creating "an ecumenical problem." The question of whether the Catholic Church might "modify her discipline and admit women to priestly ordination" was being asked not only from outside but also among Catholic theologians who had begun to discuss the matter publicly.

The document takes on the difficulties raised by some of St. Paul's teaching regarding women. "But it must be noted that these ordinances, probably inspired by the customs of the period, concern scarcely more than disciplinary practices of minor importance" that no longer obtain today. However, the doctrinal congregation viewed Paul's prescription against women teaching in the Christian assembly as "bound up with the divine plan of creation," and thus difficult to see in the context of "the expression of a cultural fact." In other words, the requirement that women cover their heads was culturally conditioned, but the prohibition against teaching in the assembly was part of God's divine plan.

"In the final analysis," says the 1976 declaration, "it is the church through the voice of the Magisterium that, in these various domains, decides what can change and what must remain immutable. When she judges she cannot accept certain changes, it is because she knows she is bound by Christ's manner of acting."

The statement seems to validate in many respects the critique by McGrath, Chittister, and others that the church's understanding of God's will—including the exclusion of women from ordination—is determined exclusively by men. The church, in matters requiring judgment about who can minister, is represented by the magisterium, which is comprised

---

10. Sacred Congregation for the Doctrine of the Faith, "Declaration *Inter Insigniores*: On the Question of Admission of Women to the Ministerial Priesthood," October 15, 1976.

only of ordained celibate males. They alone decide "Christ's manner of acting," and such decisions have always been made in a milieu in which women have no presence, much less an authoritative voice or any means for directly influencing the men's thinking. It stands to reason that if a woman is prohibited from teaching in the assembly, she will hardly be acknowledged in the upper echelons of the church's leadership.

The question for the critics of the exclusion of women, of course, is whether even questioning the magisterium's notion of its own absolute authority automatically places one outside the community. Could a woman be critical of the structure that excludes women without being seen as in conflict with "the divine plan"?

The congregation's conclusion was that the church's consistent teaching and practice is unalterable. It was "echoing" a declaration that Paul VI had made nearly a year earlier, in a letter to the Anglican Church as it was considering ordaining women, stating that the church "does not consider herself authorized to admit women to priestly ordination." Serious consideration of the reflections outlined in the document, said the congregation, would lead one to "better understand how well-founded is the basis of the church's practice." It would also lead one to "conclude that the controversies raised in our days over the ordination of women are for all Christians a pressing invitation to meditate on the mystery of the Church, to study in greater detail the meaning of the episcopate and the priesthood, and to rediscover the real and pre-eminent place of the priest in the community of the baptized." It is a position that sets the priest apart from the rest of the community because "he is—with all the effectiveness proper to the sacraments—the image and symbol of Christ himself who calls, forgives, and accomplishes the sacrifice of the Covenant."

Pope John Paul II would attempt to impose a final papal clamp-down on any discussion of the matter with his 1994 apostolic letter, *Ordinatio Sacerdotalis,* which repeats the arguments put forth by Paul VI in his letter to the Anglicans and the 1976 declaration by the Congregation for the Doctrine of the Faith, which Paul VI approved.

John Paul II wished to end any further debate over the matter:

> Although the teaching that priestly ordination is to be reserved to men alone has been preserved by the constant and universal Tradition of the Church and firmly taught by the Magisterium in its more recent documents, at the present time in some places it is nonetheless considered still open to debate, or the Church's judgment that women are not to be admitted to ordination is considered to have a merely disciplinary force.

Wherefore, in order that all doubt may be removed regarding a matter of great importance, a matter which pertains to the Church's divine constitution itself, in virtue of my ministry of confirming the brethren (cf. Lk 22:32) I declare that the Church has no authority whatsoever to confer priestly ordination on women and that this judgment is to be definitively held by all the Church's faithful.

The discussion, however, did not end. A debate remains open over what "definitively held" means. Cardinal Joseph Ratzinger (later Pope Benedict XVI) was at the time head of the Congregation for the Doctrine of the Faith and explained that John Paul II did not intend *Ordinatio Sacredotalis* as an *ex cathedra* infallible statement. The congregation said that it was, instead, to be seen as an infallibly taught doctrine because it had been affirmed by the magisterium and had also been the unbroken tradition of the church.

Theologians, scholars, and activists, individually as well as in groups, raised enough concerns about the status of the teaching that the Congregation for the Doctrine of the Faith a year later issued a *responsum ad dubium* affirming the teaching. In a cover letter to presidents of bishops' conferences around the world, Ratzinger explained:

The publication in May 1994 of the apostolic letter *Ordinatio Sacerdotalis* was followed by a number of problematic and negative statements by certain theologians, organizations of priests and religious, as well as some associations of lay people. These reactions attempted to cast doubt on the definitive character of the letter's teaching on the inadmissibility of women to the ministerial priesthood and also questioned whether this teaching belonged to the deposit of the faith.

This congregation therefore has judged it necessary to dispel the doubts and reservations that have arisen by issuing a *responsum ad dubium*, which the Holy Father has approved and ordered to be published.

The *responsum* stated that the teaching "requires definitive assent, since, founded on the written Word of God, and from the beginning constantly preserved and applied in the Tradition of the Church, it has been set forth infallibly by the ordinary and universal Magisterium." The pope, it said, "has handed on this same teaching by a formal declaration, explicitly stating what is to be held always, everywhere, and by all, as belonging to the deposit of the faith."

The Catholic Theological Society of America, in a paper titled "Tradition and Ordination of Women," raised questions regarding the Vatican's *responsum* and whether *Ordinatio Sacerdotalis* was actually an infallible pronouncement. The paper was submitted for the society's 1997 convention.[11]

"The CDF's *Responsum* does not change the doctrinal weight of *Ordinatio Sacerdotalis*. It does not raise its teaching to the level of an *ex cathedra* definition even when it declares that its doctrine has been taught infallibly," the paper states. "Canon law makes it clear that no doctrine is to be understood as infallibly defined unless this is manifestly established (Canon 749.3). Hence, whether a doctrine has been infallibly taught is a question of fact and the law of the Church requires that this fact be clearly established." It continues: "The law of the Church, it would seem, justifies Catholic theologians in raising the question whether the reasons offered by the Congregation 'clearly establish' the fact that this doctrine has been infallibly taught."

After disputing the primary rationales in the *responsum*, the theologians concluded that there remained "serious doubts regarding the nature of the authority of this teaching and its grounds in Tradition. There is serious, widespread disagreement on this question not only among theologians, but also within the larger community of the Church."

That argument has done little to change minds in the Vatican. Even Pope Francis, who seems tolerant of a range of questions and topics that previously would not have been entertained for discussion, was abrupt when asked about women's ordination during a flight from Rio de Janeiro back to Rome in July 2013. "The church has spoken and says no," he responded. "That door is closed." He referred to Pope John Paul II's *Ordinatio Sacerdotalis* and said the "no" had been spoken "with a formula that was definitive. That door is closed."

The string of Vatican documents during the late twentieth century was intended to close the case on women's ordination for good. There was nothing left to discuss, and any discussion could be seen as a violation of church teaching.

Perhaps all that the Vatican pronouncements proved, however, was that forbidding people to think about or discuss an issue was an invitation to even wider discussion and action. Groups like Women's Ordination Worldwide, Women's Ordination Conference, and Womenpriests evidence an ongoing interest in the question. The Womenpriests organi-

---

11. "Appendix A: Tradition and the Ordination of Women," in *Proceedings of the Fifty-second Annual Convention of the Catholic Theological Society of America* (1997), 197–204.

zation, for instance, began in 2002 and within five years had ordained fifty people, including six men, most of them in the United States.

In a 2007 interview with Pamela Schaeffer of *National Catholic Reporter*, Gerry Rausch of St. Louis dismissed hierarchical objections. Rausch was a board member of the Women's Ordination Conference, which, Schaeffer wrote, "supports a variety of forms of priestly roles for women, ranging from ordination to a 'discipleship of equals,' in which all symbols of power, including ordination, would be obsolete." The Women's Ordination Conference continues as of this writing, with a regular presence in Rome, to advocate for greater roles for women in the church, including ordination.

Womenpriests has reported receiving support from many male priests and adds that "three bishops in good standing have taken the extraordinary step of ordaining women bishops." Patricia Fresen, a bishop in the Womenpriests movement, said supportive priests are more common in Europe than in North America, where most of the future ordinations are expected to occur.

Fresen told Schaeffer that her ordination was "documented and notarized, with a record of those present, along with copies of the three bishops' apostolic successions (with her name at the end) signed and sealed in a bank vault whose location, in *Da Vinci Code* fashion, is known only to a few."[12]

The movement, tiny as it might be, is robust and growing as of this writing. The women involved appear realistic about where they stand—formally outside the community but in hopes of prodding it to a new understanding of ordination. In some cases, they lead small parishes that meet in a variety of settings and with different levels of ministry within those communities and beyond.

As Chittister has consistently maintained, women's ordination was never high on her list of issues, so she was surprised when she received a call in late 1999 from Sr. Myra Poole, a British member of the Sisters of Notre Dame de Namur, asking her to be a keynote speaker for a conference on the topic of women's ordination scheduled for 2001 in Ireland. Poole, one of the principal organizers of the conference, had met Chittister during one of the Erie nun's earlier speaking tours of England.

---

12. Pamela Schaeffer, "Though Church Bans Women Priests, More and More Women Are Saying 'Why Wait?'" *National Catholic Reporter*, December 7, 2007.

Chittister responded, "Oh, Myra, this is lovely of you to think of me. I don't have to tell you that I'm completely committed to the women's issue, but I'm not your person for an ordination conference because I am not an expert in the original documents. I support thisissue completely and believe strongly that the church has to face it, but I cannot provide you with the cited information that you need to help move these women and this question in the church."

She recalled there was a pause, and then Poole said, "We know that."

"Then why are you calling me?"

"Because, Joan, we do know you. We heard you speak all over England and we know that everything you do is embedded in the scriptures and in the tradition, and that's where we want to be."

"Well, you have to help me here, Myra, because I'm not really sure then what you want, because you know I'm not going to speak on ordination."

"She said, 'But you'll speak on Jesus. You'll talk about the following of Jesus.'"

"I said, 'Oh, you mean discipleship. I can talk on discipleship. My whole life is immersed in that. I can do that.'

So she said, 'That's great. That's what we want. Just start us off with this scriptural perspective on what it is to follow Jesus. That's all, and everybody else will handle it from there.'"

I interviewed Poole in July 2014 on the campus of The Catholic University of America. She was attending a meeting of her order at Trinity College, run by the Notre Dame sisters, across the street from the university. I read her the content of the conversation as Chittister had described it and asked if it was accurate. She responded, "Absolutely."

Chittister, after ending the call with Poole, found Tobin and told her about the phone conversation. "You're going to open a conference on women's ordination?" Tobin asked.

Well, not really," Chittister answered. "I'm not doing ordination. I'm doing discipleship." And that was the last that was said about it.

A year and a half went by and the trip to Ireland was just a few months away when Chittister received a call from Christine Vladimiroff, then prioress, who asked to see her the next morning in a home on 8th Street in Erie, a place where she sometimes stayed when not at the monastery.

"When I got there, I sat down on the couch." Vladimiroff was sitting nearby. She turned to Chittister and handed her an envelope, saying, "I got this letter."

Chittister noticed the Vatican stamp on the envelope. She opened it and read the letter and immediately recognized that the threat in it could upend her life. "I had known fear as a child that was physical, but I was long past that one." The letter was of another order of threat from those she had known as a child.

The letter was from the Congregation for Institutes of Consecrated Life and Societies of Apostolic Life, the Vatican agency that oversees religious orders. The correspondence, addressed to "Sr. Christine," said that the dicastery had learned that Chittister was to be "one of the principal participants at the first international meeting in favor of the ordination of women" in the Catholic Church.

"As you know, the Magisterium of the Church has been abundantly clear and constant in teaching, according to the mind of Christ, that women cannot be admitted to the ministerial priesthood. On numerous occasions, Pope John Paul II has reaffirmed this doctrine," the letter stated. It noted that John Paul had repeated his assertion in *Ordinatio Sacerdotalis* that the church "has no authority whatsoever to confer priestly ordination on women" and that this judgement is to be definitively held by all the Church's faithful.

The letter said that John Paul II's 1988 apostolic letter *motu proprio Ad tuendam fidem* had established a new version of a church statute reinforcing in law what it means that a teaching be "definitively held" and giving details about who could be punished under the statute.

Chittister's participation in a conference advocating "something which the church has consistently maintained is impossible can only cause scandal, further dissent, incite hatred towards the Apostolic See and the person of the Roman Pontiff and, indeed, even deceive the faithful and others into thinking that the definitive teaching of the church is open to alteration." Speaking at the gathering, the letter said, would constitute "an outrageous disservice to the Church in Ireland and elsewhere."

Vladimiroff was "officially and explicitly directed... to forbid and prohibit Sr. Joan Chittister by way of a formal precept of obedience from participating in this gathering in Dublin." She was also charged with conveying to Chittister "the aforementioned serious concerns of this Dicastery and the grave ramifications, not excluding a just penalty, of sustained contempt for and rejection of the Church's authoritative teaching concerning the ordination of women to the ministerial priesthood in the Catholic Church but also with actively preventing her from attending this conference."

Failure to follow "this command... will result in appropriate punishment." The Vatican officials said they awaited Vladimiroff's response "as to what measures you have enacted to ensure that this religious will not attend the meeting in question." It was signed by Bishop Piergiorgio Silvano Nesti, Secretary of the Congregation.

The letter never detailed what "just punishment" meant, but both Chittister and Vladimiroff presumed it could include such actions as dismissal from religious life for Chittister and possibly even excommunication or dismissal of Vladimiroff as prioress.

"I doubled over. I had literally been kicked in the stomach. I stayed over like this," Chittister said, bending at the waist while sitting, her face staring at the floor, "and I sat up and said, 'Christine, before there's any discussion, before we say a single word. There's something I need to tell you.'

"She said, 'Yes?'

"I said, 'I'm going to Dublin.'

"She said, 'I thought you'd say that.'

"I said, 'I'm going. These men are not going to do this. They have no right.'"

In the stark tension of the moment, the two women understood what was at stake, and it was larger than whatever disagreements might exist between them. The two had remarkably similar stories in coming to the order. Vladimiroff came from a poor family, attended St. Benedict Academy and, like Chittister, had to work there to earn her tuition. If Chittister was the first to earn a doctorate, Vladimiroff was not far behind. She was a teacher and administrator at various points in her career at the elementary, secondary, and college levels. She also served as multicultural coordinator and later as secretary of education for the Cleveland diocese and in 1991 was appointed president and CEO of the Second Harvest National Food Bank Network in Chicago and remained there until 1998, when she was elected prioress of the Erie community.[13] She had embraced renewal and reform enthusiastically and well ahead of Chittister and had spoken out herself in speeches in favor of women's ordination.

She and Chittister were the only Benedictines to have been elected president of the Leadership Conference of Women Religious, a somewhat remarkable representation at the level of national leadership for a relatively tiny community on the northern edge of the country. Vladimiroff also was elected to leadership in the order where she served as president of the Conference of American Benedictine Prioresses and as a delegate to the international organization of Benedictine women, *Communio Internationalis Benedictinarum.*

These two women—strong, ambitious, at times opponents and at other times collaborators—now faced a threat that could imperil them both and jeopardize the stability of the larger community as well.

Chittister was stunned, and she could see that Vladimiroff was also deeply upset. "It was clear. She stood up and I could see her profile. I saw

---

13. From an obituary first published at NCRonline and globalsistersreport. org, September 30, 2014.

that she was shaken, and I said to her, 'Christine, issue the order. I don't want you under pressure. I don't want the community under pressure. Give me the mandate.' I could see that her eyes were brimming with tears, even thought her face was turned toward the wall.

"She said, 'What if I can't do that?'

"I said, 'Well, in that case we're at another place, and we'll have to do it differently. I don't want this to happen to you. I don't want this to happen to the community. I'm begging you to take them out of the picture.'

Vladimiroff answered, "Well, we'll see." And that's how the conversation ended that day.[14]

For Chittister, the matter became a justice issue, and her explanation of it was, simultaneously, soul-wrenching yet defiant, the plaint of a woman who would not be ordered to be silent. "This was not a women's issue to me. This was a justice issue that happened to be rooted in the women's question. It was a matter of 'Who do you think you are that you can tell me what to think, tell me to whom I may speak, tell me where I can or cannot go? Who do you think you are, Daddy? I'm a big, grown-up girl, and I can go into this myself and, trust me, I will maintain my faith and I will be a member of the church. That doesn't make me a moral infant or an immoral woman, and if we have to shoot this out in the street, we're going to because I'm going. I am going."

She was "shocked" that someone who had "given her life to the church at age sixteen and was still there fifty years later" would hear, "You'll do this or else."

Another part of her, however, said "Why are you shocked? This is the history of this institution." It was recent history. Since Vatican II, she told herself, "they have been taking some of our best theologians and destroying them and their work. Why not you? You're nothing."

The letter, she said, was "the equivalent of mugging a woman in the alley" where the assailant will have his way. "I said to myself, 'Well, you may. You will win, but I refuse to be complicit in the silence. I will scream and I will tell, and I am not going to give in to this kind of intimidation and ruthless, brutal use of power simply because I am a woman without power. It was that simple. That's the whole story. It's right there."

---

14. I interviewed Christine Vladimiroff on November 29, 2011. Before the segment dealing with this matter, I read her the transcript of the section of my interview with Chittister in which she recounted this scene and asked if it was accurate. She responded that it was and that she would not add to or cut anything from it.

That story may have seemed simple at the moment, but it had deep and tangled roots that were wrapped around her experience as a child, and, as well, it had implications far beyond Chittister. She admitted that she felt that her mother, who had died in 1996, was in the room with her when she told Christine that she was determined to go to the event in Ireland. In fact, she said she told an interviewer for a national publication that she was doing this in her mother's name.

"No one knew what I was talking about. They thought I was saying it about women" in general. "'In my mother's name,' I said."

She said she sensed her mother there, sitting with her, saying, "You're right. Don't be afraid."

"She never cautioned me, 'Don't do this, Joan. They'll beat you up.'" Instead, what she heard from her mother was, "'You go ahead and you'll be all right. Don't be afraid,' and I never doubted it for a minute. I prayed to her during those days. I was so angry. It was just one more example of the disposable woman whom they would call disobedient because she had an idea of her own."

Asked if her father was also, metaphorically, in the room with her during that exchange, she said "No." She returned to her mother and referred to her as "brilliant," a term, she said, that she rarely uses to describe anyone. "She was brilliant and totally undereducated, and she is the icon to this day for me. I always talk about losing the intellectual resources of half the world, and I'm talking about my mother and all women like her who never had the chance, were never asked a question, never participated in any major decisions."

She recalled having had the opportunity in the late 1970s to speak to Cardinal Eduardo Francisco Pironio, then prefect of the Vatican's Sacred Congregation for Religious and Secular Institutes, a man she much admired. At the time she was president of the Federation of St. Scholastica, of the Leadership Conference of Women Religious, and of the Conference of American Benedictine Prioresses. She believes the encounter with Pironio, an Argentine who was known as a champion of human rights during his time in that country, occurred during one of the annual meetings LCWR leaders held with church officials in Rome. She said she looked him in the eye and told him: "Everything that is written about us is written without us. The only input that the church takes on the women's issue is what we do on the steps outside your closed doors. After you issue your bulletins defining us as lower and lesser kinds of human beings, we react to them. Dissent is the only ministry a woman has in the church. And when we react, you call us radical feminists and heretics."

"He listened to all of this—he was gentle and he listened." She described him as "such a beautiful, quiet man with piercing eyes. He was patient with me, he heard me out." The sisters—she wasn't certain if there was another cleric in the room—were seated with him in a circle. "The look on his face was so kind and aware. He said, 'Joan, Joan, Joan, everything you say is right, what you say is true. But you must only say it here, among us here. You must never ever say it outside. That is harmful to the church.'"

She responded that it was "all well and good for you, Your Eminence, but we don't ever get invited in here where you decide our lives. We're invisible. Yes, I am right, we are right, you know we're right. But I will never be quiet. I will not keep that law of silence. That law is sinful. That law covers the sins against half the church, and I will never agree that it's right for the church." Given that view, Chittister says, "you can understand my reaction when I received that letter from the Vatican."

Chittister left the meeting with Vladimiroff, returned to her office, and called several of her close friends, including Maureen Tobin and Mary Lou Kownacki. She told them what had happened. Kownacki said, "It had to happen. They had to get you, Joan. You have too clear a voice in this country. You keep defining the questions. They don't want questions, Joan."

Vladimiroff faced the quandary of what to do, of how to both respond to the Vatican with integrity while maintaining the integrity of the community and of Benedictine life. And she had to figure a way to do that without, at the same time, jeopardizing the community.

As she interpreted the letter and subsequent correspondence from the Vatican, church officials wanted her "to bring Joan into my office with probably a witness and tell her that she was forbidden to go, under the vow of obedience, to Dublin. That's not the way Benedictines read the vow, anyway. Benedictine obedience is not military obedience," she would explain. It is not merely a top-down matter of giving orders and having them carried out. Obedience in the Benedictine community of the twenty-first century depends more on dialogue and discernment. "We are looking at obedience from the position of people who live in this [Benedictine] tradition, and the Vatican is looking at it from a tradition of canon law. The norms are different," she told the *National Catholic Reporter*.[15]

"Plus," she told me, "I thought that this was interference with the running of a community—the internal working of the community and my authority as prioress in the Benedictine tradition. So I wrote them back as if they were requesting that I consider doing this. Of course

---

15. Patty McCarty, "Nuns Firm under Fire," *National Catholic Reporter,* July 13, 2001.

they weren't requesting me to consider, but we played that game back and forth, biding time."

"I gathered the community and kept them advised," said Vladimiroff. "I just said, 'I will consult with you as a community. I will meet with small groups. I will meet with individuals. But I want you to know the letter is addressed to me, and I will make my decision, but only after I've heard from you.'" She told them that ultimately the decision regarding whether to prohibit Chittister from attending the conference "is my decision because I'm the one that's being ordered."

Vladimiroff began consulting canonists, including Sr. Sharon Holland, a member of the Immaculate Heart of Mary Sisters of Monroe, Michigan. Holland worked in the congregation in Rome, though not in the section that would have handled such a conflict, she said in a January 2015 interview. Holland retired in 2009 after more than twenty years at the Congregation for Religious. Throughout most of those years she was recognized as the highest-ranking woman working in the Vatican. She returned to Monroe and in 2014 was elected president of the Leadership Conference of Women Religious. In 2001 she was a valuable contact because she knew how the system worked, who the people were, and what to expect in a meeting at the Vatican.

Holland in 2015 said she did not remember much about those early contacts, but does recall helping to set up a meeting at the congregation. As Vladimiroff remembered it, Holland in a phone conversation first said that the prioress probably didn't need to schedule a meeting, but could simply send a letter. But when Vladimiroff faxed Holland the letter she had received from the congregation, Holland changed her mind. "Oh, yes you have to come in," Vladimiroff recalled her saying.

Holland said that though no punishment had been spelled out, she considered the language in the Vatican letter "very severe."

Vladimiroff headed for Rome with Sr. Pat McGreevy, who served on her council. McGreevy was a canonist who had served as a chancellor for several dioceses across the United States. They met for about two hours with congregation officials, with Holland sitting in to interpret the Italian.

Even though during this meeting they had argued the case that the nub of the issue was not women's ordination but a matter of silencing somebody, Vladimiroff was uncertain as to whether that rationale would be accepted. She had to consider the possibility that the community could be harmed. She said she did not make a definite decision regarding the precept of obedience until the very last moment. In fact, the members of her council said the same. Even they didn't know which way she would finally decide until just before Chittister was to leave for the conference in Ireland.

The first Vatican letter had arrived in March. The event in Ireland was scheduled for June 30. For three months, Vladimiroff went back and forth with canonists and Vatican officials trying to find a solution that would be acceptable to everyone.

"And of course, you had someone saying we should comply because 'the pope wants us to do it,' and someone saying, 'Let's get out of this church,' and everything in between. There were people who said let's fax them to death, or demonstrate. I said, 'How can I say I'm going to have a conversation in good will if you're painting protest signs in the basement? I can't do that. That's not who I am. I have to be saying around the table, 'We can settle it this way, and I want to use the law to protect us.'" Chittister was approached during this period by print reporters and by at least one television network. "She asked, 'Can I given an interview?'" recalled Vladimiroff, "and I said, 'No. I'm working this out.'"

Vladimiroff believed the real threat was to herself, reasoning that congregation officials could remove her because it was she to whom the letter was addressed. "I'm the one they were ordering to do something. They weren't ordering Joan." They never dealt directly with the person who was causing the problem, she said, "and the only way they could touch Joan was if I gave her the precept and she disobeyed it. And they could, so that was not an option for me. Plus, it wasn't an option for me to give up my authority as prioress."

She and her council, however, did draw up some plans should she be removed. "In terms of my council, I made some strategic movements around who I thought could handle the public if I were removed and who could handle the internal community matters, and we thought about it. We weren't naive."

In the process she also considered what would happen to her if she were removed from office. She thought the community might take her in as a "residential oblate," attached to the community in a lesser way than someone fully professed. "I wasn't naïve about it. I looked this thing in the face. I had just appointed a committee to begin to plan for our 150th, and I thought, 'This committee might not even exist by that date.'"

Whether the Vatican was primarily after Chittister or Vladmiroff or both was never finally established. Miriam Mashank, who was on Vladimiroff's council at the time, said questions still remain for some about what Rome intended and who would have been disciplined. "Was it Joan or was it Christine? Joan because she went ahead and gave the talk, or Christine because she didn't stop her?"

There was a third, mostly hidden layer of threat in all of this and it was to some individual members of the community. "When you sit in the office of prioress, people will bare their souls," said McGreevy. "Christine is generally perceived as matter-of-fact, quick, and all of that, but she has a heart of gold for the person who's suffering. We have sisters who have been sexually abused and physically abused. Some of the fallout from what happened during that time was triggering a reaction in the community that could be described as what we call today post-traumatic syndrome behaviors."

Those who were experiencing such difficulties during the period of stress and conflict triggered by the Vatican threat "were able to go to her, talk to her, and she saw them through that with all of this chaos going on around her," McGreevy added. "It's not a thing that everybody knows, but I know it, and she has said it, and I know a few people that she would have said it to, but the community at large would not have any idea of how people were suffering."

If some were beneficiaries of Vladimiroff's compassion, others saw her as remote, insular, and secretive. Chittister, for one, was angry at the way the process was handled. She saw it as another capitulation to the way the hierarchy in the Vatican wanted things handled. Vladimiroff saw it as the path of least damage.

Vladimiroff described the period as "the long Holy Week." She kept the correspondence to herself. "I was always asked for copies of the letters and I never gave any of my letters out. That was intentional. I said, 'I'm not going to carry this conversation on in public. The letters were addressed to me, my letters were addressed to them." The meetings were between her and the Vatican officials, and she refused to divulge the contents of the conversations.

She said she didn't believe confrontation would work in the church. "I was of the opinion that you get their backs to the wall and you're going to get slammed. So it would be better to work through the intricacies of canon law back and forth, with appeals, et cetera, and that's what I think really won the thing."

The initial letter sent by the Vatican to Vladimiroff was the only document I was able to obtain. The rest of the correspondence is in the order's archives and, according to the current prioress, Sr. Anne Wambach, will not be available for decades. Vladimiroff's preference for handling the matter personally, prohibiting Chittister and others from speaking publicly about it, and sealing all the documents was a source of great tension. Her leadership style during this period, despite the apparent success of her tactics, became a source of deep division and threatened a split in the community in the aftermath of the faceoff with the Vatican.[16]

Mashank feels that a large measure of the tension that resulted in the community stemmed from Vladimiroff's secretive handling of the

---

16. Vladimiroff was adamant that the rest of the correspondence with the Vatican and with her canon lawyers and other documentation regarding the case be sealed. She said it was being held under a community "policy for record retention." Vladimiroff died in September 2014, and I appealed to the leadership in January 2015 to reconsider releasing the documents. Prioress Anne Wambach replied that community archival policy restricts access to such documents for sixty years.

matter. "We as council members . . . well, I think probably nobody was more surprised than we were the night Christine made her announcement to the community, when we all gathered and she was going to tell the community what her decision was, I think we left the council room thinking she was going to stop Joan from going." They went from the council room to the sanctuary of the chapel, and that's when the community found out that Christine would not deliver the precept of obedience. She would not stop Joan from going.

Reflecting on that time during our interview, Vladimiroff told me she believed that "a united community rather than a divided community would be a more difficult scenario for them [Vatican officials] to manage without looking heartless . . . I think there was a grace of coming together. It was just like a point in renewal when we said, 'I'm going to go slower and they're going to go faster because we want to do it together.'"

She said she had, at one point, written a letter that forbade Chittister from going to the event in Ireland. "And I looked at it and said, 'I can't do that.' I knew I couldn't from the beginning."

Pressed on the matter, she said, "I knew from the beginning I couldn't give the precept. I really did. I really could not do that. I would not do that. I shouldn't have said I couldn't do it; I would not do that."

In the end, she wrote her final letter and read it to the community at Vespers. "I put it on the altar and said, 'We've signed our vows on this altar. Anybody who wants to join their signature to this, I invite them to do that.' The gospel for that evening which I preached on was the woman bent over [Luke 13:10–17], so I said it's time to stand straight and be healed."

She had made arrangements for anyone who couldn't be there to appoint a proxy ahead of time, someone designated to respond in her name. All but one of the 128 active sisters signed. There is confusion over who that one person might have been. Chittister maintains that she is the only one who didn't sign it. Others contend it was an older nun who was confused by the process. In any event, what the Congregation for Institutes of Consecrated Life and Societies of Apostolic Life received was in effect a unanimous declaration of support from the community.

After the letter signing, the sisters bestowed a special blessing on Chittister and then, Vladimiroff later told a reporter, "We had dinner together. That's what families do."

On June 30, 2001, Chittister delivered a talk, "Discipleship for a Priestly People in a Priestless Period" to 350 people from twenty-seven countries attending a conference sponsored by Women's Ordination Worldwide and hosted by the group, Brothers and Sisters in Christ (BASIC) at University College Dublin. She posed the question: "What do people really need in a period when the sacraments are being lost in a sacramental church" at the same time that all questions about the nature of priesthood are "blocked obstructed, denied, and suppressed?"

She told of a trip she had made to an Indian village atop a mountain in Mexico that was visited annually by a priest. "But that was years ago. Now the mountain is just as high and the priest is fifteen years older."

She said she had spoken five years earlier in an American parish of 6,000 families. "There is no priest shortage there, however, the priests want you to know, because the bishop has redefined the optimum ratio of priest to people from one priest to every 250 families to one to every 2,000 families."

In diocese after diocese, she said, churches are being turned into "sacramental way stations, served by retired priests or married male deacons, both of which are designed to keep the church male...The number of priests is declining, the number of Catholics is increasing, the number of lay ministers being certified is rising in every academic system despite the fact that their services are being restricted, rejected, or made redundant in parish after parish."

The church may assert its changelessness, she said, but it is certainly changing. "It is a far cry from the dynamism of the early church in which Prisca, and Lydia, and Thecla, and Phoebe and hundreds of women like them, opened house churches, walked as disciples of Paul, 'constrained him,' the scripture says, to serve a given region, instructed people in the faith and ministered to the fledgling Christian communities with no apology, no argument, no tricky theological shell games about whether they were ministering *'in persona Christi'* or *'in nomine Christi.'*"

The answer to "What do people really need?" is "What they needed when the Temple became more important than the Torah. They need what they needed when the faith was more a vision than an institution ...they need Christian community, not patriarchal clericalism. They need the sacred, not the sexist. The people need more prophets, not more priests. They need discipleship, not canonical decrees."

Christian discipleship in its earliest expressions, she said, "meant the rejection of emperor worship, the foreswearing of animal sacrifice, the inclusion of gentiles, the elimination of dietary laws, the disavowal of circumcision—the acceptance of women—and the supplanting of law with love, of nationalism with universalism." Discipleship was not an intellectual or philosophical exercise, but a call to live in a way "that is sure, eventually, to tumble a person from the banquet tables of prestigious boards and the reviewing stands of presidents and the processions of ecclesiastical knighthood to the most suspect margins of both church and society."

More than a decade before Pope Francis would upend the ecclesial status quo with an example of humility and service, with his memorable instruction to bishops to take on "the smell of the sheep," and with an understanding of the Gospel that toppled many of the presumptions of political and economic power, Chittister was preaching that "to follow Jesus ... is to follow the one who turns the world upside down, even the religious world."

Living as Christ lived involves "touching lepers, raising donkeys from ditches on Sabbath days, questioning the unquestionable and—consorting with women! Discipleship implies a commitment to leave nets and homes, positions and securities, lordship and legalities to be, in our own world, what Christ was for his: healer and prophet, voice and heart, call and sign of the God whose design for this world is justice and love."

The world is changing, she told the crowd in Ireland, and women are emerging across cultures and religions to take roles of leadership previously reserved for men alone. "In India, women are beginning to do the sacred dances and light the sacred fires. In Judaism, women study Torah and carry the scrolls and read the scriptures and lead the congregations. Only in the most backward, most legalistic, most primitive of cultures are women made invisible, made useless, made less than fully human, less than fully spiritual."

Christianity is not a product of books or "documents called 'definitive.'" It is not to be discovered in "platitudes about 'special vocations,'" or "in old errors dignified as 'tradition.' The new fact of life is that discipleship to women and the discipleship of women is key to the discipleship of the rest of the church."

Chittister spoke of the exclusion of women and emphasized those moments in the life of Jesus when he overturned conventions and met and ate with those whom religious authorities at the time considered outcasts. Her words had behind them the weight of personal experience.

On April 20, less than two and a half months before her appearance in Ireland, Chittister gave the keynote address on the final day of the National Catholic Education Association (NCEA) convention in Milwaukee. It might have been an unremarkable date on her schedule except that bishops or their administrators in the dioceses of Pittsburgh, Pennsylvania; Peoria, Illinois; Lincoln, Nebraska; Tulsa, Oklahoma; and LaCrosse, Wisconsin, had called for teachers and school administrators to boycott the conference, or at least Chittister's part in it, because of her decision to go to Ireland. It was not the first time her presence at a function had been opposed by a bishop. About a dozen bishops, according to Tobin, had made it known that Chittister would not be permitted to speak on Catholic premises in their dioceses. Many of her talks took place at neutral sites or in Protestant churches. She was among a group of Catholic writers and thinkers who met such resistance during the latter years of the John Paul II papacy, when the increasingly conservative clerics he had appointed to the U.S. episcopacy applied sometimes extremely stringent rules regarding who could speak or teach in their dioceses. Prior to the Vatican objection to her appearance in Dublin, Chittister had never been sanctioned by Rome or her own local bishop.

The attempts to silence her in 2001 backfired. An NCEA official said Chittster was invited because she was well published and well thought of in the area of spirituality. The organization refused to disinvite her.[17] Teachers interviewed generally saw the bishops' actions as an affront to free speech and an unnecessary intrusion into the world of Catholic education. "It's unfortunate for the church to divide itself in this manner," said one Catholic high school principal. "We're teachers. That means we're supposed to be intellectuals. We're supposed to help our young people open themselves to ideas and opinions. How can we form an opinion if we don't hear things?"

Chittister was greeted with a standing ovation and "spoke of the irony that all issues but women's status in the church seem open to discussion today. 'We can talk about cloning, about nuclear war, about pedophilia. But we can't talk about women. At least we ought to honor their questions with some serious discussion," she said.

She repeated her conviction that she was not interested in ordination. "If you ordained women tomorrow, I would not be there," she said. "Joan Chittister has absolutely no call to be a priest." The point that she would repeat in Ireland was that the question at least should be seriously considered. Although she was not at the NCEA to talk about women's ordination, comments throughout her talk about the status of women in the church drew spontaneous applause from the teachers and administrators. She urged educators to teach students "to ask how it is that one sex can take upon itself the right to define what God wants of the other one. Teach them to ask what kind of God it is that would give a woman a mind, a soul, a baptism, and a call and then forbid her to answer it when a sacramental church is in danger of losing the sacraments."

The association had anticipated attendance of about ten thousand, but more than fourteen thousand showed up.

In my interviews and conversations with her, Chittister has repeated that she doesn't expect to see in her lifetime any change in the church's teaching on women and ordination. Her duty, she feels, is to keep "piling up documents" and "making arguments" and to join with others doing the same. The obligation, she says, is to establish such an over-

---

17. The account here is taken from a May 4, 2001, story in *National Catholic Reporter*, "Chittister Cheered Despite Boycott."

whelming case for the injustice of the exclusion of women that someday the hierarchical church will have to listen.

Her words echo the case she made in Dublin when she said, "we need a group free of *mandatums*," referring to the requirement that theologians seek approval of their orthodoxy from the local bishop in order to teach, "to organize seminars, hold public debates...hold teach-ins, sponsor publications, write books and gather discussion groups."

Despite the severe language of the Vatican's letter, the threat of punishment and the months of back and forth between Erie and the Congregation for Religious, following the conference the Vatican press office released a comparatively conciliatory statement to *National Catholic Reporter*: "The Congregation for Institutes of Consecrated Life and Societies of Apostolic Life believed that the participation of the two female religious in the women's ordination conference would not be opportune without the permission of their superior generals. The congregation has not taken—in this case—disciplinary measures into consideration."

The second nun referenced in that statement was Myra Poole, who had invited Chittister to speak at the conference in Ireland. A Sister of Notre Dame de Namur, Poole, with her superior, received similar threats in letters from the Vatican and went through a similar routine of meeting in Rome to plead her case. In the end, Poole initially obeyed the Vatican directive and remained away from the gathering, just south of Dublin, during the first half of the conference. But she had arranged for women from a number of developing countries to come to the conference and she felt the need to be there for them no matter what the cost. So she arrived on the final day to an enthusiastic welcome. "The church is in grave error on the question of women's ordination," Poole told the group. "I have been a member of my community for forty-two years. I will never leave the Catholic Church. I will never leave my community," she said.[18]

The event, and the Vatican's response, was widely viewed as a triumph for women, for women religious, and as an example of what solidarity could accomplish. One might make the argument for the effect of solidarity in the case of the Erie Benedictines. It involved fewer than 130 women in one place, a functioning community that regularly prayed and ate together, made decisions together, and celebrated all of life's big moments together. It was a family that would pull together and defend itself when threatened, regardless of internal dissension.

The case of the Sisters of Notre Dame de Namur was altogether different. The order is much larger than Chittister's community, and it is international in scope, with sisters all over the globe. Poole and her superior were, by comparison, rather alone in their dealings with the Vatican.

---

18. "Nuns Firm under Fire."

If the world outside saw it as triumph, Vladimiroff knew the other side of the process. "As I said, there are scars," she told me. "There are people who made their passionate speeches and some were hurtful. I mean, some hurt others." There were other occasions, she said, "where loyalty, whether to the church or to the community, was questioned. A human group is going to go through that."

––––––––––––

One more episode immediately related to Chittister's appearance in Ireland lay ahead for the community. The Vatican ordered an "apostolic visitation" to check on the life of the community and to answer such questions as what was being taught and by whom. It was similar, but on a smaller scale, to the wider investigation of all U.S. religious orders that began in 2008 and ended in late 2014 with a largely favorable report from the same Congregation for Institutes of Consecrated Life and Societies of Apostolic Life that wanted Vladimiroff to order Chittister not to speak at the conference in Ireland.

The investigation of the Erie Benedictines was conducted quietly in December following the Ireland conference by then-Archbishop Daniel Buechlein of Indianapolis, who was a Benedictine, and Mother Mary Clare Millea, a member of the Congregation of the Apostles of the Sacred Heart of Jesus, who would later be called on to lead an investigation of all American nuns by order of the Vatican. Again, no documentation that was generated by the Erie visitation is available. The final report has been placed in the archives and will not be released for decades. But in interviews with Vladimiroff and her council, with Chittister and other members of the community, a picture comes clear of a community that remained divided, an investigation that came up with nothing of consequence, and a brief final report that those I interviewed described as relatively innocuous and having little effect on the community's life or activities.[19]

––––––––––––

19. Archbishop Buechlein took early retirement in 2011, at age 73, because of multiple health issues, including a mild stroke and a battle with Hodgkins lymphoma and multiple surgeries. A spokesperson for St. Meinrad Archabbey, were he lived in retirement, told me in January 2015 that the archbishop was in a rehabilitation center and too ill to be interviewed. For depictions of the process I rely on interviews with members of the community, and particularly with Vladimiroff and members of her council regarding the final meeting with Buechlein. I also interviewed retired Erie Bishop Donald Trautman, who was still the bishop at the time of the investigation. He hosted Buechlein during his time in Erie.

Some members of the community wanted to boycott the visitation, others wanted to use the opportunity to convey their feelings and observations to the archbishop. Most seemed to go along with Vladimiroff's wish that the community revert to its default position, Benedictine hospitality, a central tenet of Benedict's rule.

The bishop of Erie at the time, Donald Trautman, knew nothing of the visitation until he received a call from Buechlein. Trautman said he was never informed by the nuncio at the time nor by the congregation in Rome that another bishop would be coming in to investigate a community of sisters.

While it was no secret that more than a few bishops wanted nothing to do with Chittister or the Erie Benedictines and that she had been outright banned from speaking in Catholic facilities in a number of dioceses, Trautman's endorsement was unqualified.

"The Benedictine sisters in Erie are faithful, active, prophetic people, and they have never been a problem to me during my twenty-two years of shepherding God's people here," he said. "Sr. Joan herself is a prophetic voice, and the church needs prophetic voices. I've never had to confront her on any doctrinal issues."[20] He noted that the community worked extensively among Erie's poor and underprivileged, "giving great witness."

Trautman said that ultimately the investigation came up lacking any firm evidence that Chittister had promoted anything doctrinally incorrect. "Again, no community is perfect. No individual is perfect," he said. "But I'm trying to say they're giving good witness for the Lord, and in terms of church orthodoxy, I cannot think of anything where they have gone to the extreme. They have been portrayed in the extreme, and I simply say, 'Show me an instance where they have spoken against church doctrine.' It doesn't exist."

Positing that Chittister never advocates for women's ordination would take, at minimum, a kind of Thomas More parsing of the king's oath—the words, indeed, are important and perhaps, as Trautman attested, she never comes out and says women must be ordained. In fact in our conversations, Chittister insisted that she is not lobbying for a particular answer as much as she is "looking for a discussion in the church."

"I keep saying the church cannot avoid this issue any longer. This must be discussed, because if it isn't, the church is going to break apart. As a church, we must consider this thoughtfully, slowly, carefully. I have said in public a hundred times: It is possible that at the

---

20. This quote and those following are from an interview with Trautman that I conducted in November 2012.

end of all those discussions we will say, 'There is absolutely no theological reason whatsoever, no scriptural reason anywhere that a woman cannot and should not be ordained, but we have decided that in our church we will maintain a commitment to the male priesthood for the following reasons . . .'"

"I am open to that. If the church, if the heart of the church works through this thing, I would be willing to patiently work through it, but I am not willing to have it ignored. I'm not willing to have it by fiat . . . I'm not willing to have somebody say, 'We are not able.' Oh, you're able to do anything you want to do and have for two thousand years. Don't give me that. We're not that dumb. We're not that dumb."

Asked to describe "the heart of the church," she responded: "Three percent of the church is clerical. Ninety-seven percent of the church is the heart of the church. Listen to them. Take their data. Talk in the parishes. See how people feel. The infallibility doctrine says that all a pope can do is affirm the infallibility of what the church already knows. Now how do we know what the church already knows? We have to ask. They've asked nobody."

Such a discussion is probably nowhere in the church's immediate future, but it is safe to say that if it were held and if Chittister were consulted, she would say there is absolutely no reason, in terms of scripture or theology, that women should be excluded from ordination.

The topic was inescapable in her ongoing commentaries on women's exclusion from church circles where the issues that affect women are discussed and where decisions are made—and even from church language. "It is simply not true that 'men' means 'women,'" she wrote in a 1985 column, commenting on those who maintained that male nouns and pronouns were inclusive of all. "If it does, why doesn't it mean it all the time? Why doesn't it mean it when it's inscribed over the portal of the seminary in Cleveland? The sign clearly says, 'Blessed are the young men who enter here.' Or are women welcome in that seminary and someone simply forgot to tell us?"

This business of the piling up of documents, of making the case persistently and without fail, has gone on for most of Chittister's life as a member of the Erie Benedictines. If there is hope that records of any sort will be preserved through the coming centuries, Chittister has given her reading of the times and the major questions about women as much a chance as anything.

She made the point of the importance of such preservation during a talk in 2012 to a group of archivists. She recounted in that lecture that both men's and women's Benedictine monasteries had been "the sole civic anchor and agricultural organizer of peasant populations from one end of Europe to the other" from the second through the thirteenth centuries. They were the monasteries widely credited with saving European civilization. Yet, when women's monasteries began to disappear at the hands of marauding bands and sheer poverty, she said, none of their archives was saved. "So, despite the fact that their lives and works were exactly like those of the male communities we have all been taught to revere, an entire subculture of women was simply allowed to vanish from human sight and thought: their experiences ignored, their wisdom demeaned, their contributions buried with them."

Women and their views, as much as she could help it, would not vanish in the current era—and certainly not by order of a Vatican congregation.

Most of the sisters I interviewed thought Buechlein a kind and even gentle presence, someone who listened and, because of his Benedictine background, had an understanding of monastic realities. In his last meeting with Vladimiroff and her council, just as he was about to leave, she asked him to wait and hear one last thing.

"I remember he gave the final reports to the council, and we stood up, and I said, 'I don't want anybody out of this room until you hear this.'" And then she said, "There's a human cost to this visitation. Sisters who have been abused as children and have post-traumatic syndrome, which they put aside a long time ago, are back into it because we have eighty-year-olds who don't know where they're going to sleep if the Vatican comes in here and takes the community away from them. So there has been a human cost.' He was very understanding. He really was."

The final report, given the possibilities, was rather tame. Although it remains "chapter material" and thus subject to the sixty-year restriction, Vladimiroff said the items, about ten of them, fell into the category of "you have to come up with something when you do an assessment." In her case, the recommendation was that she "make two retreats a year contemplating my authority and responsibility as a prioress" and it also recommended that "Joan should be reminded that she's influential and should use her influence for the good of the church."

Sr. Anne Wambach, the prioress who succeeded Vladimiroff, said, "I am not aware of anything that we are currently doing or long-term changes we have made because of the Vatican visitation."[21]

Vladimiroff and the community survived. But Vladimiroff's handling of the confrontation with the Vatican, her determination to keep correspondence secret, and the reaction against that by some members of the community bared other, deeper rifts over leadership style and the

---

21. This response was to one of several questions posed and answered by email in January 2015.

direction of the community. She was elected for a second time in 2002, but the turmoil in the community never abated. Rifts that were partially generational, partly over leadership methods, partly over concern about the future of the community and the direction of monastic life became so pronounced that in 2008 the community brought in a mediator and conducted discernment sessions over the next two years.

"There for a while," said McGreevy, "you couldn't have a chapter meeting that wasn't volatile because of residual anger." Referring to the need for a mediator, she said, "The Vatican didn't cause that. There are some things we have to hold ourselves accountable for, and we're not good at communication in some instances. Every now and then, you need somebody from the outside to put it in perspective."

Amid the internal drama, said McGreevy, Vladimiroff was receiving calls from other orders that also were having difficulties with the Vatican. "A lot of it was just for the emotional and professional support they got from talking with Christine." McGreevy reinforced the need to seal documents for sixty years "or during the lifetime of anybody connected with the event." She said the rule was to protect those still alive from public disclosure of anything negative or unfavorable in the correspondence.

Vladimiroff was reelected in 2006 and served as prioress until 2010. She died in September 2014, after an extended struggle with cancer.

Chittister, too, survived the confrontation with the Vatican, and in some ways her reputation and that of the Erie Benedictines was enhanced. They were seen as victorious in their stand against unreasonable demands by church authorities, a triumph of solidarity versus the abusive use of authority.

If it was a victory, it was less than complete for Chittister. Soon after she received the initial letter, she met with Christine and her council. "The question was how would the community proceed, or how would Christine, or how would I proceed. The meeting was laying things out. There were no decisions made there, at least not in front of me."

She said her position was not complicated. "I'm going to Dublin because I do not think we're doing the church any good by refusing to discuss what is a major theological question in the church. I made the point that the church discussed the nature of Jesus for three hundred years...It seems to me that you could spend a meeting or two on the theological role of women in the church twenty centuries later."

Sometime in the two months before the event in Ireland, Chittister collapsed in Erie, and doctors discovered she had an abdominal cyst that needed to be removed. She was in the hospital for nearly a month and was weak and walking with a cane as the date for her trip to Ireland approached.

She was prepared to be told by Vladimiroff not to go and prepared to take the Vatican's discipline for attending the conference. She had begun speaking with religious leaders outside the community about what her options might be. She was prepared to receive "the letter that said, 'If this is going to happen, here is your dispensation'" from the order. It never arrived.

On her return from Ireland, she said, it was clear that Vladimiroff wanted to control the story and did not want any of the documentation released. "We have no idea what's in our archives. We may know everything there is to know. On the other hand, we may not."

Chittister said she did not protest the visitation, but "went in and had a nice conversation with the bishop. "I told him the whole thing. I said, 'This is the way I feel about women. This is our historical position. I will continue to question that until the day that I die. I do not see it as deviance. I see it as an intellectual, theological imperative, that we think our way through the faith.' I was very nice. He was very nice. We had met in Rome some years before. We remembered that meeting with some great anecdotes."

She recalls the meeting's conclusion: "I said, "Bishop, I just want to make one thing very clear at the end of this discussion. I really don't care—and I'm not saying this with any kind of flippancy—you can do whatever you want to me, but don't you touch my community.'

"He said, 'I understand, Sister.'

"I said, 'Thank you very much,' and left."

Chittister never received any personal communication from the Vatican. She wasn't disciplined. She was not restricted in any way in her writing or her speaking.

NINE

BEYOND THE COMMUNITY

By the time Chittister's third and final term as prioress ended in 1990, she had occupied leadership positions in most of the major organizations of women religious for which she might have qualified. She had been president of the Federation of St. Scholastica; president of the Conference of American Benedictine Prioresses; president of the Leadership Conference of Women Religious; U.S. Councilor-Delegate to the International Union of Superiors General; and head of her own community. Her peers had validated her vision, her talent, her leadership skills in countless ways. In addition, she had been an elementary school teacher, a high school teacher and, multiple times, a published author, and in constant demand as a speaker. She was fifty-four years old, enormously energetic, and she had not a clue as to what she would do with the rest of her life.

"I told my council before I left office that I had no idea what I was going to do next." Members of the council were puzzled. Why wouldn't she continue doing what she had been doing even as prioress? Invitations to speak were arriving regularly, more than she could accept, and she certainly could go on writing. "I had some very strange ideas, both as president and as prioress. I thought that when people called me for any kind of help at all, what they wanted to know was what a Benedictine prioress thought about something." And she assumed that after she left office there would no longer be any reason for people to seek out her thoughts and opinions. "I really thought the conversation followed the prioress, so when I looked ahead to no longer being prioress, I had no idea what to do with all of that. It was really a down time for me, because I had to rethink everything. When I look back now, I ask myself, 'Why could you not see anything, Joan? What was the block?'"

Her uncertainty might have been due, in part, to her personality and the sense of insecurity that had threaded as a theme through her life, even as her accomplishments had exceeded anyone's expectations. She admitted that it had taken her more than forty years to finally smile and accept the praise when a friend said, "Not bad for a kid from Seventeenth and Peach," referring to the corner in a poor part of Erie where she had spent much of her childhood.

She admits to a certain Irish fatalism and a wariness, which has ebbed over the years, about the fact that the big steps in her life—the elections, the doctorate, the influence she has had over people and events, the accolades—were never part of any overarching plan or career path when she left Seventeenth and Peach for the simple monastery on 9th Street.

She says she never feels "quite right enough" about a talk or a book. She will tinker with speeches until the minute they have to be delivered. For years she has done the bulk of her writing during three months in winter in a cottage in Ireland that friends have invited her to use. Another friend and supporter for years has given her the use of a cottage in the Cayman Islands where, during a two-month period in summer, she does another round of writing and editing.[1] Her writing process includes consultation with a wide group of readers, within and outside the community, depending on the topic.

"I'm never quite right enough. I'm never quite prepared enough. I'm never quite finished enough," she says. During our conversation on this matter, she puzzled for a while over the question of why she felt inadequate. As we were about to move on to another topic, she said, "I just want to go back to that...there is one thing that I do think had something to do with that." It had to do with her childhood. "I did everything to please my mother. If I could make my mother happy, that's all I needed, just to know that something was good for her. She wanted me to do well in school and I worked very hard at that. Even if school came easy to me, I didn't take it for granted that it would come easy, any more than I take speaking for granted. I would bring home a report card with straight A's and my mother—where it says 'Parents' Comments'—every year of my life, my mother wrote on that, 'Joan can do better.'"

"'Joan can do better.'...I spent my whole life standing on tiptoe trying to finally get to the point where somebody would say, 'You couldn't do any better than that, Joan.'"

---

1. Erie friends William and Betsy Vosheck, who own property in the Cayman Islands, have annually offered Chittister a place to write since 1980.

Had she gotten there yet? I asked.

"No, I'm still working at it," she said.

That sense of inadequacy and the fear of letting people down were undoubtedly magnified at the end of her term as prioress. She had been elected on the first ballot in 1978 and then two more times, serving for a total of twelve years, but it was only at the very end that she discovered a small faction of the community was deeply resentful of her and angry over the direction in which the community was headed. She said she had overheard several sisters talking at a table and saying that they wanted no one from the previous administration reelected. Sr. Phyllis Schleicher, who worked apart from the community, was finally chosen after a long election process in which she was challenged by two sisters who were advocating for a complete break from the previous administration. Schleicher had been an elected member of Chittister's council during her final term.

In the intervening years, the wounds of that time for Joan and others in the community have largely healed, and if there were any doubt about the community's support of its highest profile member, it was dispelled by the unanimous backing for her during the episode with the Vatican.

Schleicher, who at the time was director of a diocesan nursing home in the town of Hermitage, some eighty miles from the Mount, emerged as the compromise candidate at the very end of the election process in 1990 and she said that from the outset she was determined to continue and build on what Chittister had started.

With the distance of years, a pattern emerges in the selection of prioresses from the middle of the twentieth century through the beginning of the twenty-first. Mary Alice Schierberl (1958–64), who began to open the door to renewal, was also capable of unpredictable volatility. She was followed by Mary Margaret Kraus, generally viewed as a steadying force who guided the community through the tumultuous years just post–Vatican II, led the community to its new quarters at the Mount, and stood firm in the face of a bishop's objections to allow women to begin moving into homes outside the monastery and to work in individual ministries.

Chittister's tenure marked a period of extremely high energy and innovation: new ministries in the inner city, an enhanced involvement with non-violence and the anti-nuclear campaigns of the era, new initiatives in the area of ecology, and all of that amid the new questions forming about the nature of religious life. The closing of St. Benedict Academy evidenced the community's most dramatic break with its past. It made concrete the need to establish a new identity for the community. Renewal involved nothing less than updating the definition of religious life for women who, less than a decade before, had been conducting their lives largely in silence, covered head to toe in garb that had been fashioned for their predecessors centuries before, and living according to a schedule that left little time for individual thought, much less for meaningful communication among members. One sister remembers another saying, following Chittister's third term, that the community would have to "see what there was after all the dust settles."

Schleicher, who now works in rural ministry in Pennsylvania, recalled in an interview that a headline in the diocesan newspaper following her election noted that she was chosen as a "quiet force" to lead the community during the next six years.[2] Indeed, her term had the effect of turning down the heat under a boiling pot. Though she worked apart from the community, she had been a member of Chittister's council and was in full agreement with the steps in renewal and the new direction of the community. Perhaps as someone who had not been immersed in the day-to-day tensions of the monastery, she was able to bring a new eye to the circumstances in-house. From the start, she intuited Chittister's situation, worked hard to keep her connected to the community, and ultimately played a major role in freeing Chittister to build a ministry of writing and teaching beyond the boundaries of the community.

Schleicher was re-elected once and served through 1998, when Christine Vladimiroff was elected to the first of three terms. She served through 2010, but after dealing with the Vatican threat in 2001, her tenure was increasingly turbulent, requiring the community to engage a mediator who led the group through extensive sessions for two years in which they delved into the divisions that had developed. She was succeeded by Anne Wambach, who, in the logic of the cycle that one community member described as "high energy, low energy, high energy, low energy," is seen as a calming and steadying influence.

"High energy, low energy," hardly covers the forces and particular challenges that have shaped both the community and its leadership from one era to the next. As another member of the community put it, the difference may have been not in the amount of energy expended but in how that energy was used. Chittister and Vladimiroff, for instance, by far the most public of the prioresses of that era, were not known as particularly "hands-on" administrators. Chittister's travel and lecture schedule, for instance, would have been more than a full-time job for most. That she was able to accomplish that and maintain confidence as prioress was no small feat. But several women interviewed said the home front at times suffered. The same claim was made by some about the Vladimiroff years. It seems, perhaps, that instead of "high energy, low energy," the difference among prioresses might better be explained as "inside and outside." Both Schleicher and Wambach maintained a far lower profile on the national front but spent much more time and

2. Interview by phone on January 23, 2015.

energy on the details of governance, the lives of those in the community, and the running of ministries.

Those delineations, of course, are far from absolute. They are as much a product of individual personality as they are of the collective personality of the community while it grew through various stages of life. If the comparison can be extended a bit, the post-renewal years during which Chittister was in leadership might well be likened to those of the teen growing to adulthood, with all of the attendant growth spurts and unevenness essential to achieving maturity.

The community that has developed through the years of renewal is not the one for which most of the women doing the electing during the past half-century and more had originally signed up. They could not have imagined as sixteen- or seventeen-year-olds, with their steamer trunks and place settings, their new black shoes and postulant habits, the changes they would witness before they even reached middle age in the community to which they'd given their lives and solemn vows.

After dozens of informal conversations and formal interviews I had with members of the community over a three-year period, I think it reasonable to say that most of the periodic eruptions within the community were far more relational, even familial, in nature than anything involving theology or essential principles.

These women had known each other, for the most part, since late childhood. They knew each other the way family members know one another—their flaws and failures as well as their gifts and triumphs. When the rules and strictures, the routines and sameness that once kept the family placid began to fall away, the community had to discover new ways to work through everyday as well as extraordinary tensions. Repeatedly, when sisters spoke of those times of dissension and unrest, they spoke of not knowing how to communicate. At least, in part, it was because they hadn't learned. Under the old regime, being polite was often enough. Rarely did anyone have to communicate her wishes or feelings.

"You didn't have to talk to anyone," said Chittister of the earlier years. "You just took the order and fulfilled it. That's all you were expected to do; it was all you were allowed to do."

A reading of the record of the community's activities during those years, from Mary Margaret's time to the present, would show how much effort and creativity the community had put into learning new skills. The women who as girls had joined the Benedictines, so many of them wishing to become just like the women who had taught them and to take on the look and the rhythm of that life, were now working even harder to become something different.

The effort was not confined to externals—to leaving behind the habit, the old space, the well-defined ministry of education; it also had to do with interior changes. It involved a spirituality that perforce had to now include a much a larger and more diverse reality in the new ministries than one encountered in a well-ordered Catholic girls' school. The spirituality now had to engage the world. The whole effort was a matter of understanding, as Chittister explained in her first hours as new prioress, not only that the community had grown up, but the reasons for growing up.

Chittister's writing would benefit from her having lived through all the struggles and changes. However, when she ended her term as leader of the community, she found herself, at age fifty-four, directionless and, in a sense, without brief. It was not an unusual occurrence at the time for superiors of religious orders undergoing such change. No precedent or template existed for what to do in these new circumstances. By chance, while teaching for a semester at Loyola University in Chicago in 1988, Chittister met a nun who had done a great deal of work in spiritual direction. During a lunch conversation, Chittister brought up her sense of feeling she was heading into a time when she would have no place or purpose in the community she'd been leading for the past decade. The nun told her it had become a familiar strain of concern for people in her position. She told her that the superiors of her generation "had no future in their heads." The old forms no longer could hold them; the ministries that once defined them had ended or were coming to an end. None of them had been asked, "What will you do next? What would you like to do next?"

In more recent years, said Chittister, that kind of self-doubt and lack of direction is no longer the case. "In interim years, the nuns have learned to adjust and become adult thinking women." Many of them, on leaving leadership, find the greatest fulfillment of their education and experience, she said, working on the margins of society with the poorest and the outcast in ministries with which the nuns of today are increasingly identified.

For Chittister, the landscape appeared bleak. She had been deeply affected by the show of opposition, a factor that lent credence to her feeling that she would not have a place in the community any longer. She felt herself "eminently unemployable" and, at her age, facing fifteen or twenty years with no clear plan for how to proceed. The weekend of the election, said Schleicher, was the last of several discernment sessions leading up to the community vote. The mediator from outside the community who had been moderating the sessions became ill and could not make it to the final session. Her replacement, said Schleicher, had not been present for previous sessions and the discussions "quickly got out of hand." Those who wanted to raise objections to what had gone on under Chittister's leadership "felt this was the time to bring up those objections—this was their opportunity. A better facilitator, one who had been with us, could have controlled that, but it got out of hand."

Tobin confirmed that the discussion became heated, but her analysis is that apart from a small faction, the mood of the community "was not so much against as it was that the community was floundering, trying to find someone who could follow Joan. I did not see it as a rejection of Joan, although she had a hard time of it and viewed some of it that way." The community's difficulty in choosing a new leader is reflected in the fact that while most elections occurred well before the scheduled end of the weekend activities, the election of Schleicher took place at the very end.

Joan described herself during that period as depressed and feeling disconnected. When she attended community functions she sat on the outer edge of things and almost never spoke. It would take her two years to begin to find a firm direction and become convinced of the encouraging promptings from Schleicher. The new prioress went to great lengths to keep Chittister engaged in the community, urging her to attend meetings and chapters. "I was trying to keep Joan with us and trying to lift her up and make her realize that she was part of us," said Schleicher.[3]

At some point early in Schleicher's term she and Chittister traveled together to a meeting of the Leadership Conference of Women Religious in Albuquerque, New Mexico. During the trip, Chittister met up with Franciscan Fr. Richard Rohr, a friend and a highly regarded thinker and writer on matters of faith and spirituality who also understood the dynamics of religious communities. Chittister and Rohr have met a number of times during their respective careers, mostly at places where both were speaking. Chittister said she trusted Rohr, whose Center for Action and Contemplation is located in Albuquerque. Recalling the meeting, but not the entire conversation, Rohr said he "certainly would have told her" that it would take "a number of years before she would be able to be integrated in a new way into the community."

"We had dinner together," recalled Rohr.[4] "I encouraged her to not let her gift be squelched by staying 'in too small a world.'" He recalls advising her to "keep some space" and return to the community "at a new level of relationship."

In 1991, Chittister was giving a talk at an anti–nuclear weapons rally in the desert near Las Vegas at the same time as the legendary Sr. Mary Luke Tobin, a member of the Sisters of Loretto, was scheduled to speak at a retreat at the Mount. Tobin (no relation to Maureen) was a

3. Interview with Sr. Phyllis Schleicher by phone on January 24, 2015.
4. Interview by phone on January 23, 2015.

prototype, if such a term might be used here, of the kind of ministry that Chittister would eventually develop. Tobin had been superior general of her order, a friend of Thomas Merton, an international speaker and activist for peace and on behalf of women, and past president of the Leadership Conference of Women Religious. She was best known, perhaps, as one of only fifteen women invited as auditors to the sessions of Vatican II and one of three women religious who were members of the council's planning commissions. Tobin, who died in 2006, had high credibility among women religious in the United States. She spoke with great authority from personal experience.

Chittister, whose talk in Nevada had been scheduled before Mary Luke had been invited to speak for the weekend retreat at the Mount, was unable to return in time for the start of the retreat. When she finally arrived, midway through, she heard her own voice coming from the conference room. Someone had managed to get a video of her speech back to the Mount before she arrived.

The visitor, said Schleicher, had an insight into what was going on with Chittister and the community. As Chittister took a seat at the edge of the gathering, Mary Luke motioned toward the screen and asked if the community knew what to do with someone who possessed such gifts. She said if she were in the community she would want that person freed to speak to the wider world and to write and publish. With that, Schleicher stood up and walked over toward Chittister,.

"I looked right at Joan," recalls Schleicher, "and I said, 'Do you hear what Mary Luke is saying? You are more than this community." She commissioned her to "be free" to speak and to write. "Please, in our name, take us wherever you go. Be free."

She told Chittister to accept invitations to speak nationally and internationally, to accept membership on committees and organizations outside the community, and to devote time to writing. Sr. Mary Grace Hanes, secretary to Chittister during her time as prioress, and Maureen Tobin, subprioress and treasurer of the community during that time, were appointed to staff a new office overseeing Joan's work. Joan, herself, was told to find office space somewhere.

Maureen Tobin took care of the scheduling and finances. All of Chittister's fees for lecturing and writing were placed in a separate Benedictine sisters' account and Tobin was responsible for accounting for those funds. Mary Grace answered the phone and handled all the correspondence. Income from Chittister's lecturing and writing covered the cost of the office, and a monthly stipend was returned to the main community financial account. The office eventually evolved into Benetvision which, in the words of the endeavor's website, "exists to encourage the development of contemporary spirituality from a monastic, feminist, and global perspective through the works of Joan Chittister." Mary Lou Kownacki was credited with the founding of the venture when she suggested that Chittister write a monthly newsletter called "The Monastic Way." Kownacki has remained a creative and behind-the-scenes driving force behind the development of Benetvision's various media platforms and offerings. Chittister's work is spread throughout the world in traditional print and in digital forms, including Monasteries of the Heart, an Internet project that has attracted tens of thousands in dozens of countries. By early 2015, Benetvision employed four sisters and three lay people.

The spontaneous commissioning ceremony became another turning point in Chittister's life. It would take years before she could, as Rohr put it, reenter the large community at a new level of relationship. In the meantime, her small house community on 9th Street, St. Scholastica Priory, and other friends helped her find the next phase in her life. She would become an internationally acclaimed writer and speaker, and her calendar for the coming decades would be filled several years in advance.

Schleicher and the community also made Chittister's career as a writer and lecturer possible in an act far less public but probably even more demanding of the community than the commissioning.

By the early 1990s, Loretta Chittister had descended steadily into the thick and puzzling mists of Alzheimer's disease. In 1992, she was living in a home for the elderly operated by the Episcopal Church and located just down East Lake Road from the monastery when the sisters at the Mount were alerted to a fire at the home. Many of them rushed to the scene to be of help only to hear that Mrs. Chittister had forgotten about oil heating on her stove. Her apartment was filled with black smoke.

It was apparent that Loretta's condition had reached the point where she could no longer care for herself. "Every week there was more and more evidence of deterioration," says Chittister. Loretta at times accused her daughter of stealing furniture and money. The old connection evaporated as one of the two who had survived so much together was no longer able to even recognize the other as her daughter.

"Other sisters had to take in eggs and bread and food," said Chittister. "Every time she saw me, she just went nuts. I came to the conclusion that that was the only emotion she had left. That was her show of excitement because she never stopped loving me. She had calendars hanging on the wall that were two-and-a-half feet long and they had huge blocks, and they were all filled in. She had pulled herself through those years by writing herself notes. Precise notes about appointments and bills, when they came in and when they had to be paid, when they were paid."

A few sisters went to the smoky apartment and spoke to Loretta. Joan was out of the country but they had contacted her and told Loretta that Joan wanted her to come and stay at the Mount until they'd figured out what to do about her apartment.

"I'm going to Joan's house?" she asked.

"Yes," the sisters told her.

"Loretta got her purse and left on the arm of one of the sisters and never again asked anything about the apartment or her belongings or what had happened to them," says Chittister. She lived with the community for the next four years, "and they were probably four of the happiest years of her life. She had started out wanting to be in a convent and now she was in one, and she was quite content."

There wasn't much to be passed on. Chittister has photographs and a few mementos of her early years. She has notes and letters, postcards and holiday greetings, birthday and anniversary cards that she wrote to her mother and has been able to preserve. Copied, they filled a thick binder, and provide, from one side of the equation, a look at the evolution of Sr. Mary Peter into Sr. Joan Chittister. Some are brief notes on new countries or states she was visiting, others are chattier excursions into where she's been or explanations of the offices to which she's just been elected. There are descriptions of the busy weeks during grad school and bits from her years as teacher. The notes never broach that other darker, hidden reality. There are a few notes to Dutch or to the two of them, but this is primarily a correspondence between daughter and mother and mostly on the daughter's terms.

There are abundant stories about Loretta at the monastery, but among the most common are those about her demands to go to the Zucker Club, a service organization she had belonged to in the past—a request that was never met—and her requests to go for ice cream, which were regularly accommodated. Occasionally she would simply make herself at home with whatever was going on at the moment, including one memorable chapter meeting. "Somebody said someone ought to take Loretta upstairs to the infirmary," recalled Chittister. But Loretta wasn't about to comply. They told her it was a sisters' meeting, and she replied, "Okay." Finally someone said there was no reason to go on about it, that, in any event, she wouldn't remember what was being said. So they let her stay and she mostly looked on without saying anything until she apparently had had enough and stood up, unprovoked, and declared it "the damndest, dumbest meeting I've ever attended at the Zucker Club."

The prioress long before who had seen much farther down the road than was possible for any sixteen-year-old had been correct, of course. Loretta, despite her best intentions, would need her only child as she became old and infirm. But what the prioress at the time couldn't see—probably could not have imagined—was how quickly and dramatically things would change, so that the community was able, at least for a while, to take in not only aging and infirm parents but foster babies and others in need.[5] In the end, Loretta moved in and became the charge of the equivalent of dozens of daughters, who welcomed her and helped care for her until she died.

Her funeral was held at the Mount in December 1966, and in her eulogy, Chittister spoke of the disease that for twenty-eight years had gradually "shrunk her life to long-term debility." The tragedy for Chittister that day was not that "someone lively and vibrant has died" but "that someone lively and vibrant had so little time to really live."

She recalled her mother's tough life as a child and young widow, her difficulties with the church as a partner in a mixed marriage. She mentioned the way she suffered as other women had in a culture that undervalued women. She was "a totally uneducated but avid reader when education had little or nothing to do with women. She was a woman who was born outside her time and spent her life instead schooling me for when that time would come."

The memories of home were happy ones in which "she gave me music lessons so I would have a good time at parties. She taught every boy I dated to dance because she had married a non-dancer and wanted to save me from the same fate. She insisted on every possible educational experience so that I would always be able to take care of myself.

"She sewed every evening gown and the wedding dress for my profession. She stayed up every night with tea and sandwiches, whatever the time, to hear every word about every activity and every date."

It was clear, in Joan's description, that Loretta had had a difficult life, but the details were never spelled out. The terror, the violence, and the man in her life were only hinted at. The goodbye would be on the daughter's terms.

One of the readings for the day was from Ezekiel, who "berates God who has betrayed kindness with pain" and brings back to life the child of his hostess.

The gospel was the story of Jesus when he cured the daughter of Jairus, "the establishment type, the institution man, the one without what

---

5. Eventually, the infirmary at the Mount was filled with members of the community. Chittister said the community also came up against the realization that taking in more people who were not members of the community would have caused legal problems because the Mount did not meet the legal requirements of a nursing home.

the purists would call a deserving 'faith,' and brought the whole community a sense of the kind of newness that comes with following Jesus."

Loretta was wrapped up in it all, in all the symbols and reality of redemption the gathered community and its sacred texts could muster. Chittister thanked the community, recognizing the work that had been done at home while she was going about her own work. "The care such a difficult patient got in this house she could not have gotten anywhere else in the world. She went years without an odor, without a bed sore, without a dirty dress, without a single hair out of place. But most of all, she got love, and hugs, and all the smiles and the friends that meant so much to her."

————————————

When Chittister was commissioned to move beyond the confines of the community, her writing moved with her. Her themes, untethered from the boundaries exclusive to religious life, became universal—what she believed, what she questioned, huge issues of faith viewed across religious traditions, explorations of spirituality. At the same time, she approached all of it thoroughly anchored in her own tradition. While her subjects took on a universal scope as her writing evolved, the expansive almost always proceeded from very particular and, often, from very personal circumstances.

Just as she had plumbed the depths of the Rule of Benedict for its relevance to a community of women at the end of the twentieth century, so she went, in her 1999 work, *In Search of Belief*, statement by statement through the Creed, essentially a pastor answering other believers, especially women, who had confided to her their difficulty in reciting the prayer. It was never enough, never quite satisfactory, for Chittister to accept something so essential as what she believed on anyone else's say so. If she was going to argue with the church about its exclusion of women, she had to wrestle, as well, with its male imagery. She had to understand, line by line and statement by statement, whether she could say, "I believe," and recommend it to others.

In her catechesis, never divorced from the realities of life and the issues of an era, "I believe" doesn't bestow on us "supernatural sleight of hand designed to save us from the exigencies of life...It is not a fantasy or a way out of life's troubles but a basis for personal development" and a guide through them. "Belief makes of life more a quest than a place," she writes. It is not "what makes it possible for us to settle down complacent in our goodness, certain that if we keep the rules we will have life without having to live it."

To say "I believe," she writes, is to say that my heart is in what I know but do not know, what I feel but cannot see, what I want and do not have, however much I have. To say 'I believe' is to say yes to the mystery of life."[6]

As we have seen, the God she believes in has also broken the restraints of old boundaries. She opens the section on God in *In Search of Belief* with the declaration: "God is the mystery nobody wants. What people covet in God is not mystery but certainty. God is what everyone seeks to be sure about. And is not."

Chittister views the opening line of the Creed in two sections, "I believe" and "in God," and describes them as "the two most developmental statements in the human lexicon." To Chittister, the phrase means "I commit myself to make God a presence in the center of my heart, in the humdrum of my days, in the dregs of my struggles. Discovering the way God works in each of those is the spiritual journey of a lifetime."[7]

But what about God, "the father"? Doesn't that put up an impenetrable obstruction across the path of argument that God is not male? Jesus, as a male, referred to his heavenly "father." Chittister argues, first, that the Jewish community in which Jesus was formed had a rich array of terms for God: "To the psalmist, God is a midwife; to Isaiah a comforting mother; in Exodus, the ultimate Being; in Haggai a wife." And in the Christian scriptures, "in Luke, a shepherd and a woman searching for a lost coin; in Hebrews, a consuming fire."[8]

Her dispute is not with God the Father, but rather with God defined solely as "father." "No single dimension engraved in gold, carved in stone, dripping with dogma can suffice for it all. Every single dimension of God, though it crystallizes our understanding of God, also limits the human understanding of God. To cling to one without proclaiming the others is to make God small."

She sees in Jesus' use of the term "Abba" the "loving parent image for God." In a legalistic culture "that featured a thundering deity," the affectionate image that Abba conjured, she writes, "broke open the current understandings of the relationship between the human and the Divine to stress the intimacy of God with humanity." She makes the case that in the increased use of the term "father" in the gospels—from 4 times in Mark, the earliest in the canon, to 101 times in John, the latest —it is obvious that "the farther away the Church got from Jesus the more patriarchal its language became again, not because Jesus was patriarchal, but because we are."

---

6. Joan Chittister, *In Search of Belief* (Liguori, MO: Ligouri/Triumph, 1999), 15–16.
7. Ibid., 22.
8. Ibid., 25.

God, of course, is father, she writes, "but God is much more than that. 'God,' clearly, is a very complex concept. To say otherwise is to come very close to denying belief in God."

She begins the chapter on "I believe in Jesus Christ," with an unsettling moment of doubt regarding the Eucharist and the church's teaching that the bread and wine are the body and blood of Christ. The childhood formulas, including the instruction to not chew on the host because it was the body of Christ, didn't work any longer. "The problem was that I wanted to believe. I wanted to understand it. Otherwise, how could I possibly stay in a monastery any longer?" She put the question to a priest, and the discussion went on for more than an hour. Exasperated, he finally asked: "Do you believe in God?"

"I looked out into the grey sky melting into the grey lake in front of us. I was about to hang my life on this question. I had to believe in something. I eyed the copse of larch behind us and the rolling fields of wildflowers along the horizon. There has to be a source for all of this, I had long ago decided."

She said "Yes . . . But that's about all I'm sure of."

"Well, then, that's enough," said the priest.

Her immediate conclusion was that the poor guy had no answer.

"But as the years went by, I began to realize that he was, indeed, right. That is the answer. That is enough to know. Whatever words we use to explain the presence of Jesus in my heart may well be wrong. But the presence is powerful."

She finds little of practical interest in the definitions of Jesus that came out of ancient councils that dealt with "problems of another age, of another group of seekers trying to understand who Jesus really is— human or divine or both—and what Jesus really did—save us or atone for us or buy us back from forces in us too deep to name, too fearsome to resist by purely human means."

Her questions, instead, "hearken back to when Jesus himself posed the problem in the two questions asked of his disciples: 'Who do others say that I am?' And 'Who do you say I am?'"

"The first question is the substance of theological seminars, and someone should go on asking it, of course. But the second question is the one meant for me that no one but I can answer. It is the Jesus of my own life and the life of the world around me that I have come to confess in the Creed. It is that Jesus I follow. It is that question that each of us must face sometime in life. And it is that Jesus who captivates me completely."

The Creed calls us to realize that the Jesus who stands before us is "the clearest, sharpest, most fulsome picture we have of the face of God. And how can we be sure of that? Because Jesus is what we know in our hearts God must surely be: compassionate, just, merciful, loving, and on the other side of every boundary. It is Jesus with the Samaritan Woman, Jesus with the little children, Jesus with the prisoner, Jesus immersed in God that I must become if the Creator-God is ever to see divinity come to fullness of life in me, as well."

And so she goes on, phrase by phrase, propelling the meaning of the Creed forward, extracting the essence and insisting, if the words indeed are timeless and intended for more than a single gender, that it can be said with integrity by a contemporary woman. The book is not so much polemic—even those segments directly dealing with the use of exclusively male image and language—as much as it is a turning of the prism through which the prayer is prayed. Insistence may be too strong a word, but there seems to be that quality to her plea that we all acknowledge that women should not be invisible in our liturgies and the prayers that define our faith.

Another foundational text deriving from her spirituality, *Called to Question: A Spiritual Memoir,* was published five years later. She describes it as her "most personal and intense writing to date." The material originated in a series of "conversations" she conducted with spiritual writers in her personal journal. In the book those conversations are elaborated on in sections: the inward life; immersion in life: the other side of inwardness; resistance: the gospel imperative; feminist spirituality: the coming of a new world; ecology: the other side of the spiritual life; dailiness: the gift of the mundane.

She sets up the significance of questions to her spirituality in the prologue of the book by recounting an incident in which, coincidentally, the Eucharist again is central. It occurred in Rome where she was with delegates representing religious orders from all over the world. The discussion was about a new Vatican document making Mass and the Eucharist an "essential element," or requirement for convents the world over. An obvious problem stemmed from the fact that increasingly convents, not to mention parishes, had no access to priests. "Daily Eucharist was simply not possible anymore," the women agreed. "Since everyone knew that," they asked the cardinal with whom they were discussing the matter, "why require it?"

The cardinal told them that if they were not able to receive the Eucharist itself, "then you must teach the sisters the Eucharist of Desire."

But what was the point, the women responded, if it is impossible to have daily Eucharist?

"Because," the cardinal insisted with some degree of irritation, "if you desire the Eucharist, you have the Eucharist!"

A priest assistant, attempting to clarify the matter, told the gathered nuns that the cardinal was really saying "that it is not the Eucharist you lack. What you lack is simply the priestly presence."

"The silence in the room spoke a language of its own...Apparently, we had been getting up at six o'clock in the morning every morning of our lives more for the presence of the priest than for the presence of Jesus."[9]

That day, she says, when "I heard that I could have the Eucharist without having it but had to go to it, nevertheless, when a priest was there—was the day I began the conscious, perilous journey from religion to spirituality, from the certainties of dogma to that long, slow, personal journey into God."[10]

Religions, she writes, are intended to lead us to the divine and along the way they "provide a kind of landmark...We can see the cross, or the star, or the lotus, or the half-moon before us, calling us on. Or, we sense that [they are] behind us, calling us back. Or we come to feel that [they are] beside us, giving us strength as we go" with their definitions and boundaries and traditions. "Religion is meant to bring us to spirituality," she says. "But spirituality brings people to religion, as well."

Each serves the journey to a life with God, who is "greater than religion" and "the spiritual within us that calls us to the deep, conscious living of a spiritual life. God is the question that drives us beyond facile answers...the invisible vision that drives us to the immersion of the self in God."

No one begins at that level of mysticism; most come through the standard paths, as she did, of religion and all of its externals. She recognizes that, "What forms us lives in us forever. The important thing is that it not be allowed to stunt our growth."[11]

The sense of movement in her understanding of belief and the spiritual life is constant, even relentless. Commitment itself—something she surely has demonstrated in a lifetime lived with this community by the shores of Lake Erie—"is something that happens on a daily basis, not once and forever. It is something we grow into, not something we come to full-blown." It is not a call to a "static state of life," but rather a call "to move always toward the best self we can possibly be."

That last, however, is not a prescription for the self-absorbed pursuit of personal comfort. She rejects the "spiritual culture" that says that something, once started, must be finished regardless of the cost, as well as its opposite—that "once a thing begins to get difficult" personal happiness requires us to move on regardless of the effect of this on others. The conviction, stated earlier, that splits in communities rarely served

---

9. Joan Chittister, *Called to Question: A Spiritual Memoir* (Kansas City: Sheed and Ward, 2004), 3.

10. Ibid., 3–4.

11. Ibid., 21.

to better the circumstances, runs strong. At the same time, for Chittister, commitment means something more than simply gutting out difficult circumstances.

One reaches a point of personal growth, she writes, "at which I become myself, become free, become open to the world. Then commitment has done its thing. Then I do not stay where I am because I must. I stay where I am because where I am has brought me to a point of concern beyond the self. There are 'the responsibilities of the years,' those obligations that emerge from the awareness of my place in the world." The commitment becomes right "not only for my own development, but for the sake of the development of the world around me." In her journal, puzzling over this matter of commitment led her to question whether her pilgrimage would end in "silence, alienation, or abandonment. Will I remain in this holy vessel of endless sin and sexism called the church? Or will I choose to follow my own sins instead?"[12] The obvious in this instance I yet find a pleasure to record: she remained.

Chittister started out intending to write a book on spirituality, perhaps a history of spirituality, and wound up writing a book full of questions. Her experience, she writes, is an indicator of "the sanctifying nature of mistakes and miscalculations." Sanctity does not lie in "questionable certainties," but in the pilgrimage to a full life in God. "Once we empty ourselves of our certainties, we open ourselves to the mystery. We expose ourselves to the God in whom 'we live and move and have our being.' We bare ourselves to the possibility that God is seeking us in places and people and things we thought were outside the pale of the God of our spiritual childhood."[13]

Having opened herself to questions beyond the monastery, and freed to accept the invitations of the wider world and to carry the community with her to the ends of the earth, Chittister's exploration went on virtually unbounded.

Yet for all of the controversy over some of her views and the questions and critiques she poses of the all-male clerical culture, she has said and written little about the cultural issues that have proven so divisive in the wider culture and in U.S. politics. A search of the NCR files revealed few references to abortion, and in those instances, her opposition to abortion on demand was always mentioned in the context of a seamless garment approach, as one in a range of life issues from womb to tomb.

---

12. Ibid., 80–81.
13. Ibid., 29.

In a 1984 column for NCR in advance of that year's presidential election, she wrote:

> Morality is obviously at a crossroads. Personal sin is the least of the world's evils. I stand with those who oppose abortion on demand. But I stand most of all with the 23 brave bishops who pointed out that "to claim that nuclear war is only a potential evil and that abortion is actual neglects a terrible reality. For indeed, there can be no possibility of exercising moral responsibility against nuclear war if we wait until the missiles have been released."
>
> To avoid both threats, the peace movement, the pro-birth movement and the pro-life movements are going to have to join to build a new coalition of American values.

In a 1991 NCR column on humility and the rise of extreme individualism, she writes: "We view with alarm the rising number of poor in the richest country in the world. We are overwhelmed by the calloused approach to the subject of abortion by those who would far rather pay for the elimination of a child than for its lifelong development."

"I have never written anything major about abortion," she told me. "Not a half a page. It's never been my issue, because I think it is basically unresolved, and I don't want to add to the division. I know that doctors are working on it, theologians are working on it, and moralists are working on it, and I believe it will take that convergence of disciplines to come to what is really a Godly answer."

Nor has she given any extended treatment to the other divisive "culture war" issue, homosexuality. It is clear, however, that she was an early supporter of gay rights. In 1997, she was a principal speaker at a national meeting of New Ways Ministry, cofounded by Sr. Jeannine Gramick and the late Fr. Robert Nugent to advocate for greater acceptance of gays and lesbians in the church.

In the wake of the May 1999 attempt by the Vatican to silence Gramick and Nugent, Chittister composed a "Prayer in Honor of Those Whom Jesus Loved." Gramick continues to lead New Ways Ministry. Nugent returned to parish work. He died in 2014.

The text of the prayer, which is distributed by the Erie Benedictines:

> Jesus who loved the Samaritan woman,
>   outcast proclaimer of your name,
>   let us love and support all those who proclaim
>   your name to the gay and lesbian community.
> Jesus who loved the lepers
>   whom others called unclean,

let us see the glory of creation everywhere,
    in everyone.
Jesus who loved the one condemned with him
        and promised him heaven by virtue of his faith,
        give us the faith to broaden our vision
        of the reign of God.
Jesus who loved the hemorrhaging woman,
            long ignored and thought to be intrinsically disordered,
        give us hearts large enough to embrace
            those whom the world calls bent.
Jesus who loved the tax collector the community feared,
        enable us to put down our fear of those
        who are different from ourselves.
Jesus who loved the Roman soldier,
        foreigner and oppressor,
        help us to love those who make exiles of
        our gay and lesbian brothers and sisters.
Jesus who loves us in all our humanness, all our glories,
        enable us to love those
        whose glories we have failed to see.
You who called women disciples in a male world,
who confronted leaders of the synagogue
        with their sins of injustice,
who sent out your disciples to the whole world,
give us the courage to stand with
        our gay and lesbian brothers and sisters,
their families and those who minister to them.
Give us the grace to confront their rejection,
to ease their loneliness,
to calm their fears and
to belie their sense of abandonment.
Give us all the grace to own our sexual identity,
        whatever its orientation,
as another manifestation of your goodness.
Give us the vision to recognize and reject
the homophobia around us and in our own hearts, as well.
May we and the church of Jesus open
        our hearts and homes and sanctuaries
to the gay and lesbian community,
to the glory of God they bring in new voice,
with different face.
Let us bless the God of differences.
Amen

It would require volumes more to do justice to the effect of Chittister's public ministry, as it were, but a few highlights will suffice to establish some of its dimensions.

During her years as prioress she was already keeping to a fairly full travel schedule, both to fulfill obligations for the organizations of women religious in which she was active and on behalf of other groups, such as peace organizations and women's groups. She had even traveled to the Soviet Union with a Fellowship of Reconciliation delegation prior to the fall of communism.

A defining trip that placed her squarely in the middle of the international movement for women's rights was a grueling journey in 1995 that began with a twenty-three-day train trip from Helsinki to Beijing. The Peace Train, as it was called, carried 230 women from forty-two nations through nine countries, meeting with women in each of them, and arriving in China for the UN Conference on Women. The conference ran from September 4 to 15 and gathered nearly 40,000 women from around the world. Chittister's trip and reports on the conference were carried by the *National Catholic Reporter* (NCR). Those reports as well as the entries in a personal journal kept throughout the entire length of the journey were included in a book, *Beyond Beijing: The Next Step for Women*.

The Beijing conference was the fourth in a series on women that had been convened by the United Nations. The first had been held in Mexico City in 1975. A quarter of a century on from that original meeting, wrote Chittister, the issues had become "boringly obvious." Apparent as that might have been, problems associated with those issues had only become worse over the years. "The feminization of poverty, personal and public violence against women, political disenfranchisement, disempowerment and personal disregard mark the lives of women everywhere, are everywhere considered normal, even godly for women. Everywhere women are 'respected,' and then respectfully overlooked," she wrote in a column for NCR.[14]

Chittister kept personal journals—all beautifully handwritten in old-style Palmer method cursive and easily readable decades later—for years, even during her travels. (She moved easily into the digital age, toting around laptops when they came out, and later an iPad.) The travel journals contain depictions of events, descriptions of places and people, and endless questions that were provoked by everything from conferences and meetings to sightseeing. What is extraordinary to this reader is that most of the travel entries, remarkably well formed for

---

14. *Beyond Beijing* (Kansas City, MO: Sheed and Ward, 1996), 161.

first drafts, were composed on the run, in planes and trains, without a delete button and with very few things scratched out.

A sampling from her Beijing journal:

> Today I saw two worlds come together in one long human clang. We had breakfast, fresh rolls and coffee at "The Vie de France." And there, sitting in the tiny little table next to us in turned-around baseball caps and "Johnies" T-shirts, sat a crowd of young college students from St. Joe, Minnesota, who know me from their class reading list and seemed to take for granted the fact that we would all be in Beijing together. Tell me again how large the world is? When I was a kid, I never expected to leave town, let alone Pennsylvania. Now young people consider world travel a given, meet you in Beijing and talk to you about things you said before they were born. I was happy—and proud—to see them. They were wholesome, straight-thinking young people. Maybe the world will someday be too small a place to destroy itself, thanks to generations like them.[15]

In numerous spots in her columns and journal entries from Beijing, Chittister considers whether it was all worth the effort, the expense, the time. In real terms, the world for the first time recognized women's issues "as societal issues, girl children have been singled out for particular protection from sexual exploitation, and recommendations to make violence against women a criminal offense in all its forms has been accepted as necessary and just."

Since, however, the UN can mandate nothing, was the effort worth it? Chittister finds an answer in the sheer persistence of those who have organized around the cause of women over decades and in the fact of the gathering in Beijing. "In a country where the Taoist symbol for the female is water, a Chinese proverb teaches: 'Water wears away the rock.' . . . In a world where, 20 years ago, most of the countries of the world had no idea how women spent their time, how they sustained themselves, whether or not they could read, or even how many of them there were on earth, this conference drowned in information about refugee women and old women and little girls. The invisible woman is coming into focus."[16]

She has been of mixed mind about travel and speaking since the start of that ministry, even before she was commissioned. It is alternately, and sometimes simultaneously, energizing and exhausting. The trip to Beijing, for instance, was grueling for someone who finds it diffi-

---

15. Ibid. 124.
16. Ibid., 166.

cult to climb steps or walk long distances because of the consequences of childhood polio. And yet, that journey and other countless jaunts to corners of the world kept deepening and widening her understanding of the poor, of the difficulties of women, of the state of the church and religious life in other cultures, and of the complexities of pursuing peace on a global scale. In addition, she gained a greater appreciation for other religious expressions.

In a personal journal entry from April 26, 1981, her birthday and roughly a year before she had to decide whether to stand for reelection as prioress, she writes first of a party the community has given her and of the gifts, which included a fishing tackle box and a handmade suit. She describes "a marvelous family-style dinner, a beautiful Vespers, the community dance and so much gentle love. It all amazes and embarrasses me. It's also things like this that make next year's election decision harder."

She had just returned from a trip to visit an abbey in Massachusetts and would leave in several days for a meeting in Minneapolis before traveling on to California to give a talk. "I'm prepared for none of them," she wrote. "I'm also tired of running uphill unprepared all the time. But I don't know how to break the pattern."

She was also concerned at the time about the opening of Benetwood, an apartment development for the elderly just south of Mount St. Benedict Monastery. Work of the project had begun under Mary Margaret with detailed research and reports to the leadership of the community and the formation of a lay board and ultimate approval by the Congregation Council of St. Scholastica, of which Chittister was president. That body approved the plans and the project went forward, but there were several delays over technicalities in applications to the federal Department of Housing and Urban Development.

The units were finally opened in June 1981. Within four months, the seventy-five one-bedroom apartments were filled and a waiting list was started. The community continues to operate and manage the complex today. At the time, however, Chittister had some "misgivings" because the development "will tie up the land with buildings, obligate us to a 'ministry' that will actually involve few of us...and keep a mortgage over our heads for years."

That note is followed up with an entry on May 28 as she is giving a "directed retreat" to Msgr. Jack Egan, a celebrated Chicago priest who was an outspoken advocate for social justice. "A man of his stature and experience needs more than I can give him. The first sessions were really difficult but tonight was better." She said she didn't know Egan until he arrived in Erie and that she didn't see herself as a "retreat-giver." She wrote that "therefore, God must be doing a special thing in both of us. (Maybe that's what everybody says to justify misperception and ineptness.)"

Without any further transition, the day's entry switches to thoughts about a demanding upcoming research project on ecumenism that she will undertake the following summer, with a book that will result. Before that happens, "there are presentations coming that I have no time to give good attention to: The bishop's meeting at N.D.; the LCWR Past-Presidents' Meeting and National Assembly; the vocation conference."

She writes, "Way down deep I want it all to end: the speaking, the traveling, the position of prioress. There is not enough spontaneity or privacy in my life. There is too constant a feeling of responsibility, of pressure. There is too much fatigue; too much mail; too many meetings.

"I wonder if the whole world is whirling out of orbit."

On the following page, however, she finds an uplift to the routine as she recalls the trip that she and Tobin took to California. "I enjoyed being able to do something for her that she liked and that got her away from the routine for awhile. She handles all the details so well and so faithfully."

Her presentation on "Turning Points and Tensions in the Church" was given in an Episcopal church in Pasadena. It was well received and she received a standing ovation. The talk, she notes, was to be printed in the magazine, *Missiology*.

"The big thing about the day, though, is that I attended Mass and received communion there before the Forum [where she delivered her presentation]. Five or six years ago I would have insisted on going to a Roman Eucharist to 'fulfill my Sunday obligation.' Now I have no doubt that being in that Protestant congregation did just that."

In August 1989, Chittister traveled with a Pax Christi delegation to Haiti, where she met Jean Bertrand Aristide, then still a Salesian priest, who had developed a reputation as a radical and a forceful proponent of liberation theology. Aristide, who had criticized bishops as well as the state for their disregard of the poor, had been removed from his parish by the time Chittister arrived and was working as a chaplain to nuns and running a clinic for the poor. Chittister described him as "a figure to be reckoned with."

"He has denounced the government . . . and challenged the bishops to speak for the poor. As a result, he has enemies in multiple places." She described his assignment as chaplain as an attempt "to neutralize his power. After all, with no pulpit to preach from, what threat is he with the crowds? . . . Jesus didn't have a synagogue to operate from either, and Merton didn't have a position, and Dorothy Day was not an institution woman."

Aristide would win a campaign for president the following year and serve, at different times, three brief periods as president, interrupted by coups and U.S. intervention.

On the plane's approach into Port-au-Prince, Chittister had written in her journal: "I am much too tired. Much too busy, much too intellectually scattered to be here, so why am I here? Bonhoeffer writes: there is a meaning in every journey that is unknown to the traveler. So I will have to let Haiti itself teach me why I'm here."

Three months later, she was making her way to the Philippines. In the Los Angeles airport, just a third of the way on a nine-thousand-mile journey, she writes: "I'm dreading this trip with a special kind of dread. It's too long, too intense and too broken up...I've been force-feeding Phillipino [sic] literature for nine hours and all of it is depressing. Every day, everywhere, the cry of the poor gets louder and more insistent and more frustrating."

Closer to her destination, she writes that she almost hates to see the flight end, "because when it does, the thirty days of strangers start and the speaking starts and the heat starts and the fear starts. Why do I do these things? Even I don't know. Somehow it is my only gift. What would I do if I didn't do it? What would I be? What would the world be if some people didn't begin to step over national borders to explain one group of people to another group of people? It comes down to being a necessary behavior that I really do not want. That is the definition of a dilemma or a paradox or a schizophrenic situation. It is the definition of me."

She had no idea at the time of how intense this trip would become.

It is another country with "miles and miles and miles of corrugated shacks, one balanced against another." She describes them as "corridors of pain" that "run right through the main streets of town, along the beach, under the Hilton Hotel, next to the College of St. Scholastica itself."

She had been invited to present seminars and workshops for the entire month of November on the Rule of Benedict for the Missionary Benedictine Sisters in the Philippines. The group wanted help in their efforts at renewal. A week into the sessions, Joan writes that the nuns "have been coming in droves, alone and in groups, to thank me for the conferences. Some have come grateful to have been confirmed; some to acknowledge a conversion; some to confess that they have been hard on their own who have a social vision; some have come simply to beg me to go on talking—a message that has real meaning in my own life right now; some have come to thank me for giving them back their vocation to the Rule." She is stunned, she writes, at the reaction and to learn that the sisters have been meeting "all over the house in groups after each conference to discuss it and lay their own plans for change. It is really very humbling."

At some point on December 1, Chittister had a private, forty-five-minute meeting with President Corazon Aquino, "whom she later described as a strong, articulate woman, a peacemaker."[17]

Six hours later, rebel troops began staging one of the most serious threats Aquino would face to her presidency. An attempted coup took shape as the antigovernment forces began bombing the palace only eight blocks from St. Scholastica Convent, where Chittister was staying.

"Five days is, at one level, not a long time," Chittister wrote at the beginning of a breathless entry in her journal. "At another level, when bombs are bursting around you and planes are doing strafing runs overhead and nuns are going into bloody streets to take food to soldiers and people you know are trapped at bridges and barricades and the news goes from bad to good to bad again constantly, and facts change from hour to hour and anti-Americanism is high and you don't really know when or how or if you'll ever get out of this...it all has a telling effect on the soul. Time stands still and important things—freedom, love, God's presence, the psalms, home, truth—get more important and little things—schedules, speeches, plans—get smaller and smaller."

Back home in Erie, her sisters held an all-night vigil in the chapel, a "sign of solidarity with Joan and the people of the Philippines." The Filipino sisters, for their part, used every connection they had and worked every angle to get Chittister on the first plane possible out of the country. She arrived back in Erie on December 5. The following year, in the last issue of "The Leaven" before she stepped down as prioress, Chittister noted that the Benedictine sisters in the Philippines had sent a letter thanking her for a $3,000 donation from the 1989 Christmas collection at the Mount. The money paid for ten four-year scholarships awarded to poor students at secondary schools run by the sisters throughout the country.

———————

Chittister's imprint on the international arena took on a more permanent form in the Global Peace Initiative of Women (GPIW), an organization that was formed following the World Summit of Women Religious and Spiritual Leaders at the Palais des Nations in Geneva in 2002.

Dena Merriam, the gentle voice and determined force behind GPIW, had organized an earlier conference, the Millennium World Peace Summit of Religious and Spiritual Leaders held in 2000 at the United

———————

17. That detail and others about the trip are taken from a brief description in Sr. Stephanie Campbell, *Vision of Change, Voices of Challenge: The History of Renewal in the Benedictine Sisters of Erie, 1858–1990* (Xlibris, 2015), 382–83.

Nations.[18] The intent of that conference was to build a partnership between religious leaders and the UN on matters of peacemaking. She had sought out as many women as possible but had difficulty recruiting them in part because some religious traditions, Catholic among them, don't allow women leaders. The women who came together for that conference were dissatisfied that there were not more women. "We had maybe 10 percent women, if that, and many of them were public figures, not religious leaders." Then–UN Secretary General Kofi Annan, with whom Merriam had worked on the initial conference, encouraged her to convene a session just with women religious leaders at the Palais de Nations, the UN headquarters in Geneva.

Although Chittister had been invited to the first event, she was unable to attend because of a scheduling conflict. But she was able to make the Geneva event. Merriam recalls meeting with a Vatican representative at the time to discuss the event and being told that it was a good idea, "but don't bring women who are angry."

She met resistance from UN people in Geneva who didn't want her to use "religious leaders" in the title of the conference. "No, call it the role of women in the faith communities," they said.

Merriam responded, "If I can't have a meeting of women religious leaders, I'm going home. There's no point. So we stuck to that title and we had a lot of opposition."

"Many of the religious communities said, 'We don't have women religious leaders.' End of story. So I said, 'I'll find them. I'm sure you've got women religious leaders.' We had women from seventy countries."

Chittister and the Rev. Joan Brown Campbell, former general secretary of the National Council of Churches and then–director of religion at the Chatauqua Institute, an adult education center and resort in Chatauqua, New York, were invited to speak at the general assembly. "Both of them did," said Merriam, "and the three of us bonded right away."

Almost immediately, the new organization received a request "to come and help dialogue in Israel and Palestine. Both Joans were committed to this and said yes." So they decided to form an organization. "Initially we were called the Global Peace Initiative of Women Religious and Spiritual Leaders, but when we tried to raise money, nobody wanted to touch religion, so we shortened it to "Global Peace Initiative of Women." Merriam was founder and convener; Chittister and Brown Campbell were co-chairs.

They received a grant to bring Palestinian and Israeli women to the Nobel Peace Academy in Oslo, Norway. They originally thought this would be a one-time event, but soon they began to travel to Israel and

18. Interview with Dena Merriam on May 7, 2013 in GPIW's New York offices.

Palestine. "I went many times with both Joans to Israel and Palestine," said Merriam. "We went through checkpoints. We met with the Palestinians. We met with the Israelis. Then we took them to Norway for a meeting, and then we came back and had a follow-up meeting in Jordan. So we began doing this peace work, which was to bring spiritual religious leaders—women—to these areas and hold dialogues."

Merriam and "the two Joans" also went to Lebanon and Syria following the war between Lebanon and Israel for meetings with religious leaders. They have conducted dialogues with Iraqis and Afghans and with Sudanese. Eventually, the group began to shift its attention from primarily conflict areas "to the issues that were creating stress, like climate change, that could lead to conflict. So we organized spiritual forums at the UN Climate Change Conference in Copenhagen. Joan came to that and spoke." They traveled to Egypt in November 2011, months after the January uprising in Cairo's Tahrir Square. A number of the delegation intended to visit a mosque and a church nearby, but Chittister headed for the Square. "I sent a few guys with her, men from India, and I said, 'You be back by dark.'" Before long, they saw men racing to the Square. "A crowd was gathering. Joan was in the middle of it, and she was speaking to these guys who were gathering around her... They were asking her about the U.S. She was speaking there to the crowd as it gathered, and I was so worried about her."

Merriam, a Hindu and long time student of Paramahansa Yogananda and a practitioner of Kriya Yoga meditation, has deep respect for monastic traditions and said the friendship she and Chittister forged has allowed each of them to see more deeply into the other's tradition. "She brings the depth of tradition and the ability to reach the deepest places within a specific tradition. Yet, she can still see the universality of it. She can sit with a Buddhist nun and she can see the common points between them. She can speak in a place of total unity with that Buddhist nun because she has had that experience and has experienced the discipline, and what the discipline brings."

The fact that she has remained faithful to the Catholic tradition, even through troubled times, increases her credibility with some, said Merriam. Other religious leaders have left their orders or traditions over one issue or another. "She's deeply committed, and yet she's not willing to compromise her principles." Merriam mentions the popular theologian Matthew Fox, a former Dominican priest who left over disputes with Rome and his order. "He can do certain things because he has left," she said. "He can speak whatever he wants but there's also value because Joan has stayed. There are certain people who will hear her who will not hear him."

Chittister's meaning to the organization and the genuine respect with which she is regarded by leaders in other traditions was on display during a gathering celebrating the tenth anniversary of the Global Peace Initiative of Women held in March 2012 in Kenya.[19]

It would have been a demanding and at times even grueling trip for most, but especially for a contemplative nun with a bum knee dealing, as always, with the results of childhood polio. She set out for Nairobi on February 27 from Ireland with her good friend Gail Freyne, a lawyer, family therapist, author, and wife of the distinguished and influential Irish theologian Sean Freyne. Sean Freyne (who died August 5, 2013) had called Chittister in 1991, while she was conducting workshops in Dublin. He and his wife had read some of Chittister's work and were impressed by it, and he was inviting her to dinner at their home that night. That was the beginning of a long friendship among the three of them.

The following year, Joan was again in Ireland on a lecture tour, and the Freynes invited her to drive with them to a cottage they owned in the Dublin Mountains. Along the way, they asked where she did her writing. "Well, that's always a problem. There isn't a place. I look every year," Joan said. The need for "a place" had become more intense as she had become more and more a public figure. In Erie it was difficult to carve out the necessary space and quiet. "Well, don't look anymore," the Freynes said. "Just come here." And she has during the winter months ever since, writing a book a year as well as preparing lectures.

"Gail and I left Kerry on Thursday for Cork. It was a sad leaving. I hate to leave my writing and the silence and the smallness and beauty of that place," she wrote in her travel journal. "It is so wonderful to write there. Having to leave just reopens the question of what I really should be doing at this period of life. There will not be much time left for writing. If I keep allowing things like this to interrupt it, I will end up having done nothing of value in life at all. It is such a tension for me."

They arrived at a hotel in Nairobi on February 28 of a leap year. The following day she met with some local Benedictines and the conversation turned to a community health clinic the sisters ran. They told her that the basic issue they faced was AIDS, "particularly among pregnant women who had been infected by their husbands; the pregnancies were difficult, the mothers often died, the babies were prone to be infected as well," she recorded in her journal.

"How is it," she asked, "that my church can forgive pedophile priests so easily but won't even discuss the use of condoms for married men in order to save their wives and children?" She records that she regretted making the remark without first considering cultural differences.

---

19. Portions of the following account appeared previously as an article by the author in the April 13, 2012, issue of *National Catholic Reporter*. Other portions are from a personal travel diary Chittister kept during the trip.

"What does that say about the church's acceptance of the full humanity of women? My voice was taut and full of pain and a touch of personal anger. I was staring into space in the lobby as I said it. And then I looked up: both sisters were crying. They know as well as we do what is going on. They know how the church views women, never really condemns men—boys will be boys after all. Never cares about a woman's questions. It was the deep, quiet tears that got me. In the United States, most nuns will at least say that that is wrong. Here, they don't dare say a word. But they know."

The first day of the eight-day conference, "Awakening the Healing Heart: Transforming Communities through Love and Compassion," was held at the United Nations Information Center in Nairobi. In opening remarks there, Merriam said, "The human community is at war not just with each other, but with the Earth. We must end the war." That connection, an unbreakable link between human-on-human violence and violence toward the rest of creation, became both a presumption and a point of discussion for the rest of the week.

In a bit of hellish irony, it also became a kind of script for days of brutal violence on the game preserve where much of the conference was held. In the weeks following the event, poachers who kill elephants for tusks to be traded on the black market reportedly set fire to nearly half the acreage as an act of retaliation against the preserve's patrols and its owner, Kuki Gallmann.

In remarks to the group on the first day, UN Undersecretary Achim Steiner, an environmental expert, pointed out that in the same room in Nairobi he had "seen decades of delegations coming together to describe their differences" and only occasionally did he witness a breakthrough to "common ground." The Global Peace Initiative of Women event, he said, provided an opportunity to celebrate what is being done.

Poverty, he noted, "is the greatest enemy of the environment." He urged those attending to "look for underlying causes" to those events "we describe in dark images."

And just as strongly as the group was urged to look outward, Zarko Andricevic, founder of the Buddhist Center in Zagreb, Croatia, voiced an alternating tug inward. Andricevic emphasized Buddhism's offering of "the experience of interconnectedness." It is more than theory, he said, it is an experience "that has transformative power to change from within. If there is not inner change or transformation," he added, one "can't do the work outside."

Chittister then placed the question in rather stark terms: "What can possibly be done on issues so great by the likes of us? By people with little money and even less official power?

"And yet here we are—you and I—in one of the great struggles of human history. This struggle is for the very preservation of the globe,"

Chittister said, referring to environmental degradation and the growing threat of climate change. "To make wrong-hearted decisions now, to choose denial over a determination to reverse this debacle, may well end existence on Earth as we know it. We are a people with the chronicle of time in our hands," she said.

She said humanity has come "face to face with the consequences of what it means to ravage the Earth—to choke off its air and poison its waters, to destroy its rain forests and rape its resources, and to decimate its animal life for fur coats and ivory artifacts and face creams—and most of all for money and profit and power."

The consequences, she said, can be seen in exhausted resources, disappearing animal species, growing desertification, and rising oceans. "How do we explain that kind of moral suicide to people who look to us for answers to the great questions of life? We religious professionals who love to talk about morality and spirituality and sanctity and salvation, nirvana, enlightenment, creation and the will of God.

"How can this devastation of global life possibly be the will of God, and why did we never know that?"

Religion itself and its theologies of human domination have led to excessive consumerism, she said, and given justification for "rapacious greed that fueled that inordinate accumulation."

It is time, Chittister noted, for those "who call ourselves 'religious' to think again about what God is really saying in all our scriptures about creation, about human agency, about human responsibility, and begin to teach it differently."

That difference was modeled, if only for a week and amid a tiny but diverse sampling of humanity, during sessions held at the Laikipia Nature Conservancy, a remote one hundred thousand acres in the northern part of the country near the Rift Valley, thought by many to be the birthplace of humanity. It was a seven-hour drive north, a climb out of Nairobi, which is situated at an elevation comparable to that of Denver, along bumpy roads, at best, and rutted dirt roads at worst, in a caravan of vans the springs and shock absorbers of which had evidently reached their limits of wear many miles before.

If the gathering in Africa gave any indication of the group's purpose, then at least part of it was to sustain a conversation between deep interior spirituality—a richness of meditation and contemplation across traditions was evident throughout the program—and some of the bleakest human rights abuses and violent circumstances on the planet. A subtext to the conversation was evident in occasional exchanges between an outward kind of Western pragmatism and the more meditative and internal orientation of many of the Eastern traditions.

So, on an African plain, representatives of many of the world's religions as well as of the nonreligious gathered where lions made a noisy early morning visit to a meadow as participants slept in safari tents, where trumpeting elephants were heard during an evening meal, and where zebras and impalas moved across a near horizon at breakfast. The more than sixty people from twenty-five countries who attended included lay practitioners of Buddhism and Hinduism as well as Buddhist monks and nuns, Hindu swamis, Catholic nuns, Protestant ministers, Muslims, a Jewish social anthropologist, a Palestinian psychosocial therapist, African physicians who practice traditional Western medicine, as well as a traditional healer, an African chief who was an herbalist and spiritualist, humanists, at least one theosophist, and a fair sampling, in religious terms, of none of the above. Many of those attending could also be described by the remarkable work they do advocating and working for justice and human rights, often among some of the most unjust, not to mention complex, situations on the globe.

There were moments when the conversations grasped at the ethereal. A caution from Freyne, for instance, against the "deep environmentalist" inclination to wipe out distinctions among species, brought a long response on sentience. Sraddhalu Ranade of India, a scientist and a specialist in the teachings of the late Indian sage Sri Aurobindo, described in an extensive discourse scientific experiments that recorded the activity of molecules in animal and plant life and other objects that demonstrated, he said, that even in what we consider inanimate forms there can be expressions of anxiety and fear to perceived threats.

But the conversation was never far from the more recognizable and often horrific threats to humans. A woman who worked for the Sudan country office of the African Leadership and Reconciliation Ministry (ALARM), may have left her newly established country of South Sudan for a few days, but the heartache of its struggles wasn't far away. On the first day of the conference, Kenya's *Daily Nation* newspaper contained a special section with a cover story headlined, "The stain on South Sudan: Inter-ethnic fighting and failed promises put Salva Kiir's administration on the spot."

Peace and reconciliation are simultaneously compelling needs and often distant dreams in such places. Stories of ethnic and tribal killings, unimaginable brutality against women and children were always close to the surface. Dealing with the aftermath is a long and difficult slog.

Dr. Célestin Musekura, founder of ALARM, who was born and raised in Rwanda, witnessed the 1994 genocide in which the majority Hutu population killed an estimated eight hundred thousand Tutsis. He received a seminary education in Kenya and at Dallas Theological Seminary, where his doctoral research was on contemporary models of forgiveness. At the time of the conference, ALARM had a ministry of fifty-four full-time staff training church and community leaders in Burundi, Congo, Kenya, Rwanda, Sudan, Tanzania, Uganda, and Zambia.

The Rwandan pastor and Hutu whose extended family included Tutsis, said he had lost family members as well as about seventy Tutsi members of his congregation, and he had had to wrestle in the aftermath with the realities of forgiveness. "I believe the concept of love and forgiveness is not something from outside," Musekura said, because each individual must call on those qualities. Loving one's neighbor, he pointed out, is a matter of "loving enough to not cause harm. Men and women in the community who taught love and forgiveness," understood that it is not imposed by anyone else, but occurs because it is human.

Forgiveness, he said, doesn't occur quickly or easily. It also doesn't mean wiping out or trying to just get beyond what has happened. "To begin to explain forgiveness, we must make people understand that what was done to them was evil," he said. "Otherwise, we will be misunderstanding what forgiveness is. You begin by judging what was done to you as evil, as inhuman, you allow people to be angry." He explained that this is the reason ALARM does counseling for trauma—people express how they feel. "Those who are counseling from a Christian perspective," he said, must understand that "forgiveness is not just a microwave solution."

Many there seemed to answer Chittister's question about what people with little money and no official power can do. A woman from Congo who was president of the Federation of Protestant Women in the Ecumenical Church of Democratic Republic of Congo described workshops the organization gives on peace-building and seminars for couples on gender issues, and how it advocates for an end to violence against women.

Jessica Okello of Uganda was general secretary of Pan African Christian Women Alliance and headed the Women and Children Department of ALARM in Uganda. She described her work with many women affected by the twenty-three-year civil war in northern Uganda.

Dr. Sakena Yacoobi seemed to exemplify the possibilities of the individual against great odds in the extreme. The sixty-one-year-old from Afghanistan came to the United States as a lone teenager just out of high school in the early 1970s at the encouragement of some U.S. Peace Corps volunteers who, she said, recognized that she had potential and that it would not be fully realized in her home country.

She stayed with an American family in Michigan, took intensive language courses and, though accepted at Stanford, UCLA, Davis, and Berkeley, accepted the family's advice and went to the smaller University of the Pacific in Stockton, California, where she took pre-med courses. She eventually completed a master's in public health at Loma Linda University and later earned a doctorate in that field. A Muslim, she said she remembersed her time at the Seventh Day Adventist university in Loma

Linda as among the best periods of her life. "I learned so much from them," she said.

Along the way, she worked four jobs simultaneously, at times to supplement scholarship money. In 1987, after her family escaped during the Soviet invasion of Afghanistan to refugee camps in Iran, she was able to purchase a house in Michigan and served as sponsor to thirteen members of her family who came to the United States.

Once they were settled, she took off for the Afghan refugee camps in Pakistan and began seeking out the uneducated women who sat idly and bringing them into schools she had founded. She's continued to this day doing that work, under the aegis of the Afghan Institute of Learning, which she founded. She said she had established hundreds of schools for girls throughout Afghanistan.

Throughout the week, Chittister led workshops and was often looked to as someone who could wrap up a discussion or provide a balancing insight. A good example is one incident in particular that took place on the last day of the conference during a workshop on economics. Several speakers were dealing with the issue in terms of the economic collapse of that period and exploring the possibilities of understanding those on Wall Street who were at that time being widely vilified. Could the critique of greed be separated from the individual? Could these individuals be seen as decent people caught up in a system? In the very mixed group, heads began to nod when Chittister, as one of a panel, essentially preached from the gospel story of the Good Samaritan as a model of those who, ignoring social and class distinctions, lay down their lives for others.

On her way back to Ireland, she judged that the week "had been a great experience; it was not an easy one."

"But GPIW seems to have grown up," she wrote. "It is a name now with a huge network of people from all around the world who really take it seriously...It is a very small model of the human conversation that is more spiritual than political. God knows, the world needs that. Politics and economics have done more harm than good too often."

In Amsterdam, she wrote: "The worst part of the flight is over. One more hour to Cork, three more hours to Kerry. Then, back to work full bore. There is so much of the rest of my life to do...In fact, how many lives do I live? One, the community; two, the writing; three, Monasteries of the Heart; four, a public life. Too many for any one monastic, I'm sure."

TEN

INTO UNCHARTED WATERS

During one of my visits to the Mount in 2012, I interviewed Sr. Phyllis Weaver. She was eighty-nine at the time and still full of enthusiasm and welcome. We spoke at length about her time as a sister and about the changes that had occurred during her more than seventy years as a Benedictine and for which she expressed a great deal of fondness. She had been a teacher, with a master's from the University of Notre Dame and certification to teach languages, including Latin, French, and Spanish.

She was among the legion of sisters who made religious life what it was in the years between the mid-1940s and mid-1960s. That was the period when the church in the United States, particularly in the Northeast and Upper Midwest, saw record numbers of young men heading to seminary and young women going into religious orders. That period, though short-lived, created iconic images of Catholic culture that exist today as a measure of the health of the church. That previous period of full rectories and convents is for many the permanent standard of success. In the same way, the current period of decline implies failure.

Weaver had an interesting perspective on the numbers. The morning after our interview she wheeled up to me in her electrically powered scooter as we were leaving morning prayer in the chapel and said she'd had a thought overnight that perhaps I'd find helpful. "In 1941 when I entered the community," she said, "there were a hundred in the community and no postulants. Today, we have a hundred members and one postulant."

What was her conclusion from that data? "Perhaps we're too worried about numbers," she said.

Weaver, who died in December 2014, was making a point from personal experience that demographers and others had been making when viewing the data in a broader context. Not that the drop in religious vocations is not worrisome. When Weaver entered, the community was far younger than it is today and would only continue to grow for the next two decades. Today, the median age in the community is seventy-three, and the expectation is that the decline in numbers will be swift and significant over the next decade.

The Center for Applied Research in the Apostolate (CARA) at Georgetown University estimates that if current trends continue—and CARA's Mark M. Gray parenthetically notes "and they may not"—the number of religious sisters in the United States would drop to fewer than a thousand by 2043.[1]

In fact, Chittister, when asked about Weaver's observation, said she had been making a similar point for years. When she was prioress, she said, she did a study of the numbers entering the community from the year of its origin in Erie in 1856 through the early 1940s and discovered that the average number entering during that time was one and a half persons a year. Then, as occurred throughout much of the U.S. Catholic Church, the numbers jumped until the major exodus of the mid-1960s.

It is necessary to walk deeper into the thicket of sociological data to understand the numbers in a broader context. They have too often been used to fashion facile arguments on the state of religious life and of the church in general. But, delaying that walk for a moment, it is equally important to ask about the nature of religious life: What is it? What is its purpose? How are the charisms of religious orders best expressed and carried out in the twenty-first century?

Chittister's self-described "manifesto" on religious life, *The Fire in These Ashes: A Spirituality of Contemporary Religious Life,* was published in 1995 and, she writes, had been thirty years in the making. The book was based on a lengthy piece, "Religious life is still alive, but far from Promised Land," that ran in the February 18, 1994, issue of *National Catholic Reporter.* Chittister entered religious life just as the

---

1. The Center for Applied Research in the Apostolate, which celebrated its fiftieth anniversary in 2014, has accumulated a wealth of sociological data on the Catholic Church in the United States. Some of the data here was posted online on August 26, 2014, "Sister Statistics: What Is Happening?" Other data and analysis for this section is contained in *New Generations of Catholic Sisters: The Challenge of Diversity*, by Mary Johnson SNDdeN, Patricia Wittberg, SC, and Mary L. Gautier, senior research associate for CARA (New York: Oxford University Press, 2014).

numbers nationally were reaching their apex, and she has lived most of her life in the community in the era of decline. She was one of those who considered, as we've seen, departing the community, not because she wanted to leave religious life but because she felt religious life had left her, gone on to be something for which she'd not signed up.

She stayed, and *The Fire in These Ashes* is the condensed wisdom and vision, often passionately dispensed, of her individual and the community's collective struggle through the work of renewal and revitalization. It is interesting, but perhaps not surprising given Chittister's knack for turning the prism of a question a few degrees to come at a subject from a different angle, that her "manifesto" is not so much about strategies for recruitment as it is a deep plunge into the meaning and purpose of religious life. Answer that, she seems to say, and you'll find the norm, in terms of numbers and the way the life is lived, in any age.

Hers are different considerations from the worn questions that have largely driven the conversation about the future of religious life: How can we recruit more people? How can we get nuns to look like nuns again?

"Surely," Chittister writes, "the consuming question for religious life in our day must be more than what shape religious life shall take in years to come. Frankly, who cares? That we must live and think in such a way that we make the future possible is one thing. That we should abandon a consciousness of the energizing quality of the present in order to live in the far-off-but-not-here is entirely another."

What is of present value? That question is much more difficult to answer, she writes, than asking whether the past was good or the future is possible.[2]

If there is purpose in the present, she asks, what is it? "Can religious life be revived? Should religious life be revived? Is there any fire left in these ashes?"

The image is taken from an Irish term, *Grieshog*, which describes the practice of burying warm coals under ashes at night to preserve the embers so that a fire can be started quickly in the morning. "It is a holy process, this preservation of purpose, of energy, of warmth and light in darkness. What we call death and end and loss in our lives, as one thing turns into another, may, in these terms be better understood as *grieshog*, as the preservation of the coals, as refusing to go cold." The responsibility of today's nuns and sisters "may simply be to stay religious till the day we die so that religious life may live long after we do."

---

2. Joan Chittister, *The Fire in These Ashes: A Spirituality of Contemporary Religious Life* (Kansas City: Sheed and Ward, 1995), 36ff.

She turns the argument back on those whose analysis rests on numbers and who blame the decline on the loss of old disciplines and garb and on too much involvement in the world beyond convent walls. "Religious life will not die in the future unless it is dead in religious already. Each and every religious alive today is its carrier. Each of us is its life."

To understand what religious life will look like in the future one need only "look in a reflecting pool: Is there energy of heart shining out of the eyes there? Is there a pounding commitment to a wild and unruly gospel there? Is the spiritual life aglow there? Is there risk there? Is there unflagging commitment, undying intensity, unequivocal determination to be what I say I am? Or has the old glow gone dull? Is life now simply a matter of enduring the days and going through the motions? Or is religious life in a brand new arc demanding more discipline from me and giving more life through me than ever?"[3]

According to CARA's calculations, between 1943 and 1965 the number of women religious in the United States jumped 47,400, a 35 percent increase, to a total of 179,954. Since then, through 2014, there was a loss of 131,500 to 48,554. Of that population, according to CARA, 11 percent were in their nineties, 26 percent were in their eighties, and 32 percent were in their seventies. The estimated total number of women religious in 2043, should trends continue, "would be similar to the number of sisters in the middle of the nineteenth century."

The question, then, is what represents the norm? Was it the nearly one hundred years prior to the explosion from the 1940s through the 1960s? Or was it the two decades, played out in select portions of the country at the apex of Catholic immigrant experience and fixed in a certain generation's memory as how the church was and should always be?

The farther one gets from that period of greatest numbers, the more it appears to be a short-lived anomaly and that the norm will be found somewhere below those figures. The same might be said, again, for the number of priests in the United States, which peaked in 1970 at a total of 59,192 and steadily declined to 38,275 in 2014. Of that total, 26,265 are diocesan priests; fewer than 20,000 are available for active, full-time ministry. Of those, more than 6,000 are priests who have been brought in to the United States from other countries, and almost all of those countries are, on the basis of priests per number of Catholics, far worse off than the United States.

The data seem to be pointing toward an unsettling reality, that a phase of church life in the United States, particularly the way it was structured, is coming to an end. No less a traditionalist figure than

---

3. Ibid., 38.

Cardinal Timothy Dolan of New York has described the situation in dramatic terms in a book-length interview: "I'm developing a theory that one of our major challenges today is that American Catholic leadership is strangled by trying to maintain the behemoth of the institutional Catholicism that we inherited from the 1940s and '50s."[4] At another point in the conversation with John L. Allen Jr., Dolan states that bishops "are exhausted by maintenance, and we have forgotten the mission, not to mention the mystery and the message. As important as structures are, few people are going to surrender their lives to a structure."

As major archdioceses like Boston and Philadelphia sold off chanceries and residences that once symbolized the church's prominence in society, and as parishes closed and merged and other properties were "repurposed" into retreat centers or sold to other denominations or to non-denominational congregations, it became increasingly clear that an end of an era was at hand. In the first decade of the twenty-first century, the realization was inescapable that the Irish/European project of some 150 years was over. The United States version of that project, with parochial "plants" so heavily dependent on high densities of Catholics in the inner cities and high numbers of priests and nuns, had become unsustainable.

The fact that the model could no longer be maintained as it had been for decades in no way suggested that the church was crumbling. Quite the contrary. It only meant that its population centers were shifting to the South and West; that the numerous old, and often large, churches of the past could no longer be supported; and that its cheap and abundant labor force was disappearing. The rub here and in some other English-speaking countries where the same historical trajectory applied was that no one at the hierarchical level dared imagine what a church of the future might look like.

The changes occurred mostly out of necessity and not by design. One of them, a partial fix at best, was importing foreign priests. Another of the partial fixes to the priest shortage was an enormous upsurge in the number of permanent deacons, mostly married men, ordained between 1975, when there were 898, and 2014, when there were 17,464. The number of parishes without a resident priest pastor has increased from 549 in 1965 to 3,496 in 2014. At the same time, the number of parishes, after rising from 17,637 in 1965 to 19,620 in 1990, has subsequently dropped to 17,483, below the 1965 number, in

4. John L. Allen Jr., *A People of Hope: Archbishop Timothy Dolan in Conversation with John L. Allen Jr.* (New York: Image Books, 2012), 35–36.

2014. The 2014 number reflects the closing and merger of parishes in the old Catholic centers. At the same time, new parishes are being built in the South and West, where often construction (and the number of priests needed) can't keep up with population growth. The Catholic population of the United States has increased during the past half century from 46.3 million to 66.6 million, according to the *Official Catholic Directory*.

Another phenomenon in the contemporary church has been the emergence of lay professional ministers, non-ordained and non-vowed Catholics, whose numbers have grown from 10,674 in 1995, the first year for which CARA has such figures, to 21,424 in 2014. Since 1990, lay ecclesial ministers involved in parish ministry, including vowed religious and other lay persons, jumped from 21,569 to 39,651 between 1990 and 2014.[5] The point of wading into this sea of statistics, (and this is a small sampling) is to note the importance of placing the data about nuns in a larger context. What the figures begin to demonstrate is that the church in the United States has changed dramatically over the past half century—in many ways, not just in the number of nuns and priests—and often because of forces well beyond the control of bishops, cardinals, and pastoral planners.

————————————

One often accepted explanation for the drop in religious vocations, particularly among women, is that they took reform too far and were too affected by the libertine spirit of the 1960s and by the feminist movement, allowing themselves to be led into "dissent" from magisterial teaching and a distortion of the intent of the Second Vatican Council.

Elements of truth can be found in all of those assertions, of course. The great drop-off in vocation numbers did, indeed, begin in the 1960s, a period of self-examination, turmoil, and reform for a host of institutions. It would have been impossible for religious orders to remain unaffected. It is arguable, however, that the renewal of religious orders was as much, if not more, a result of the mandates of Vatican II as it was of cultural upheaval. Feminism, and its awareness of the historic subjugation of women, as we have seen, certainly affected the thinking within religious orders. But Chittister would also maintain that a kind of feminist thinking among women religious emerged from new understandings of scripture and a realization of how much religious life for women has been determined historically by men.

————————————

5. See CARA website under "Frequently Requested Church Statistics."

As mentioned earlier, journalist and author Ann Carey has written an important book, a detailed treatment of the changes in U.S. religious life that leans heavily toward the conservative perspective. *Sisters in Crisis: The Tragic Unraveling of Women's Religious Communities* was first published in 1997 by Our Sunday Visitor Publishing Division and reissued by Ignatius Press in 2013 as *Sisters in Crisis, Revisited: From Unraveling to Reform and Renewal.*

As a history of the arc of change in religious life in the United States, it is an invaluable source with its attention to dates, details, documentation, influential actors, and such. Whether one agrees with the conclusions the author reaches regarding the path of renewal of most religious orders in the United States is a matter of one's point of view and probably where one falls on the ecclesial spectrum on a range of issues that have been under debate in the church for the past half century.

Chittister, in Carey's view, would represent an influence that has led religious life down the wrong path, the one that leads to what she would term the "unraveling."

She quotes a claim Chittister made in her contribution to the book *Midwives of the Future: American Sisters Tell Their Story*, that the work most religious orders came to the United States to do had been completed with the election of John F. Kennedy as president. "Through the school system, the faith had been preserved in a strange land; Catholics had been inserted into a Protestant culture; the church had a tightly organized catechetical base and major institutional system. But whole new pockets of poor and oppressed people have arisen in this society and women Religious are attempting to start all over again with the same bias toward the poor of this generation."

In Carey's analysis, Chittister had "rationalized" that the only way the poor today could be helped was by the "deconstruction of the traditional forms of religious life." As an alternative example, Carey raised the model of Mother Teresa and her Missionaries of Charity.[6] It is noteworthy, perhaps, that Mother Teresa's congregation was started only after she saw a need to which her previous order was not responding. Mother Teresa and Joan Chittister would likely disagree on a number of issues having to do with religious life and challenging the status quo in both church and state, but interesting parallels exist. Carey notes that canon law stipulates that in order for a community to take on apostolic work different from that for which it was established, it needs the consent of the local bishop. In terms of the Erie Benedictines, it

---

6. Ann Carey, *Sisters in Crisis, Revisited: From Unraveling to Reform and Renewal* (San Francisco: Ignatius Press, 2013), 220.

took Mother Mary Margaret Kraus some correspondence with the papal nuncio to persuade the local bishop to approve of individual ministries, not that the Benedictines, in any strict sense, were established to run girls' academies. Chittister built on that instinct and ultimately gained consensus to give up the academy, which was severely draining the community's resources, in order to concentrate on the new poor in the community. In Mother Teresa's case, she didn't attempt to change the direction of her community. Instead, she lobbied the local bishop until he gave her permission to leave the Loreto Sisters and her ministry teaching high school. She left behind her order and its disciplines and distinctive habit, adopted the sari, far more in line with the garb of India, and took up a daring ministry among the poor and dying in the streets of Calcutta.

Could one person's deconstruction be another's leave-taking?

One finds little daylight between Carey and Chittister in their characterization of pre–Vatican II religious life and the need for renewal. Indeed, early in her book, Carey speaks of sisters in the years immediately preceding Vatican II as "underappreciated and overworked." She goes through a list of old disciplines and practices that had become either meaningless or unnecessarily burdensome, including "the tyranny of some mother superiors," an horarium dictating life for each hour of the day, censored mail and restrictions on the number of letters a sister could write. "Little courtesies, such as offering a cup of coffee to a visitor, had to be cleared through the superior in some communities, and most orders did not allow a sister to venture outside the walls without a sister companion."[7]

Carey understands the need for change and renewal; she just disagrees with the manner in which much of it occurred and the lengths to which it was taken in many cases. "Sr. Joan's philosophy has been echoed by other women who answered the legitimate call of Vatican II to make religious life less authoritarian, but rather than implementing reasonable reforms, they threw off all semblance of authority and eventually discarded most of the traditions of their institutes, even the reasonable ones, including the apostolate that the institute had always performed."[8]

For Carey, Chittister's influence represented a total undoing of everything that had preceded it. "Gone with the structure and traditions was the specific end or purpose of the institute, even though Vatican II decrees stressed that the purpose of the institute must be preserved."

She is distressed that the habit was not merely altered and updated but abandoned in most cases, and she takes on at length the develop-

7. Ibid., 27–36.
8. Ibid., 220.

ment of the Leadership Conference of Women Religious (LCWR), an organization that, in her view, is engaged in dissent, willful defiance of the hierarchy, and various forms of theological and spiritual chicanery.

Any act of social renewal involving tens of thousands of people in hundreds of distinct groups discerning new paths over the course of two decades is bound to, at times, go down wrong paths and entertain ideas that ultimately are scrapped. At the same time, isn't it more than coincidence that so many communities of women were reaching similar conclusions? Can we grant the reformers the benefit of collective wisdom and even of a continuity with such women as Hildegard of Bingen, Catherine of Siena, Mary MacKillop, and Mary Ward—all strong-willed and daring innovators who, over the centuries, bucked bishops, bullied popes, wrote in ways the Christian world had never seen, faced excommunication, and generally dragged religious life free from domineering clerics and rules that had become useless?

The judgments of Carey—and hers are considered here because she is perhaps the best representative of a point of view—are just that, judgments. How Vatican II documents are interpreted is still a matter of debate, and the deliberations about them are likely to continue until Vatican III. One settled matter that emerges from the turmoil and uncertainty of the period of reform and renewal is a deep sense of loss. Across the country, for instance, the number of Catholic elementary and high schools has plummeted in recent years. It is incorrect to blame all of it on disappearing nuns. Not an insignificant amount was caused by white Catholic flight from inner cities to suburbs and some of it was due, as was the case in Erie, to increasing costs as well as a change in ministry. Chittister's life gives evidence of the fact that the reality of closing down their school ministry was an enormous event for the community. The members went into the chapel together in tears, having decided that remaining a community in service of the gospel was more important than disappearing because of an insistence on remaining with the one task they had known.

Only time will tell if that was the correct decision, but it was one not taken lightly or in haste or for frivolous reasons.

The future of religious life, of course, will be decided well after the generation that has waged such contentious debates about its course has walked off the stage. Writers such as Charles Morris and Peter Steinfels believe the feminist movement had as much as any other force to do with the diminishment of religious orders.[9]

---

9. See Johnson, Wittberg, and Gautier, *New Generations of Catholic Sisters*, 7–8.

Meanwhile Kenneth Briggs, author of *Double Crossed: Uncovering the Catholic Church's Betrayal of American Nuns,* makes the case that, among other reasons, it was the hierarchy's unreasonable restrictions on religious institutes that caused the exodus, while George Weigel claims the split in religious life went neatly along the division between those who wear habits and favor a traditional way of life and those who have given up the habit and older practices. Weigel, a noted conservative, further contends that the traditionalist communities are growing and that the progressive orders are dying out.[10]

That is a claim that Carey also makes and one that deserves challenge since it has become part of a widely accepted narrative in the discussion of religious life. That assertion ignores at least several dimensions and, at worst, misrepresents the data.

The authors of *New Generations of Catholic Sisters* note that sociological studies of religious life over the years have "listed changes in society and the church as reasons why fewer people were entering religious orders." Researcher Sr. Marie Augusta Neal, SNDdeN, "pointed to several of the internal policies the sisters had adopted: requiring candidates to have some college and/or work experience prior to entrance; failing to invite vocations from new immigrants; and the reduced probability of young women coming in direct contact with sisters."

Other sociologists, said the writers, attributed the drop in numbers to "the declining power of traditional Catholic beliefs...and the deep erosion of the power of traditional Catholic symbols and sacraments."

Yet another researcher cited listed "such factors as the new collegial approach to authority articulated by Vatican II, expanding secular opportunities for women, declining birth rates, credentialism in professional associations, and the rise of feminist ideologies in the society."[11]

The temptation is to be flip and conclude that most of the forces of church and society are aligned against the success of religious orders. Suffice it to say, for the sake of this discussion, that it is a complex issue with more than one cause.

It is true that two main groups of women religious exist in the United States and that they divide between more progressive orders in the LCWR, by far the larger of the two, and those that have maintained a more traditionalist outlook as members of the Council of Major Superiors of Women Religious (CMSWR). The reality is probably less rigidly dualistic than the shorthand normally used for the two groups, but the generalities apply. So do differences in characteristics of those

---

10. Ibid., 8–9.
11. Ibid., 7.

entering religious life. Mark Gray, summarizing the work of the authors of *New Generations of Catholic Sisters*, writes, "One of the key differences between those attracted to LCWR institutes is that they are more likely to be over the age of 40, whereas those attracted to CMSWR institutes tend to be younger." The younger recruits in the more traditional orders also tend to find eucharistic adoration, common meditation, and other devotional prayers more important than those in LCWR congregations, and they "are also more likely than older sisters to be attracted to their institute's fidelity to the Church and its practice regarding a habit."

Consideration of multiple factors is important because, as the authors note: "Some commentators, for ideological purposes, attempt to create generalized typologies that mask the complexity of the religious reality, arguing that all new entrants go to traditionalist institutes and few or none go to LCWR institutes... Such stereotypes are not only inaccurate but dangerous, because they contribute to the increasing polarization of Catholics in the United States and hinder attempts to address the real challenges faced by religious sisters in this country."[12]

In 2014, when *New Generation of Catholic Sisters* was published, the writers noted that "an almost equal percentage of LCWR and CMSWR institutes have no one at all in formation at the present time (32 percent and 27 percent, respectively). One of the most striking findings regarding new entrants is that almost equal numbers of women have been attracted to institutions in both conferences in recent years."

The breakdown on those numbers: in 2009, LCWR institutes had 73 candidates/postulants, 117 novices, and 317 sisters in temporary vows; CMSWR institutes had 73 candidates/postulants, 158 novices and 304 sisters in temporary vows/commitments.[13]

Because LCWR represents more than 80 percent of the religious orders in the country, the number of new entrants they attract are spread out over a much larger base, thus making any calculation of new sisters by percentage of the whole, a tactic often used to make a point, virtually useless as a comparison. An increase of two new sisters in a community of twenty will always register as a much larger percentage jump in growth than a new class of four in a community of hundreds. Thus, the apparent claim by Carey contained in a question in her introduction, "Why are the orders that have embraced the classical model of religious life attracting the most vocations?"—a claim barely supported by the data, has been endlessly repeated as established

---

12. Ibid., 17.
13. Ibid., 18.

fact in discussions of the future of religious life. In real life, the draw is about equal.

The clearest point in all of this seems to be that two of the most important pillars of the old structure of parochial Catholicism—priests and sisters—have an increasingly diminished presence in the church at the beginning of the twenty-first century. The demographers see no quick fix. A corresponding diminishment in the number of Catholics has not occurred. Quite the opposite. The questions are pressing: How will sacramental life be sustained? How will the faith be passed on to new generations?

The challenge, it seems, lies well beyond any regret that the 1950s church cannot be resurrected. It lies instead in imagining a realistic church of the future, a task yet to be undertaken in any serious, coordinated fashion by the U.S. bishops.

———————————

If the nuns will not be around in great numbers to run Catholic institutions, then what's the point of religious life? Chittister has a different starting point from those who equate the health of religious life with maintaining apostolic works.

"The first sign that something has gone wrong with religious life," she writes, "is when work, any work becomes more important than the quest itself and what it demands of us here and now. The work of teaching, the work of healing, the work of pastoring, even the work of being a religious itself is not as important as the seeking."[14]

What compels Chittister to continue in religious life could be difficult to reduce to a recruitment poster, but her motivation might be a defining characteristic—in lieu of running schools and hospitals—of religious life in the future. Regardless of the work, she writes, "the religious falls so completely into the arms of Christ, the mind of God, that nothing will suffice except to become what one seeks: the merciful One, the loving One, the truth-telling One, the One who says, 'Go you and do likewise.'"

Younger people who come to religious life "looking for social security in a place that purports to follow the Jesus who was hounded by the synagogue, feared by the state, thought crazy by his relatives, rejected by his neighbors and loved only by the outcasts of society come to exactly the wrong place."[15]

———————————

14. *The Fire in These Ashes,* 52.
15. Ibid., 60.

Living the life in the present is paramount, and she would go so far as to say that preserving religious life is not the obligation of women religious today. "Our only obligation is to go to the grave being religious ourselves. We must stop looking for reasons, accepting excuses, telling ourselves the self-fulfilling prophecies that enable us to run in place." Such living, moving beyond running in place, requires risk, which Chittister defines as "faith unbounded by reason." It is an animating principle, an element that was largely tamed out of religious life over decades. "Risk walks with God as its only sure companion. The religious congregation that risks its reputation for the sake of new questions and its benefactors for the sake of peace and its clerical support for the sake of women and its lifestyle for the sake of the ecological stewardship of the planet and its retirement monies for the sake of the poor walks the way of holy risk."

Such risk can make life difficult, "but there is no other way if the life is to be real, if the fire is to be rekindled from the flame of its past."[16]

———————————

How those ideas play out in years to come, whether they inspire or define a new kind of religious life, will be left to future analysts to consider. But it is reasonable, even necessary, to wonder if, indeed, an ember still glows beneath the ashes.

The Erie Benedictines are, in ways today, as different as one might imagine from the community the sixteen-year-old Joan Chittister joined in 1952. The sisters no longer run the schools that once served as a kind of feeder system for the community. Their identity in the city is no longer tied to a girls' high school. The "risks" they've taken have certainly resulted in a new model of community since at least 1990.

Chittister, however, believes the reshaping goes beyond new ministries. "Religious communities were once the education centers of the Catholic Church. They brought up generation after generation in the Baltimore Catechism and what we needed to be absorbed by a white Anglo-Saxon culture. That was great, but that's gone now," she said in an interview. "So do religious women have a recognizable, definable and conscious role in both Catholic society and the larger society at the present time? I would argue vehemently, Yes! And what is it? I believe religious communities must become centers of spirituality and spirituality centers."

———————————

16. Ibid., 65.

The older structures that once provided young men and women an introduction to spirituality are disappearing. "Even the parish system has broken down. It is not the same parish as it was when it was church in the Irish or Italian or whatever ghetto and everyone knew everyone; everyone we went to school with and ate supper with, we knew. Now parishes are collections of people who are looking to be able to fill gaps in their own personal spiritual lives." She makes the case that the "metamorphosis of religious communities into retreat centers, spiritual direction centers, liturgy centers, hospitality centers—those are the components of centers of spirituality and spirituality centers."

Mount St. Benedict serves as her best example. Benedictines, she says, are always home. People from outside now often crowd the chapel for liturgies, especially on special feasts. Exposure to life at Mount St. Benedict and to the work of the sisters profoundly affected Alyssa Harpst and Carrie Parsons, two young women who eventually converted to Catholicism and became oblates of the community. Oblates, though not professed, relate to the Erie community in a special way.

In some future era Harpst and Parsons may be counted in the sociological data showing the evolution of religious life from the early twenty-first century onward. For the moment, they are part of the lived reality, shaping the anecdotal information that might point a way to the future and, at the least, providing evidence of the residual heat in the embers of Catholic institutions at this point in history. When I interviewed them on separate occasions in 2013, they were both twenty-four and had recently begun working full time with the community. They were still there two years later.

By very different paths—and professing at the time no strong faith or commitment to any denomination—they both wound up at Canisius College, a Jesuit institution in Buffalo, and quite by chance also found themselves roommates.

Each credits the Jesuits and the campus ministry program there with providing opportunities for contact with Catholic spirituality and sacramental life. Eventually they both went through a program at the college called Rite of Christian Initiation of Adults, preparation for joining the Catholic Church.

One of the big influences in their spiritual journey was contact with the Erie Benedictines. The first exposure came for Harpst on a service trip that lasted a week. She lived with the community, attended morning and evening prayer and Sunday liturgy, and was able to rotate through a variety of ministries throughout the week to get a sense of the community's work. Parsons did the same service trip with Harpst the following two years.

Parsons had never met a nun before arriving at Erie. "You start at the beginning of the week timid and wondering what this place is, and by the end of it you don't want to leave. You feel so engrossed in it because they just welcome you so fully," Shortly after, she signed up to lead the group her senior year, "to bring a team down here and introduce them to it, I loved it so much. I said, 'I want to share this with people. I want to bring people here and see them experience it like I did.'"

By the time of graduation, Parsons had done a number of service trips and had, like Harpst, changed her major to sociology. As she looked toward the future, the stark choice was between a year of service—during which most of her college loans would be put on hold—or plunging into the work world to begin dealing with that debt.

The pair decided to spend the year after graduation as participants in the Benedicta Riepp program, named for the first Benedictine woman in the United States. During that year they became immersed in the community, living at the monastery and working in the community's ministry with young children. That led to a longer commitment, to their acceptance as oblates, and, finally, to a determination to stay in Erie.

Becoming fully professed members of the community is not in either woman's future. Both look forward to marriage and families; both were engaged to be married as this book went to press. Each has made clear to her boyfriend that the Erie Benedictines will always be their family. The men have also been put on alert that they are being watched by "the family"—about a hundred nuns.

Speaking about her feelings regarding her connection to the community, Parsons said: "The simplest way probably to describe that is, I want a family someday, and I value them [the Erie Benedictines] so much as a part of my life. But I know the desire to be in religious life has to be all-consuming. It's got to be that thing you just can't kick, and that's not what I felt...It was never, 'I could do this for my whole life. I could commit my entire life to what they say and do.' I want to be part of it in some way; I will always consider them my family. I stay in Erie because of them."

Both Parsons and Harpst are aware that they are seeing the demise of the order as it has been known for more than half a century. They are committed to helping the community branch out and preserve its charism. "Anything they asked of me, I'd do it," said Parsons, "but especially to preserve them because I don't want to see a world, I don't want to see an Erie, without them. I don't want to see the day come when they just don't exist anymore. Even if physically they all pass and are gone, I want to make sure that then their spirit—what they lived for and worked for their whole lives—stays here because that is what keeps this city alive in whatever way it is, and that's what binds us all together."

She sees her job now as an oblate as helping to carry on the mission. "They gave me so much and taught me so much that I need to take that and do something with that, not just sit on it."

Harpst has the same view. The nuns, she has told her friends and family, have become a "non-negotiable in my life." The nuns have become family. "They are my sisters and they mean just as much to me as the family I grew up with for twenty-three years. I don't know how else to explain that either...I would like my children to grow up knowing the community."

The community's reaction to them, she said, was expressed by a sister when she had dinner with them just before our interview. "She said, 'Would I be the first one to welcome you in if you said you wanted to enter? Yes. Do I think that's going to happen? No.' She said that she really sees how we have taken what we lived last year—what we learned, what we experienced—and how she sees us as monastics out in the community."

What is missing from their story is probably as significant as the tale itself. While both Parsons and Harpst have come to know Chittister and to admire her, treasuring the time they've been able to spend with her and the long conversations they've had with her, Chittister was not the initial draw and she is not what keeps them in Erie. In fact, neither of them knew anything about her, had not read a word of any of her books before becoming involved with the community. It is what the community has become, what it has grown into, that initially attracted them, and it is the depth of the community life, its spirituality and the way that spirituality is expressed in ministry, that sustains them and keeps them in Erie.

————————————

As this book goes to press, the Erie Benedictines count one hundred in the community, ranging in age from forty-nine to ninety-seven, with a median age of seventy-three. Those figures include two postulants, one novice, and one scholastic, all obviously in different stages of formation that normally lasts five or six years. Sixty-three live in the monastery and others live in fourteen small-group houses in Erie, with a half dozen sisters ministering within a hundred miles of Erie.

Since 2000, nine women have joined the Erie Benedictines in addition to the transfers from other communities, and a total of fifteen have participated in the year-long Benedicta Riepp program begun in 2001.

Geography is no longer a determining factor. All four of the women in formation in 2015 are from out of state.

The fastest growing segments of the community are actually extensions of the fully vowed life. Oblates are a branch of the community instituted in the 1950s that have grown significantly since the 1980s. They can be men or women "who enter into a distinct relationship with a Benedictine monastic community," who choose a life "based on the Rule of Benedict" while living and working in ordinary circumstances. In 2015, there were 270 oblates, who commit to Benedictine prayer and values. Nearly a third of the oblates live in the Erie area and the majority are within 125 miles of the city. Others are scattered throughout the country, with a few in foreign countries, including a small group in Merida, Mexico. They relate to the community through an email system just for oblates and also through mailings, through the community website, and through visits to the monastery. Some, who live close by, visit the monastery weekly; all are invited to participate in community weekends and the annual community retreat. Some work in community ministries, and the community hosts separate gatherings, such as Lent and Advent reflection days, at the monastery.

The second area of expansion is Monasteries of the Heart, a program that owes its existence and reach to the digital age and its attraction to what Chittister, in her 2011 book *Monastery of the Heart*, describes as "the search for God" that "stalks every soul." The book, in Chittister's description, is both a guide and invitation to fashion a life different from "the maze of empty promises, seductive dead ends, and useless panaceas the modern world, a spiritless culture, has to offer." It is her attempt, after fifty years in the monastery, to pass on, in a book-length reflection on the Rule of Benedict and the Benedictine way of life, the best of monasticism to be lived, not apart from the world but deep within it.

Benedict's response to the vapid and chaotic superficiality of his own age was, in Chittister's understanding of things, to live the spiritual life, and that entailed "simply living this life, our daily life, well. All of it. Every simple, single action of it." He "lived the life everyone else lived—but differently," and so it has gone on, evolving and changing, through the ages, meeting the needs of different eras but ever anchored to that ancient wisdom.[17]

The project that was rolled out at the time the book was published was described as providing "an opportunity for anyone—regardless, or

---

17. Joan Chittister, *The Monastery of the Heart* (Katonah, NY: BlueBridge, 2011), Introduction.

even in the absence, of faith tradition—to live Benedictine spirituality and values with online communities or in face-to-face groups of family, friends, neighbors or fellow churchgoers."

Describing the establishment of Monasteries of the Heart, Kownacki told the *National Catholic Reporter* that it "is not a vowed religious community or canonical religious order, and there's no intent to make it one." At the same time, she said, it offers a new way of living out religious life, including the Benedictine values of community, prayer, and work.[18]

In the years since, Monasteries of the Heart has drawn the attention of thousands of members from around the globe who go to its website for daily prayer and Benedictine spiritual practices. Members engage in on-line discussions, are invited to (and attend, virtually, in great numbers) occasional video presentations and discussions, receive a weekly newsletter, and are able to connect with like-minded seekers on line.

Sr. Anne Wambach, prioress of the community in 2015, was elected in 2010 following the last term of Christine Vladimiroff, and is herself indicative of the changes in the community since the days of renewal. Wambach is a native of Philadelphia, not Erie, began her life as a religious with the Sisters of St. Joseph of Chestnut Hill in Pennsylvania, and transferred to the Erie Benedictines in 1992. A musician by training (keyboard is her primary instrument, but she picked up oboe again when she joined the Benedictines), she met some members of the community while studying liturgy and church music at St. Joseph College in Renssellaer, Indiana, and began to visit them in Erie. She has nothing but warm memories of her formation with the St. Joseph sisters, but other elements, particularly the smaller community, the monastic life, and the sung prayer, kept drawing her to Erie.

She knew of Chittister before she transferred, had found her book, *Wisdom Distilled from the Daily,* important in her previous order. She has a deep regard for her predecessor as prioress and believes now that "Joan takes the Erie Benedictines to the world and then brings the world back to us." But, even for her, it was not Chittister but the community's life as it had evolved that attracted her.

Wambach, the first prioress to have a virtual monastery as one of the community's offerings, understands that the vowed community is diminishing, and the funeral services for members are becoming more frequent. At the same time, however, the community is increasingly a hub

---

18. "New form of religious life offers laity a Benedictine pathway," *National Catholic Reporter*, May 13, 2011.

of hospitality for visitors, including quite a few younger women who come to spend time with the community. They want to immerse themselves in Benedictine life and spirituality, but may have no intention of becoming vowed members of the community. The community still has many members in their sixties "who could be very vibrant here...I don't think we are going to be out of business. I really don't. I feel right now a new energy and some new life, and I do think certainly religious life might look different in the future, though I don't know what that is. But I think here, right now at Mount St. Benedict Monastery, there's definitely interest in who we are and what we're doing and how we're doing that."

Chittister turned seventy-nine years old in 2015. Sixty-three years of her life have been spent with the Erie Benedictines, fifty-eight of them as a fully professed member. She might be testing the very wisdom of her own writing as she faces some of the exigencies of age. She had surgery in 2011 to repair damage to both of her thumbs, surgery to repair a knee in 2013, and in early December 2014, a major operation to repair a hiatal hernia. Less than a month-and-a-half later she was headed to Ireland to do her winter-season writing, in this case the completion of two manuscripts soon due for publication. Before the surgery, she had spoken in three states in the space of several weeks and traveled to the West Coast to tape a segment of a television appearance with Oprah Winfrey. A schedule of travel and speaking appearances that someone half her age would find demanding continued to roll out in front of her.

Her "manifesto," her analysis of religious life and what it is at heart, has provided some of the fundamental language and outlooks for discussing religious life as it heads into an uncharted future. Mercy Sister Theresa Kane, who earned a certain fame for her 1979 remarks to Pope John Paul II, beseeching him to include women "in all ministries of our Church," said she believes Chittister "is probably one of the most influential women religious we have, not only nationally but internationally—and not only for sisters but for the Catholic community."

Kane, who followed Chittister by four years as president of LCWR, called her "a great leader. I mean, she just had to stand up in front of you and look out at the audience and say two words, and you were, 'Joan, tell me what you want me to do and I'll do it.' That kind of leadership that she had, it was very persuasive."[19]

---

19. Interview, November 5, 2013.

Whatever the future holds for Chittister's public life, she continues a ministry that has remained rather hidden. At some point in her career, as she looked around at her community and saw her sisters serving soup, taking care of refugee babies, educating the poor, helping immigrants find their way, she asked herself: "What do I do?" And she decided that she would write back to everyone who wrote to her. In addition to endless emails, there are on file more than ten thousand letters she's written to people all over the world.

"I made a private vow, sitting in the back of chapel years ago, that I did not want to be separated from life, that I did not ever want to allow myself to get wrapped up in me, my ideas, and my activities . . . So I made up my mind that every single piece of mail that I got I would answer, and I have. 'My husband beats me,' 'I left the Church,' 'I can't deal with my kids.' This mail is confessional.'" She is, in many ways, pastor to a far-flung congregation.

In checking some details with the Country Club Christian Church in Kansas City a few years after Chittister delivered her talk on the evolution of her thinking about God, the Rev. Carla Aday, senior associate minister, made a point of noting Chittister's pastoral gifts.

"I had the chance to watch her interact with people afterward, and I saw she is a great pastor. Something else occurred in the months following her visit here—I can't tell you the details without violating pastoral confidences, but it was then that I realized what a pastor she is. We need great public speakers, but not all great public speakers are also great pastors. Few are able to pull that off. What she did spoke to me of her authenticity and integrity."

During one of her several visits to Australia, Chittister was giving a talk in a basketball gym in Perth and, just as she was about to begin, a young man and a young woman arrived, dressed as if they'd just come in from the bush. "I thought to myself, 'What are these kids looking for? They're in the wrong room,' but they sat down and they stayed. So we got to a coffee break and I couldn't stand it. I wound my way around and went straight to the kids."

She asked them where they were from, and they said, "Alice Springs. We're up in a sheep station in Alice Springs," some fifteen hundred miles north of Perth.

They said they had walked, taken a train, a bus, and walked some more to get to her talk. When pressed on why they had taken the trip, the young woman pulled a clear folder out of her backpack and held up a piece of paper with a symbol that Chittister recognized. "I know it's Benedictine," she said to the young woman, who replied: "I wrote to you seven years ago when my mother died, and I didn't have anybody to talk to. You wrote me back this two-page letter, and I framed it. On her death anniversary, I read it every year. When I heard that you were here, I said to him, 'I'm going to get there. I don't know how, but I'm going.' All I remember of that whole Australian trip was that conversation, because I walked out saying to myself, 'It was a good decision, Joan. That is your ministry.'

"I write to prisoners and I write to everybody because they're my connection. That's what I do. I don't serve soup. I don't get to stay in one place long enough to serve soup, but I can write to them on planes. I can stay up at night writing . . . I've got an iPad now. I'm really dangerous."

During my time with Joan in Kenya, a woman from South Africa told me she had written to Chittister years before thanking her for something she had written, not expecting a reply. But she received a letter, and that was the beginning of a correspondence that had continued. Now, she said, she writes to Chittister to tell her about her family, her husband, her children, what's going on in her life.

On another occasion a young Buddhist nun told me that she had had long exchanges with Chittister about her life in community and that the older nun had helped her stay in her community.

Her commitment to that kind of correspondence continues even as she speculates, as this project heads for publication, that life might be demanding a slower pace. She isn't certain whether there will be more books or whether she will be able to keep up with the demands of travel. Yet, the example of her life militates against any great slowing down if she is able to get around. It is the acceptance of new challenges, she writes, "that make the later years a spiritual adventure as well as a psychological stumbling block. Some of us meet its demands with the joy of the climb, others are more disposed to move in place. It is the difference between life and non-life, between seeing a beckoning God everywhere and coming to the end of the search."[20] Perhaps there is some middle ground between the kind of passionate, all-in approach she has taken most of her life and coming to the end of the search. Evidence of nearly eighty years would suggest that Joan Chittister will continue always to see a beckoning God everywhere.

If the world needed proof that God could be a God of surprises, it received it with the resignation of Pope Benedict XVI in February 2013 and the election a month later of Pope Francis. With his election, the global Catholic Church experienced a tectonic shift of historic proportions.

In the relocation of the papacy from the palace to two simple rooms in a modest guest house and his insistence on the need to engage

---

20. Joan Chittister, *The Gift of Years: Growing Older Gracefully* (Katonah, NY: BlueBridge Publisher, 2008), 13.

in the art of encounter with the poor and marginalized, Francis was re-calibrating Catholics' notions of authority, leadership, and what it means to be authentically Christian.

His elevation of the God of mercy over a God of orthodoxy seemed to open significant avenues for a new tolerance of groups such as gays and lesbians and the divorced and remarried, who had been kept at a fair distance from full acceptance in the church.

His language to the cardinals following a consistory in February 2015 appeared to fairly turn on end the old criteria both for leadership and for who is considered worthy of inclusion in the community. He spoke of two ways of "having faith": "We can fear to lose the saved and we can want to save the lost." He said the church was today at the crossroads of those two approaches.

"The thinking of the doctors of the law, which would remove the danger by casting out the diseased person," is one approach. The other is "the thinking of God, who in his mercy embraces and accepts by re-instating him and turning evil into good, condemnation into salvation and exclusion into proclamation." He identified "the way of Jesus" with "the way of mercy and reintegration."

It is the work of the church, he said, "to leave her four walls be-hind and to go out in search of those who are distant, those on the out-skirts of life."

He had earlier criticized church leaders who "obsessed" over such issues as abortion and homosexuality, and he continually pressed the case of encountering and walking with the poor and those considered outcasts. "Jesus responds immediately to the leper's plea, without wait-ing to study the situation and all its possible consequences. For Jesus, what matters above all is reaching out to save those far off, healing the wounds of the sick, restoring everyone to God's family."

He made great strides during his first two years in reforming the corrupt Vatican bank, in reforming the curia, the Vatican bureaucracy that had become stuck in the palace culture of an earlier century. In the two-part synod on the family that he convened, questions that for three decades had been prohibited were back on the table. There was nothing the assembled bishops could not discuss, and he wanted it all discussed with frankness and rigor.

Francis's language has the ring of Chittister's sense of risk, of "faith unbounded by reason." Charity, he said, "is infectious, it excites, it risks, and it engages!" His agenda seems far closer to that of the nuns who have taken to the streets in service of the poor and disenfranchised than to clerical careerists making certain that the pure faith is not sul-lied by those who fall short of true orthodoxy or who ask unsettling questions.

"I have great hope in this man," Chittister said of Francis. "I believe in his honesty. I honestly think he is the face of the church I look for.

"However," she said in an interview in January 2015, "he is seventy-eight years old, and I think he doesn't know how much time he'll have, and I certainly don't either. So one thing we can probably be sure of is that everything he would like to do will probably not get done. But the way he is going about it is itself a message."

There are no perfect popes, and one of Francis's blind spots, in the view of many women, is the subject of women. Though he has spoken powerfully in condemning violence against women and the need to see women incorporated into decision-making in all levels of church and society, there has been little real movement within the church. His language in speaking about women is often awkward, his metaphors dated, and they can even, at times, seem demeaning. There is, however, an authenticity that overrides the objections, even for Chittister. His comments about women, she says, can be "sexist," "disgraceful," "totally unacceptable, except from a man with a good heart, like your grandfather, and you say he doesn't know, he just doesn't know.

"However, if he's as honest as I think he is, it doesn't make any difference where he goes into the terrible scandal of social issues today, he will wind up at the women's issue. Women are the bottom of the bottom, the worst of the poor, and they will always bear the weight of any injustice more than any other part of society, except for children. So, if he's honest, he'll find it and something will happen. And I believe he's honest, but he's not there."

She has great hope, she says, "because, I'm telling you that I wasn't there either. What got me there—my heart and my honesty."

Some may find her comments exasperating, far too patient for one who can bring such passion and insistent clarity to articulating the way women remain invisible in the church. But she long ago settled the question of how patient she might be. She is in it for the long haul.

In an essay written in 1996 for the magazine *Lutheran Woman Today*, an essay that remains one of the most requested pieces of her writing, she jokes about being asked during a talk why she stayed in the church. "'Because,' I answered, 'every time I thought about leaving, I found myself thinking of oysters.'"

What did oysters have to do with it, the questioner asked?

"Well," Chittister answered, "I realized that an oyster is an organism that defends itself by excreting a substance to protect itself against the sand in its spawning bed. The more sand in the oyster, the more chemical the oyster produces until finally, after layer upon layer of gel, the sand turns into a pearl. And the oyster itself becomes more valuable in the process. At that moment, I discovered the ministry of irritation."

The larger point is the process. It fits with her conviction that nothing remains static, that the pursuit of holiness is not something done within the confines of a monastery where rigid practices and layers of rules eliminate the need to think and any possibilities of real conflict.

The essay about why she stays begins with images of motion and journey. She quotes the writer Ursula Le Guin: "It is good to have an end to journey towards, but it is the journey that matters in the end." That is the explanation, she said, for "how it is possible, necessary even, for me as a Roman Catholic to stay in a church that is riddled with inconsistencies, closed to discussion about the implications of them, and sympathetic only to invisible women. The fact is that I have come to realize over the years that church is not a place, it is a process. To leave the church may, in fact, be leaving part of the process of my own development. And so, intent on the process of grappling with truth, I stay in it, when, for a woman, staying in it is full of pain, frustration, disillusionment and, far too often, even humiliation. Both of us, this church and I . . . need to grow. The church needs to grow in its understanding of the Gospel, and I need to grow in my understanding of myself as I strive to live it. It is, in other words, a journey of conversion for both of us."

The essay is a finely crafted statement of fidelity, the deeply considered answer to the kind of "why" questions she asks of so many others. Her model, she writes, is the Jesus who wept over Jerusalem, who taught in the synagogue and presided over the seder on Holy Thursday, "Jesus proclaiming his truth whatever the situation, whatever the cost; Jesus grappling with the depression that comes from failure, from rejection; Jesus trusting the truth, living the faith, and hoping to the end."

She stays in, she said, especially as a woman for women because "the sexist church I love needs women for its own salvation. The truth it holds, women test for authenticity. We are sanctifying one another, this church and the women who refuse to be silent, refuse to be suppressed." But it is not all in one direction, she concedes. An understanding exists, she writes, that "what each of us sets out to convert will in the end convert us as well. Women will call the church to truth. The church will call women to faith."

ACKNOWLEDGMENTS

When Sr. Joan Chittister answered my early question, "Why now?" with, "It's time," there was, of course, a more complex back story. "I never wanted to hurt anyone in the family," she said, as the project was under way. "I didn't want to hurt my mother. I didn't want to hurt Dutch. I didn't want his family to be embarrassed. So why was I willing to talk to you? Because most of those people are gone." There's no one alive, she said, who can be hurt by the details of "the childhood thing."

Now especially, she said, her mother "can't be hurt." She described Loretta as "the perfect icon for the silent woman. The neighbor who would never say she'd been beaten up the night before though she knew they'd heard it. She had to know they heard all that. She worked hard all her life to maintain her dignity. And I really believe he was a good man. But he was hurt, corrupted by the society as well as by the drink."

She said she also felt she owed it to the untold multitudes who have bought her books, attended her lectures, joined her online seminars and workshops—and especially the women—to recount those details of her life.

Unanticipated elements of timing and simple luck, then, saw me in the right place at the right time, and I am forever grateful to Joan for her trust and candor. Once committed to the project, she never failed to make herself available for more rounds of questions. From far spots on the globe, while recovering from major surgery, amid her own writing projects, by phone, Skype, and occasionally in person in Erie, she never balked at more questions, at going deeper into certain episodes, at clarifying what at times must have seemed like unimportant details.

Much more will be written in the years ahead as historians, theologians, and academics of other disciplines pore over her extensive archives. The Eberly Family Special Collections Library at Penn State, The Helen Boyle Memorial Archive in Honor of Joan D. Chittister at Mercyhurst University in Erie, and the Benedictine Sisters of Erie have arranged to cooperatively preserve and make accessible items that represent the Joan D. Chittister Archive.

Her contributions to the archive are hardly complete. As this book went to press, she had several book manuscripts under way, had just returned from two weeks in Iran with the Global Peace Initiative of Women, and faced a full lecture schedule into the next year. In addition, there are countless documents of personal correspondence in the files and personal journals that will not be made public until after her death.

Joan and the Erie Benedictines are, in real life and in the telling of this tale, inseparable. My deep gratitude certainly extends to those members of the community, only some of whom appear by name in this text, who sat for hours answering questions and providing invaluable insights into the history and other details of the community. A major benefit I received while doing this work was the opportunity to experience the hospitality of the Erie Benedictines, to be able to pray with them, share meals, and engage in countless informal but very valuable conversations. Charism can be an airy and imprecise term, but it took very clear shape in my experience of the rich and gracious texture of the Erie community, led by Prioress Sr. Anne Wambach, in its various expressions.

Two members come in for special thanks. Sr. Susan Doubet, mathematician by training and archivist by necessity, has Olympian organizational skills matched only by a kindness and generosity borne out by her willingness to find and send an endless stream of documentation between Erie and Maryland. I am also indebted to her as a reader whose questions, corrections and insights were essential to the integrity of this book. If errors crept into the telling, they are mine alone.

Sr. Maureen Tobin is a living, breathing information center. The person who for years has kept track of Joan's travel and lecture schedule and served as her confidante and advisor was ever available as a check on details, the nature of conversations recalled, and the chronology of events.

My interviews included several with Benedictines outside the Erie community, and I am especially grateful for the time given by Sr. Esther Fangman of Kansas City, Missouri. In addition to two long interview sessions, Fangman, who has a doctorate in psychology and has worked at times as a guide and mediator for the Erie community, read the opening chapters of the book. Her feedback was both affirming and instructive in helping me more precisely understand Joan and the community.

I am more indebted than they could know to readers Melinda Henneberger, who found time in her busy life as a reporter for the *Washington Post* and then Bloomberg Politics to look over the manuscript; and Mercy Sr. Anne Curtis, a member of her order's leadership team. They helped ease the anxieties of this male writer over the challenge of taking on the biography of such a powerful woman and feminist.

Finally, thanks to friend Sr. Linda Romey, a member of the Erie Benedictines and a former colleague at *National Catholic Reporter*. Her initial encouragement and verbal tour of the community and its recent history was key to my decision to do the book.

The suggestion by my longtime friend and colleague Tom Fox that I go to Erie to "freshen up the file" is but the first in a long list of reasons why this book would not have been possible without *National Catholic Reporter*.

Among the most obvious are the generosity of colleagues who tolerated my occasional disappearances during research and writing that spanned more than three years. Editor Dennis Coday, who in this digital age oversees the equivalent of at least three publications, faces more demands than any of his predecessors. He does it with a remarkable equanimity and calm and, in my case, a generosity of spirit that allowed me the time and space to deal with the requirements of this book. Also quite meaningful and reassuring was the consistent encouragement I received from NCR president and CEO Caitlin Hendel.

Less obvious but by no means less important reasons lie behind the claim that this book would not have been possible without *National Catholic Reporter*. During its half century of existence, NCR has been singular among Catholic publications for its independent reporting and commentary. Sr. Joan Chittister was but one of many voices that would not have been heard in Catholic circles on a regular basis had it not been for NCR. She and others who were often banned from speaking on "Catholic ground" because they raised questions and discussed issues that had been deemed out of bounds found limited welcome in an often fearful Catholic world.

Pope Francis has largely lifted that fear. In fact, he's encouraged full and robust debate. No one is being censured for asking questions or raising issues that once would have seen editors fired and the orthodoxy of theologians and others called into question. The critique embodied in the reporting and commentary of NCR these past 50 years— of clericalism, of an over-centralized Vatican, of curial arrogance, of the utter corruption evident in the clergy sex abuse and money scandals— have become, for the moment, the critique of the Vatican itself. This is, indeed, a green time. But we all know that the green inevitably turns to the dry again. When it does, NCR will continue to do what others will be constrained from doing. Its independence is a quality that I've come to treasure over the course of my more than twenty years with the publication as I've learned, also, to never take it for granted.

Similarly, I owe a debt of thanks to Orbis Books and the gentle and ever-patient direction of its publisher, Robert Ellsberg. Orbis is another of those places that has kept alive the thinking of theologians and others who otherwise would have found limited welcome in the Catholic publishing world. I am also most grateful for the care given the manuscript by editor Celine Allen and Orbis production coordinator Maria Angelini.

To my dear wife Sara (most know her as Sally), my gratitude goes well beyond thanks for the kindness, patience, and unwavering support she showed me during this demanding project. Long ago she was among the first to direct me on the path of understanding that women's issues are, at their simplest yet most profound, human issues.

INDEX